12

DATE DUE

Allen J. Fromherz is Assistant Professor of History at Georgia State University. He was previously Assistant Professor of Middle Eastern History at Qatar University. He received his PhD from the University of St Andrews in Scotland after graduating from Dartmouth College in New Hampshire and was awarded a Fulbright Research Scholarship to Morocco. In 2010 he was awarded the Gerda Henkel Stiftung fellowship to pursue research on the history of nationalism in the Middle East. He is also the author of *The Almohads: The Rise of an Islamic Empire* (I.B.Tauris) and *Ibn Khaldun, Life and Times*.

'Allen J. Fromherz has written an excellent book on Qatar based on a thorough knowledge of historical sources and enriched by his own experience in the country. This book will be essential reading to anyone interested in Qatar and useful to anyone interested more broadly in the dynamics of the Arab Gulf states.'

—JILL CRYSTAL, Professor of Political Science, Auburn University, and author of *Oil and Politics in the Gulf: Rulers and Merchants of Kuwait and Qatar*

'*Qatar: A Modern History* fills a major gap as it provides for the first time the necessary historical basis for understanding this Gulf state in all of its contradictions and importance.'

—G. R. GARTHWAITE, Jane & Raphael Bernstein Professor Emeritus in Asian Studies and Professor Emeritus of History, Dartmouth College

QATAR

A MODERN HISTORY

ALLEN J. FROMHERZ

Georgetown University Press

Washington, DC

First published by I.B.Tauris & Co Ltd in the United Kingdom

Library of Congress Cataloging-in-Publication Data

Fromherz, Allen James.
  Qatar : a modern history / Allen Fromherz.
    p. cm.
  Includes bibliographical references and index.
  ISBN 978-1-58901-910-2 (hardcover : alk. paper)
  1. Qatar--History. 2. Qatar--Economic conditions. 3. Qatar--Politics and government. 4. Qatar--Foreign relations--Middle East. 5. Middle East--Foreign relations--Qatar. 6. Qatar--Strategic aspects. 7. Khalifah ibn Hamad Al Thani, Amir of Qatar, 1929- 8. Al Thani, Hamad ibn Khalifah. 9. Petroleum industry and trade--Qatar. 10. Gas industry--Qatar. I. Title.
  DS247.Q35F76 2011
  953.63--dc23

                                                                                    2011037928

15 14 13 12 <3-m space> 9 8 7 6 5 4 3 2 First printing

Printed and bound in Great Britain by T.J. International, Padstow, Cornwall

Contents

Acknowledgements

I could not have completed this book without the support and inspiration of my colleagues, students and mentors in Qatar. Although I was able to remain in Qatar for only one year, it was long enough to enjoy the hospitality, warmth and graciousness of the Qatari people. I was also inspired by the many hardworking expatriates, the men and women from all corners of the world who left their families and friends and who travelled so far to make Qatar such a remarkable place.

My editors at I.B.Tauris, especially Dr Lester Crook, Joanna Godfrey and Cecile Rault, must be thanked for their patience and perseverance. Thank you, Iradj Bagherzade for contacting me about this project in 2008. I want to thank the anonymous reviewers contacted by I.B.Tauris and by Georgetown University Press for their many helpful comments and suggestions.

I acknowledge my colleagues at Georgia State University in Atlanta, Georgia and my family in Oregon for encouraging me to continue writing despite the temptation to be distracted by other projects. My grandmother Lois is always an inspiration. I want to thank Robin, Rebecca, Amy, and Allen for supporting me from afar. My friends in Atlanta, especially Joe Maxwell and Glenn Faulk, have made the life of the non-fiction writer much more bearable.

I am fortunate to have the continuing support of mentors and colleagues including Professors Gene Garthwaite, Dale Eickelman and Dirk Vandewalle at Dartmouth, Brian Catlos at the University of Colorado, Jinnyn Jacob at Harvard, Hugh Kennedy at SOAS, Steven Wright, Sheikha Misnad and Sheikha bint Jabor at Qatar University, Amira Sonbol and Mehran Kamrava at Georgetown. Of course, any errors of fact or interpretation in this book are entirely my own.

This book is dedicated to the loving memory of my best friend and colleague, Dr Mickie Mathes. Dr Mathes, who was named associate dean of Qatar University after one year as a Fulbright fellow, passed away in 2011 during her valiant struggle with cancer. Mickie devoted her life and boundless energy to bridging the cultures of America, Qatar and Japan. Her unflinching belief in the power of universal human kindness and understanding made her not just a friend to Qatar and Qataris who grew to adore her and treat her as family, but an example of the power of perseverance and love.

Mickie left the world with too much to be done. Mickie, 'In Sha Allah' we will have another, heavenly dinner and share our stories once again. I hear there is an open reservation for you anywhere in Qatar.

The completion of my manuscript was supported by a generous fellowship from the Gerda Henkel Stiftung.

Al-Thani Rulers and Princes

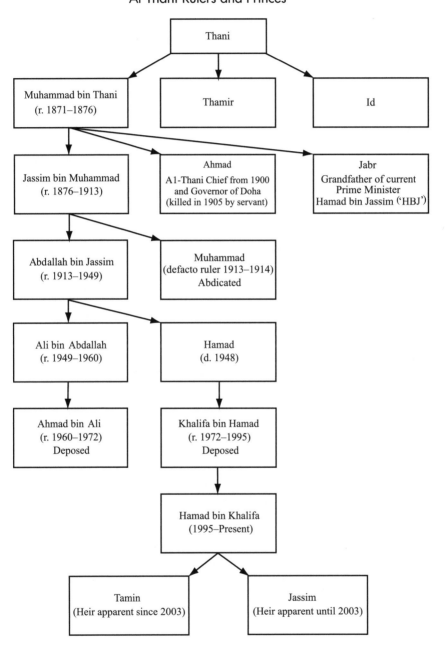

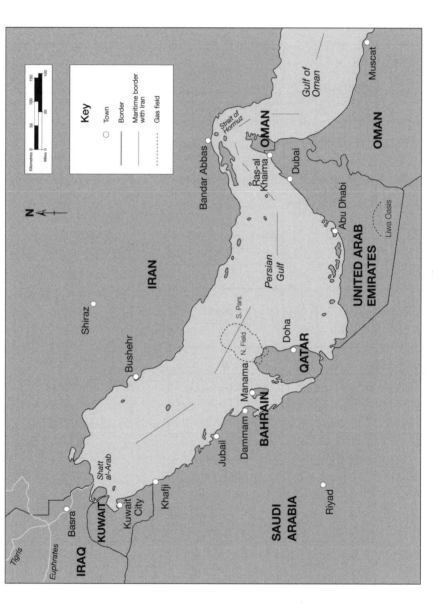

Persian Gulf

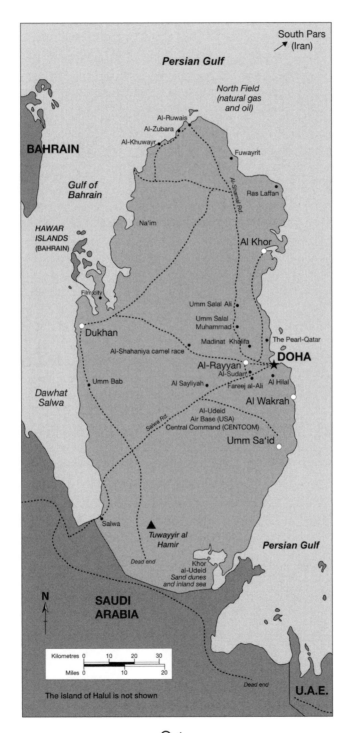

Qatar

1

Qatar – A New Model of Modernity?

S o rarely has a country of so few seemed to change so quickly over such a short period of time. Qatar's rise from an economically devastated backwater to the world's richest nation per capita in a matter of decades appears unprecedented. This rise is even more striking since Qatar's previous status as among the poorest of poor nations is within the living memory of the older generation of Qataris. The pearl price collapse and the disruptions of the Second World War had harmed the traditional exports of the Gulf. Yet even by dismal Gulf standards, Qataris were more marginal, more economically underdeveloped than the poor citizens of Kuwait, Bahrain or Dubai. In 1940 the British Political Resident provided a glimpse of Doha, capital of Qatar:

> [Doha is] little more than a miserable fishing village straggling along the coast for several miles and more than half in ruins. The *suq* consisted of mean fly-infested hovels, the roads were dusty tracks, there was no electricity, and the people had to fetch their water in skins and cans from wells two or three miles outside the town.[1]

The entire population of Qatar had fallen to 16,000. Entire villages that had survived for centuries were depopulated as tribes emigrated en masse to neighbouring, more prosperous shores. In 1944 only 6,000 fishermen were engaged in the pearl harvest as opposed to 60,000 some 20 years before.[2] In stark contrast to today, many Qataris were in dire straits. The one thing that may have made it better than equally poor places on earth was the fact that it was not a theatre of war.

Only some 15 years after 1950, the end of the 'years of hunger', however, a visitor could remark that Doha had become:

> [A] Sprawling city of concrete buildings, traffic lights, ring roads and soda stalls; air conditioning is the rule; the waterfront area has been reclaimed, and much of the filth removed; a large merchant class has grown up and social life has become conventional and 'big city'.[3]

From a place of poverty in the 1940s to an 'overgrown fishing village' in 1955 to a large city in 1965 and a growing capital in the 1970s, Doha is now the capital city of one of the most economically successful countries in the world. Qatari citizens, who endure the world's most stifling heat and who were at one time forced to survive on brackish water and reduced to starvation by the collapse of the pearl market, can now live almost perpetually in an air-conditioned, climate-controlled bubble, moving between five-star hotels, five-star shopping malls and even five-star universities imported *profectus in totum* from abroad. Qatar's population has boomed, far outpacing government predictions. It is now at around 1.7 million, more than 80 per cent of which consists of expatriate workers from around the world, servants and employees of the relatively small, and – depending on the job – somewhat unapproachable Qatari population of around 225,000. For comparison, this is approximately the population of Baton Rouge, Louisiana or Plymouth, England. Businessmen from abroad often wonder at the fact that weeks, months, even years can be spent in Qatar without even meeting a Qatari, so high are Qataris on the pyramid of economic development that has shaped their success. Much of this development, much of this disorienting, feverish change, a change in the physical environment so visible to the outsider, obscures what has not changed within Qatari society. To understand Qatar it is important to understand not just the image of rapid change and progress projected to the outside world, but the much-slower moving internal structures of Qatari society.

In much the same way that Dubai had, until recently, so skilfully adopted the branding of its success, Qatar has created an externally digestible narrative, even a brand of economic boom and opportunity where a range of opinions and beliefs are welcome. In Qatar, people are able to debate differences in internationally publicized venues such as the BBC's *Doha Debates: Qatar's Forum for Free Speech in the Arab World*.[4] According to this projected image of Qatar, an image actively promoted through Qatar's tightly controlled international media outlets such as Al-Jazeera, there are virtually no internal problems. In the marketed image of Qatar, all Qataris accept being ruled by the Emir, and always have done. In the idealized vision of Qatar, the image projected to the outside world, there is no politicking, there are not always even clear positions on international affairs, except a position defined by security, development and prosperity. Qatar seems full of venues for dialogue that enhance Qatar's image and the image of the ruling Al-Thani family. Yet this idealized narrative obscures a much more complicated and interesting local history, a history that lies just beneath the five-star hotels, international news channels and premium airport lounges. Qataris themselves have not forgotten this history, even as they are concerned that new generations will not remember the way of life that defined Qatari culture. Expensive and widely publicized attempts to showcase Qatari and Islamic culture in Doha attest to this concern with the preservation of the image of cultural authenticity. It is unclear, however, if these massive cultural projects, projects such as the building of the new Qatar National Museum and the Museum of Islamic Art designed by I. M. Pei and completed in 2008, will achieve this aim of authenticity. Yet Al-Thani family's concern with the apparent loss of visual and public authenticity does not mean that Qatar has broken completely from its past. In fact, this book argues that the traditional, underlying structures that defined Qatari life for decades remain remarkably resilient.

Qataris are the privileged citizen elite of a booming, modern state. There is little indication that Qatar's prosperity and rapid growth will be checked in the near future. Unlike other Gulf States such as Dubai, that have seen the dramatic bursting of their economic bubbles, Qatar's economy continues to expand rapidly. Qatar's economy is the fastest growing on earth with 19 per cent growth.[5] Qatar relies primarily on long-term natural gas contracts that are not subject to the same short-term price fluctuations as crude oil. Yet, despite these riches and the stunning pace of development, there are still a surprising number of similarities between Qataris of today and the impoverished Qataris of 1940. Wealth has transformed Qatari society in some ways, but not nearly to the extent that it has been transformative in the Qatari economy or built environment. In fact, economic modernization has done little to damage long-established lineage loyalties. The names, loyalties and social networks of the past, a past that in some respects has actually been artificially deepened, somehow dug into memory as deeply as the gleaming new skyscrapers of the skyline are high, and they are still important for understanding Qatar's present and future. While Qatar's present economic success was created in recent decades, the future of Qatar lies as much in its historical particularities as it does in the deceptively impressive, emerald towers of glass that symbolize Qatar's wealth and prosperity. Some of what seems to have changed so quickly has not, in fact, really changed much at all.

Briefly, the history of the Naim tribe is instructive. Long a rival and even outright enemy of the dominant Al-Thani Sheikh of Qatar, most of the Naim left Qatar decades before the oil boom, leaving their vast grazing lands, or *dira*, that cover much of the north of Qatar behind them. When they returned in the 1950s, their ancestral claims remained untouched. Indeed, many Naim could claim that their tribal chief should rightly be called an Emir, as he had been in the recent past.[6] In fact, the legitimacy of the claims of Al-Thani and of Qatar over inland areas and over the Qatar national border is tied to their association with Bedouin tribes such as the Naim. This was especially true because of the 'importance Ibn Saud [ruler of Saudi Arabia] attached to tribal territory as a basis for defining state boundaries'.[7] In the midst of territorial disputes, urbanized rulers such as Al-Thani actively competed to lure Bedouin into their territories as citizens.

There are other ways that tribes like Naim have been able to maintain a sense of internal coherence despite state intervention, changing cultural influences and the growth of state-licensed property ownership. The non-ruling tribes of Qatar remember their past

3

and they are careful to transmit that past even to the most 'Westernized' of their sons. While genealogy in the West has lost its functional meaning, becoming an internet hobby of ancestral Facebook, genealogy and ancestry in Qatar is still functional – an important indicator of social position, status and rights. As much as some in Al-Thani elite may want it to do so, development and modern education has not caused deep memories of historic rights to disappear. The chiefs of the Naim still have a throne; they still have the trappings of independence within their own group and social dynamic. Anie Montigny-Kozlowska, an anthropologist writing in French, observed in the 1980s that only very recently have Al-Thani appropriated the title of 'Emir' exclusively for themselves within Qatar.

[Only recently,] the names of the heads of groups evolved. Now there is only one Emir who directs the state. Traditional Emirs, chiefs of tribes or a sub-division of tribes have been renamed by the now, official state function they occupy as Rais al-Baladiyya (President of Municipality or Mayor) or Emir al-Qawm (Chief of the Village). Nevertheless, the old titles have not been forgotten.[8]

A similar pattern of tribal groups being incorporated into the state while also losing some of their formal power, if not the memory of that power, prevailed for other Qatari tribes and lineage groups as well. Al-Sudan and Al-Ainain, for instance, were in Qatar long before Al-Thani. They were also chiefs of Doha and Wakra before Al-Thani, a fact even Al-Thani recognized this when they gave Al-Sudan tax-exempt status during the pearling years. Modernization and rapid economic change has not destroyed either these memories or the lineage groupings and consequent cultural attitudes and norms of Qataris themselves as quickly as might be expected in classic Western models of development. While the devastation of the 1940s may have created a gaping hole that makes the present development that now plugs it seem even more impressive, Qatar is not a place 'without a past' or 'without a culture' as it has been described in popular literature.[9] Ironically, anxiety about a lack of historical roots appears to be felt more by visitors to Qatar than by Qataris themselves. Perhaps expecting exotica, adventure and orientalized Arabness, the expatriate is disappointed by the modernity, by places that look 'Western' or 'just like home'. Many Qataris, in contrast, rarely express the same level of postmodern angst. The environment has appeared to change, but many fundamental human relations remain the same for a Qatari. From their perspective, they are still bound by many of the same social rules and strictures as their parents, even if the built environment often appears Western and modern. Even so, the strictures and social rules are changing, albeit at a much slower pace than the rise of the skyscrapers.

It is not simply that the Western visitor does not see the 'real' Qatar, or that the elusive 'real Qatar' as experienced by Qataris cannot, in fact, be experienced by the vast majority of visitors. In fact, explanation for the feelings of 'inauthenticity' experienced by the Westerner or Westernized visitor in Qatar comes from the intellectual, social philosophies shaped by the particularities of Western history, particularities that seem obvious to the Westerner but do not easily apply to Qatar or to the way Qataris experience their country today. First, there is an assumption among many in the West that modernization is exhilarating yet painful, necessarily leading to historical loss and to the collapse of a past identity. There is a deep assumption in Western literature and thought that an essential conflict must exist between tradition and economic modernity.[10] This assumed, 'inevitable' conflict, experienced so vividly in the West, has been foisted upon the Middle East. According to this classic theory, Qatar should be a boiling stew of problems brought about by the conflict between tradition and modernity, but it is not. Instead, many of the same social structures, many of the same arrangements of lineage remain in the midst of apparent modernity. Qatar is a stable country and many political scientists, at one time predicting its fall, now predict a long-term future for Qatar's existing political system. The old political system is usually the first to go after the forces of modernity and tradition have clashed. Yet Qatar remains a monarchy and many social structures remain unchanged. What explains this?

The answer is to be found in Qatar's history. Only through history can the differences between the historical experience of modernity in Qatar and in the West be explained. Although often assumed to be universal, or structural, the limitations of Western philosophical and sociological perspectives about tradition and modernity are evident in Qatar. From a Western perspective, Qatar should be doomed to what the nineteenth-century sociologist Émile Durkheim called 'anomie': the devastating situation that arises when cultural norms shift too rapidly. Anomie occurs, he said, when a 'social type rests on principles so different from the preceding that it can develop only in proportion to the effacement of that preceding type'. The new economic principles, the division of labour perpetuated by the endlessly expansive, assimilative amoeba-state, fundamentally alter social relations.[11] It is easy enough to witness this erasure of non-work-related identity in post-industrial USA. What you do is who you are. One of the first questions that most new acquaintances ask in the USA is what do you do, where do you work? This appears to Americans as the most reliable way of knowing somebody. In many cultures, however, what you are, that is what you are in terms of inherited relations with others, is more important than what you do. Indeed, the extended names of Qataris, 'Muhammad bin Khalifa bin Ahmad bin...', for instance, reflect a long string of ancestors rather than the merely one in the case of Western names. The transfer of identity from what one is to what one does can create tremendous fissures in society. In fact, Durkheim, with typical French flair, identified this erasure of the traditional self with suicide. According to Durkheim, 'anomic suicide' both individually and culturally, the self-erasure of a culture's essential existence and the self-destruction of people who feel 'rootless', occurs not only when a society is devastated by economic depression but also during economic boom when the possibilities are limitless. Most Arab countries also experienced a particularly pernicious form of anomie: not only was modernization a threat to traditional values, it often seemed to originate from an outside, Western culture that was associated with a much more invasive form of colonization than that experienced by Qatar. Qatar was never really colonized, especially not in a way remotely similar to the colonization of states such as Algeria or the Congo.

This relative lack of anomie is new for the Arab world. The renowned scholar and Arabist G. E. von Grunebaum could remark in the 1960s that 'it is the near impossibility of painless accommodation to culture change which is causing much of the unrest that is today tormenting the world outside of the core countries of Western civilization.'[12] Fifty years later, modernization is no longer equated with Westernization. Indeed, technocratic, one-party rule in China has become an alternate model of development. The leaders of Qatar and other Gulf States can choose from an expanding buffet of choices when it comes to selecting their culture of modernization. Grunebaum would be criticized today for suggesting that 'the West' is the only relevant core style of modernization. Also, modernization, whether Western-style or Chinese or Indian, need not immediately break those traditional bonds that Durkheim felt so vital to the social psyche.

According to the classic Durkheim model, Qatar should have experienced the particularly pernicious whiplash of both forms of anomie, from depression in the 1940s to an endless economic boom, accelerated to a white-hot pace in the last decade. Yet the expected feeling of anomic rootlessness, while real in many circumstances, is deceptive in others. Just below the gleaming surface of commercialized modernity, the political, social and cultural realities of Qatar remain deeply rooted despite the seeming anomic whiplash of economic change. Even if some of the past has been or refashioned as sanitized, state-controlled 'heritage', the social structures, beliefs, and fundamental values and motivations of Qataris are still shaped by historical and social forces that have persisted and are often more profound than recent economic changes.

Durkheim's theories, so useful for the sociology of Western industrialization and modernization, simply do not apply as well to Qatar. This does not mean Durkheim's theory was fundamentally flawed. But rather, it means that Qatar cannot be explained by the same modernity-tradition paradigm used in the West. Reasons for this can already be grasped a few sentences later in Durkheim's work.

> In effect individuals are here grouped no longer according to lineage, but according to the particular nature of the social activity to which they concentrate themselves. Their natural milieu is no longer the natal milieu but the occupational milieu. It is no longer the real or fictitious consanguinity which marks the place of each one, but the function which he fills.[13]

In Qatar, despite enormous economic changes, individual Qataris are still grouped according to lineage, or a largely 'fictitious' if authentically felt consanguinity. Although the word 'tribe' has become problematic, a term often associated with categorizing, orientalizing tendencies in Western scholarship, the creation of and adherence to 'tribal' lineage is an internally recognized social form in Qatar. As the anthropologist Richard Tapper noted, 'Administrators – and many academics – still take a highly positivist view of tribes in the Middle East. They expect them to be mappable, bounded groups with little membership change, and they want an exact terminology for classificatory and comparative purposes.'[14] This desire to map out tribes into a manageable and unchanging human taxonomy is problematic and does not reflect the history of lineage and myths of lineage in Qatar. This simplistic approach must be avoided. Yet ignoring tribes is itself a form of politically correct, neo-orientalism: it means ignoring the major self-identified groupings of Qatar's society, whether imagined or not. The risk of over-categorizing is less than the risk of ignoring a major part of Qatari society. While certainly not experienced as a positivist category, one's *qabila*, one's extended 'tribe' or family, remains the fundamental determinant of an individual Qatari's social position and future. This remains true even if that ancestry is in some ways imagined, created or politically repositioned. As the historian and master at tribal negotiation Ibn Khaldun observed while living among the tribes of North Africa, 'When the things which result from (common) descent are there it is as if (common descent) itself were there ... In the course of time, the original descent is almost forgotten.'[15]

Viewing the world from the context of a nineteenth-century industrializing society, Durkheim assumed that economic changes always led to severe social disruptions of lineage. For Qataris, however, the necessity of work and the central focus of labour in life are important but not existentially pressing – thereby eliminating the need to distance one's self from lineage as the primary basis of social organization. Compared with industrializing Europe or America, wealth has come without the disruption of actual, industrialized 'work' and its many environmental and social ills. The division of labour is not a threat to the division of lineage in Qatari society since labour is not really an issue – most labour is taken care of by guests. Although in the 1950s and 1960s there were some Qataris who worked on the oil fields and even some protests against the excesses of Al-Thani, these protests quickly subsided and were never substantial enough truly to threaten the traditional nature of Qatari social and political relations. Oil is not a particularly laborious industry, nor did it require many Qataris themselves to do the work. In fact, the ruling Al-Thani learned early on about the risks of riot and resistance from the few Qataris who did engage in the oil industry in its first stages.[16] Resources, employment, the future itself, are all provided by the state, ruled by Al-Thani sheikh, or, more locally, by the tribe – contained and reinforced by the massive, wealthy, extended family compounds that dot the Qatari built landscape. Despite the expected anomie, almost the opposite has occurred. Tribes, lineage, consanguinity, whether imagined or not, remain remarkably strong in Qatar; they are still the primary ways individuals organize their lives.

It fact, it could be argued that the hold of tribal 'tradition', especially in relation to the marriage practices of women, traditional dress and expected social roles, is often *increased*, not decreased by wealth and the pursuit of acceptable social status within an extremely wealthy but still extremely lineage-based society. Similarly, the designation and proliferation of spaces and buildings and compounds for family groupings and tribes, impossible during times of poverty, create the new social and geographic forms in real estate. While before the 1960s Qatar's families lived in mud-brick homes, they can now live in family compounds with their own mosques, their own cohort of servants, their own self-sufficient systems. Instead of erasing the past, the distribution of wealth in Qatar to an elite citizen class can serve to magnify certain aspects of history and lineage. Only the expatriate labour, grateful for employment, largely single, male and tied to their culture in their home countries, need experience the anomie of the division of labour. Even in this instance, however, anomie is usually expressed in social consequences in the guest's home country (for example, a maid's own family left behind in the Philippines while she attends to a wealthy Qatari's child), not in Qatar. It seems at first glance that Qatar has bought itself out of the possible ill effects of modernity.

In 2009 there were more than 1.2 million males in Qatar compared with some 350,000 females. Most of these males are single, temporarily rootless expatriates from south Asia with no investment in the country or married men who have left their families at home.[17] Similarly, non-Qatari females are also predominantly single when in Qatar. Even Western expats and diplomats who are allowed to bring their families rarely stay longer than a year or two and they send their children to specially designated schools. Especially when compared with the expatriate population that surrounds them, Qataris are not 'rootless' but incredibly well rooted and seemingly oblivious to the significance of massive changes that have only begun to creep inside the family compound. Postmodernism and attempts to critique and reflect upon the limitations of the modernization process are rare.

A SHEIKHA'S POSTMODERNISM

Perhaps this seeming lack of change within the fundamental structure of Qatari lineage groups and the continuity of Qatar's political system is one explanation for a particularly intriguing and enigmatic statement I heard from one of Qatar's most respected educational leaders. Professor Sheikha Abdallah Al-Misnad is president of Qatar University, close to Mozah, the favourite wife of the Emir, and the woman most in tune with the sentiments and desires of Qatar's youth.[18] Granted an interview in 2008, I asked Sheikha Misnad what she thought was the most significant challenge for Qatar. Impeccably and conservatively attired, Sheikha Misnad did not seem to feel the need to display material signs of wealth in her dress. Her status was self-evident and clearly known not only within her own circle but among all Qataris. Contemplating her response, she looked into the distance at the bustling construction and development, at the endless cranes, the sea of glassy blue limitless on the horizon. After staring out of the window for what seemed a prolonged period, Sheikha Misnad mused that the biggest problem in Qatar is not water shortages, not rare political threats, not even education *per se*, as I had expected her to say. The biggest challenge to Qatar is 'the lack of postmodernism', the fact that 'Qatari youth, have no sense of postmodernism', no sense of angst or anomie in response to Qatar's red-hot development. Sheikha Misnad's concerns are striking. They seem to reveal the extent to which Qatar has 'developed' but not developed at the same time. External change, fuelled by petroleum rents, fuelled by the state and the Emir, had not led to those fundamental changes in mentality that are often associated with the excesses of modern consumption.

Yet even if there is no obvious anomie, some of the consequences of modernization still seem to seep through. Many visitors and reporters in the Gulf have commented, sometimes rather insensitively, about the sudden, severe problem of obesity and diabetes among wealthy citizens over the past decades, medical conditions that were almost completely non-existent before the oil boom.[19] These observers seem to feel that the diabetes, an inability of the body to absorb glucose because of lack of insulin, is analogous to a deeper intellectual and philosophical problem existing in the social fabric of Qatar: the inability to digest and process the meaning and possible negative consequences of modern change. The issue is not an inability to digest change but a persistence in not facing the negative consequences of change in a meaningful way. Instead of dealing with internal issues, there is sometimes a tendency to blame the 'phenomenon' of expatriate labour, even the dependence on expatriate labour for the ills of globalization, so that far from it being simply an economic issue, it has come to be a means of avoiding, delaying and deflecting the negative consequences of modernization.

EXPATRIATES AND ANOMIE

This creates a twist of logic. Even as the most poor and vulnerable expatriates are asked to absorb the anomie of change, they are also blamed for being a threat to authentic heritage and culture.[20] Officials of the Gulf Cooperation Council, the council of wealthy Gulf countries including Qatar, have said that 'expatriates' are a 'danger worse than the atomic bomb'.[21] Similarly, if slightly more diplomatically, Sheikh Hamad of Qatar has blamed expatriate labour for a host of ills in statements tailored to Qataris.[22] As he remarked in 2009 in one of his official addresses:

> [The] requirements of completing the building of the infrastructure and improving the
> public services, including education and health, led to a number of forms of exhaustion
> in our national economy represented by continued rising of the consumer price indexes,
> the increase of the cost of projects and the delay in their completion dates. A number of
> bottleneck areas have risen in the economy, caused by the big increase in expatriate labour.[23]

In this speech Sheikh Hamad equated the decline in Qatar's economy and fundamental structural problems with increases in expatriate labour. By this logic it is expatriates, not the decisions of the government who should be blamed. Although Sheikh Hamad may have been scoring political support from Qatari citizens by blaming outsiders for economic decisions and real estate policies that are determined by the government, expatriate labour does pose several fundamental, even existential problems for Qatar. Indeed, conflict with expatriate labour runs deep in Qatar's modern history. Although almost no Qatari would be expected to engage in manual labour today, in the 1950s most oil workers were Qataris. Several strikes pitted Qatari nationals against Dhofaris from Oman and Pakistanis who undercut their wages and appeared to be taking their jobs. Pointing to the 'problem' of expatriates has something of a civic history in Qatar.[24]

There is little internal criticism, however, of internal policies and structural imbalances that have caused the surge in expatriate labour. True, the 'price' of modernity in Qatar is the existence of an expatriate culture. However, this expatriate culture is kept subservient in terms of rights and access to Qatar's economy. Gulf citizens and their governments have failed to consider that they are themselves a source of the decisions that have led to the rise of expatriate culture, and with it the challenge of integrating that culture into Qatari society. There is little motivation for such introspection. The misplaced fear of expatriates is useful to the elite – it deflects attention from the failures of the government to bring its people honestly and willingly into the depths of modernism or, in macro-economic speak, the failure of the government to make its people 'marketable' in the global economy. This failure to make Qataris marketable is directly related to a system that denies active, internal participation in effective rule even as it promotes an agenda of freedom abroad. The aim of Qatar's new focus on creating world-class education for Qataris at Education City is not to create a larger ruling-class that is a source of criticism of the ruling Al-Thani family. Instead, education is viewed as a means of creating marketable, international skills; education is focussed on connecting Qatar to the outside world, not on the issues of governance and society within Qatar itself. Various attempts at 'Qatarization', or the enforcement of quotas for Qataris in expert positions, have only yielded limited results, and can be no more effective in the long term than attempts to fix pricing with an inflating currency. It is unclear, in fact, if it is even in the long-term interests of the Emir and his immediate family to develop a dependence on the labour of Qatari citizens, as opposed to a migrant labour class whose destiny is ultimately in the hands of the government as guests of the Sheikh.

TOO MANY EXPATRIATES?

Although this book will explain Qatar's history and the rise of Al-Thani before oil and the expatriate influx, the current state of Qatar's demography should always remain in the background. While it could be argued that the appropriate, singular focus for this book would be the extraordinary rise of Al-Thani elite and their co-opting of Qatar's tribal system, the broader history of Qataris who are not from this elite, and of non-Qataris who created much of Qatar's infrastructure in the last 50 years should not fade from view. The modern history of Qatar cannot be fully understood without understanding the history of expatriate labour in the country. As the most visible dilemma of growth in Qatar, the history of the expatriate community and its interaction with Qataris deserves to be dealt with at some length in this introduction.

The dilemma of expatriate labour is particularly extreme for Qatar. Although Qatar relied on imports of basic foodstuffs and supplies long before the discovery of oil, there was only one South Asian expat living in Qatar in the 1930s – a barber from Baluchistan.[25] Since the British claimed the right to intervene for colonial subjects, all other South Asians had been expelled. South Asians now make up the largest portion of Qatar's population. The 39 per cent of Qatar's population that were considered 'foreigners' in 1939 were mainly from Africa. Most of these African residents, originally slaves, became honorary members of tribes, adopting the names of their former owners. The only truly independent group of foreigners were 5,000 Persians involved in merchant activities. The Qatari population itself visibly dominated society with Qataris engaged in basic tasks at all levels of the economy. Both the Persians and the Africans were historic expatriate populations; Qataris had known about and traded with both groups for centuries. They assimilated fairly well into the dominant, Arab Qatari society and did not seem to pose any major cultural or identity crisis.

The Second World War and the 'years of hunger' caused by falling pearl prices led to a significant decrease in the number of expatriates and even an exodus of Qataris. Compared with Bahrain and its much more established labour tradition dating to 1932 when oil was discovered, the influx of expatriate labour only really began in Qatar in the late 1960s.[26] By the late 1970s, however, the numbers were rapidly increasing. Qatar had a severe housing shortage. Sheikh Khalifa's industrialization projects only compounded the demand for expats. A similar situation obtains today. Even Education City, established to train Qataris for high-end sectors of the global economy, has led to the need to import large numbers of professionals from the USA and Europe. The fact that 90 per cent of Qatar's food supply comes from overseas is symbolic of this general dependence on the outside, a dependence that has become an obsession of Qatar's political elite. According to the Emir, Hamad Al-Thani, 'We established the Qatar National Food Security Programme in 2008, which aims to reduce Qatar's reliance on food imports through the realization of the principle of self-sufficiency.'[27] Although functionally impossible even if Qatar could devote all of its desert territory to agriculture, the dream of self-sufficiency certainly appeals to the Qatari citizen elite, especially with the 'years of hunger' after the Second World War still in living memory. Recent investment in 'food security' is in the same vein as Qatarization, the attempts to increase the number of Qataris participating in the labour force.

Part of the challenge of labour in Qatar today is that there is little incentive in a distributive rentier economy, an economy where revenue comes from natural resources, not from taxes, for an individual Qatari to choose or be compelled to choose the full, frightening package of modernity with all of its anomic risks. This failure to address modernity head-on, as much structural and part of the cultural package of a highly rent-based economy, as it is conscious, has occasionally surfaced into something of a panic, only to subside again like a glacier sinking into glassy waters.[28] A recent scandal over the hiring of Saudi Arabian Muslim women as maids for Qatari households reveals the true nature of this anxiety. The fear of these protestors is not of expatriates; the fear is of some day being treated like them. The deep-seated fear of expatriate culture is merely a projection of the fear of facing a long-term anomic debt, a debt of the ills of modernism, a debt only compounded by a looming fear over the soundness of economic progress in a 'rentier' or natural resource exporting economy. If Saudi Arabians, Qatar's close relatives could be brought to these depths, why not, in some dreaded future, Qataris? The sheer outrage at the notion of Saudi maids even as reports of serious human rights abuses against Sri Lankan maids emerge without such protest by the local population is telling. The fact that Saudi maids are feared for their powers of traditional 'black magic', a power that non-Arab maids presumably do not have, is yet another indication of an externally projected anxiety.[29]

Despite rather disingenuous messages against expatriates and other attempts to distract the public from systemic failures, Gulf monarchies have begun to reassess the future. As Al-Thani seem to implicitly realize with their new educational initiatives and somewhat failed attempts at Qatarization of the labour force, the only real hope of a remedy to this deficit of globally competitive Qataris can come from the education and employment of Qatar's youth, not simply for the creation of more consumers of Western products. That said, the billions invested in educational initiatives such as the Qatar Foundation for Education headed by Sheikha Mozah, the Emir's wife, may not work unless critical thinking, not memorization, not even simply the acquisition of foreign language ability or sundry facts about the world, permeates and is nourished throughout all of Qatar – a change that will require much more than an investment in 'Western' educational institutions used by expats and the children of Al-Thani elite. Even as Education City expands, many non-elite Qataris continue to be educated at Qatar University with largely traditional methods.

While Durkheim correlated anomie with the destructive tendencies of modernization, there is a positive side to anomie: *internal* criticism of those negative aspects of the social status quo. With lack of postmodernism and lack of social anomie comes a lack of self-reflection, a lack of fundamental concern about the consequences of unbridled development. Although there are some exceptions, most Qatari youths, exposed and bombarded by the same endless plethora of ambiguous and confusing Western trends as American youth, remain remarkably, even disturbingly, composed in their identities. They do not feel that the external modernization and development of their country is somehow unnatural or outside 'God's plan'. In fact, many Qatari in my classes as a professor at Qatar University in 2007–8 said to me that they support the Emir because he allows for some development to occur faster than they, themselves, would think to allow or promote. This attitude, perhaps more than anything, is a sign that anomie has not taken hold in Qatar.

CHANGELESS CHANGE?

So much has changed in the infrastructure and physical, built environment of Qatar. So little has changed within the Qatari citizen's basic social milieu. It is not that no change has occurred within Qatari society but that these changes have not become significant enough to change Qatari society from its current system of governance and patronage. Perhaps the best predictor of fundamental change in Qatar, whether desirable or not, will not be when there is a huge change in oil prices or when there is some internal political disruption within the house of Al-Thani. The best indication of significant change may even be the creation of a Qatari intellectual tradition, an articulated opposition to the particular manifestations of 'modernity' in Qatari society. Fundamental political change in Qatar will probably only occur when the superficial effects of modernity, so striking to the visitor but still comparatively irrelevant to the deep-set cultural, social and political realities of the Qatari, finally leaks into the deep roots of a still prevalent neo-traditionalism, when a true sense of postmodernism arises among the youth, a postmodernism that uses modernity not only to advocate external change but a complete reformation of internal, social structures. To be real and effective this postmodernism must not be a postmodernism of blame, or of projection onto an expatriate other, but a postmodernism of introspection. Then, and perhaps only then, could a sturdy and coherent intellectual craft of critique set sail onto the teaming ocean of social or political change. That said, as the next section will discuss, Qatar's history and future is not merely the continuation of a deep-seated status quo: Qatar is still vulnerable to changes within the prevailing social paradigm even as Al-Thani elite has continued to concentrate power.

MODERN HISTORY OR HISTORY MODERNIZED?

This book began with an analysis of the ways Qatar and Qataris have reacted in unique ways to modernization. Rather than following the typical, course of angst and anomie normally associated with rapid modernization by Western theorists and sociologists, Qataris have instead maintained tradition or, at the very least, constructed neo-traditional notions of identity. Shielded from the most ravishing consequences of modernization by enormous wealth and by a dependence on a massive expatriate community, Qataris can maintain a bubble of culture and internalized authenticity. It is no mere fashion that leads all Qatari men to wear their traditional *thob* at all times in Qatar, moving through Western spaces and even influences while maintaining lineage and family as the primary determinant of destiny. The Emir and his government have perpetuated these neo-traditional myths of culture and authenticity, allowing the creation of a citizen aristocracy of Qataris even as they have slowly and steadily appropriated power from truly pre-modern, traditional elites, replacing the segmentary system of power by lineage with a centralized, unitary state where the continuity of Al-Thani is so entrenched as to appear inevitable.

Most books on the history Qatar are themselves products of the manufacturing of cultural tradition. A comprehensive study of the bibliography on Qatar will reveal several studies sponsored, if not outright financed and published by, the Qatari government and Ministry of Foreign Affairs.[30] These glossy publications and annual reports glide over social problems and political differences, presenting a society of serene contentment and wealth and a state that is a friend to all. Even Rosemarie Said Zahlan's well-researched and standard account, *The Creation of Qatar*,[31] although very useful in many respects and highly respected, praises Al-Thani somewhat uncritically and contains numerous prognostications for the unconditionally 'bright future' of Qatar. Other books on Qatar include guidebooks and even children's books. There are some exceptions to the lack of serious scholarship on Qatar such as Jill Crystal's informative work on merchants and sheikhs in Qatar and Kuwait,[32] but even these studies do not focus primarily on Qatar. The lack of scholarly work on Qatar seems stunning, especially considering Qatar's rising regional and global prominence, a prominence that, unlike Dubai's which has received much more attention, is not ephemeral but is based on truly deep reserves of natural resources and economic potential. Works in Arabic proliferate but focus almost exclusively on the pre-independence period. In the same way that the Qatar-based Al-Jazeera satellite station is allowed to report on other regimes but is limited in its ability to report too critically on Qatar itself, the writing of national history and the presentation of history to the world is almost completely monopolized by the state and the Emiri Diwan (executive council). Even images from the nineteenth century, such as the nineteenth-century paintings that line the walls of the new Museum of Islamic Art, images that would seem starkly orientalist to heroes of cultural criticism such as Edward Said, are embraced as archival portrayals of a legendary past.[33]

It is not simply with mountains of glossy publications that Qatar celebrates a sanitized and controlled heritage. As the national day of celebration on the day of the birth of Jassim clearly implies, the nation is Al-Thani and Al-Thani is the nation. Nationalism, a fundamentally 'modern' concept based on historic claims, is conflated with monarchy, a fundamental 'traditional' concept that is, in fact, the heart of innovation and power.

This is even more surprising when the history of Qatar reveals the truly contingent, chance nature of Al-Thani rise to power in the nineteenth century. In fact, the 'modernization' of Qatar in recent decades has meant less the abandonment of tradition than the creation of new claims to tradition and history. The Qatari experience of 'modernization' is, in many ways, distinct from the experience of modernization in much of the capitalist West which has experienced a much longer process of industrialization, state-sponsored education, specialization, division of labour and a focus on internal change.

According to Michel Foucault and Baudelaire, oft-cited theorists of Western modernity, the typical experience of modernity should, first of all, be characterized by a feeling of disruption and discontinuity:

[Modernity, for Foucault, is] a break with tradition, a feeling of novelty, of vertigo in the face of the passing moment. And this is indeed what Baudelaire seems to be saying when he defines modernity as 'the ephemeral, the fleeting, the contingent'. But, for him, being modern does not lie in recognizing and accepting this perpetual movement; on the contrary, it lies in adopting a certain attitude with respect to this movement; and this deliberate, difficult attitude consists in recapturing something eternal that is not beyond the present instant, nor behind it, but within it. Modernity is distinct from fashion, which does no more than call into question the course of time; modernity is the attitude that makes it possible to grasp the 'heroic' aspect of the present moment. Modernity is not a phenomenon of sensitivity to the fleeting present; it is the will to 'heroize' the present.[34]

It may seem extraordinary to claim that Qataris, citizens of one of the most economically advanced, technologically savvy and wealthy societies in the world have not experienced the modern in the Western sense perpetuated and defined by Foucault. Yet it is precisely this that this book claims. The 'heroic' in Qatar is associated not with the 'now', a now dominated and built by expatriate labour, but with what is 'behind it' – a past reconstructed and reconstituted into nationalized historical moments associated irrevocably with the right of Al-Thani to rule and the right of the Qatari citizen to enjoy all of the benefits of modern materialism at the service of reconstituted, neo-traditional identities. Even as culture, heritage and tradition are highly praised and tribal lineage becomes the basis of symbolic forms of representation, they are at the same time being slowly eroded and disempowered, slowly changing the largely independent tribal emirs into citizens, and citizens into dependent subjects. Although there have been instances of serious protest against the unitary state, such as the famous protests of Abdallah Al-Misnad in 1963 against the decline of powers of the tribal chiefs, Qataris have largely acquiesced to this diminution of their traditional political powers as the state allowed them to retain control over their own internal affairs. In some, but not all respects the story of modernization in Qatar is reflected by wider trends in the Islamic world.

In his study of Islamic modernism, Leonard Binder suggested Islam itself was a way of shielding against the consequences of modernism. According to Binder, this wrestling with the cultural price of modernity through the adoption of Islamic alternatives is a phenomenon characteristic of the Middle East and north Africa:

From the time of the Napoleonic invasion, from the time of the massacre of the Janissaries, from the time of the Sepoy mutiny, at least, the West has been trying to tell Islam what must be the price of progress in the coin of the tradition which is to be surrendered. And from those times, despite the increasing numbers of responsive Muslims, there remains a substantial number that steadfastly argue that it is possible without paying such a heavy cultural price. There are two important issues here, and not one. The first is whether Islam poses a substantial obstacle to modernization and development, and the second is whether Islam proposes a radically different and possibly much better social order than that which is adumbrated in the Western theory of development. The first issue assumes that Islam may be the barrier to development, while the second assumes that the West may be the barrier to development in the Islamic world. The first question identifies Islam and tradition, generically, while the second denies that Westernization is the only form of modernization.[35]

In a theoretical sense, Leonard Binder's observation applies to Qatar, to Qataris and indeed to Muslims of any nationality in Qatar at any level of society. What matters for the particular history of Qatar, however, is not that the conundrum and problem of modernity and tradition exists, but how it is projected, how its fundamental challenges are either met or not met. Binder's generalization does not fully describe the particular experience of Qatar. It is not simply Islam itself but a distinct, newly nationalized notion of Qatari history, citizenship and obligations of lineage that is maintained, even strengthened in some ways, in the face of modernity.

A FUTURE OF CRITICAL REFLECTION?

Although Qataris are fabulously wealthy, this delaying of the 'vertigo' of modernity has not come without a price. It is not expected that Qataris will need to pay the debts of change any time soon and that the tide of comfortable neo-traditionalism will continue to rise. Yet it will inevitably crest – whether instigated by a revolution in petroleum demand or a fundamental rupture in Qatari society caused by the over-centralization of Emiri power, or even by an imponderable external force (of these possibilities there are always many in the Gulf). Qataris will someday come out of hiding and be seen not merely in boardrooms and the play palaces of the world but in the deep, horrid and heroic avenues of the 'now'. It is at that point that Qataris will begin to consider their own history critically, to write not according to the agenda of nation and Emir but the agenda of self-realization.

The lack of a fully experienced modernity amongst Qataris also means the lack of critical history, or at least the lack of the critical, allegedly 'objectively detached' modern form of history that has come to dominate the study of history in the West. The current lack of available written histories on Qatar is not a result of the irrelevance of history to Qatar – quite the opposite. The lack of recent, critical histories on Qatar by Qataris is due to sensitivity about history as a critical enquiry and a challenge to a prosperous status quo. In a society whose comfortable, traditional assumptions are perpetuated and shielded by billions in wealth and hundreds of thousands of expatriate servants, history in its modern sense as a synthesized narrative pursued by professionally trained historians using source-based scholarship, could seem only likely to cause disruption. Whereas the many histories based on local claims to Qatari identity within Qatari society can abide together underneath a very lightly constructed non-confrontational official history that explicitly supports the Emir.

When Qataris begin writing a critical, modern history, not an 'official' history but a history that opens the inner doors of Qatari society, it will put anything that I have written in this book as a guest and observer of Qatar in a different light. As the philosopher Heidegger claimed in *Metaphysics*,

> Only as a questioning, historical, being does man come to himself; only as such is he a self. Man's selfhood means this: he must transform the being that discloses itself to him into history and bring himself to stand in it.[36]

The critical examination of history and neo-traditional assumptions could finally mean the birth of the modern and postmodern Qatari self. We will now introduce some of the central historical myths of Qatari origins and how these myths support current power and social structures in Qatar in ways that obscure history.

AL-THANI NARRATIVE OF HISTORIC POWER

Al-Thani dynasty was founded after the dynasties of the Emirates, Kuwait and Bahrain.[37] Until the discovery of oil Al-Thani only really controlled the area around Doha (or Bidaa), a city of about 12,000 inhabitants in the pre-oil period. Bahrain claimed Zubara and other prominent tribes, Al-Naim and Al bin Ali, claimed much of the land to the north and Wakra, the only other significant urban settlement. It could be said that the current power of Al-Thani family and especially the Emir, Hamad bin Khalifa Al-Thani, has no fundamental historical precedent outside of British interference. As such, the history of Qatar became highly symbolic and significant as a means of constructing such a precedent. Contextual documents of the British and Ottoman powers, both of which were interested in legitimizing Al-Thani rule and ignoring or sidelining the rival claims of other tribes, largely support a narrative of complete co-dependence of the rise of Qatar and the rise of Al-Thani. As Zahlan observed, 'the rise of one [Al-Thani] has heralded the independence of the other [Qatar]'.[38] Nevertheless, this narrative of co-dependence, something of a royalist historical narrative, ignores the more complicated history of Qatar and Qataris. As the scholar J.E. Peterson aptly observed:

> Until comparatively recently, states in Arabia were minimalist, whether considered in terms of structure, functions, or their relationships with their citizens. In rural areas, the tribe was central to the individual's existence: in many ways, it formed something of a self-contained entity, politically, economically and certainly socially. Allegiance to a larger state structure was ephemeral, produced either by force or transitory self-interest.[39]

What is remarkable and unexpected about Qatar and Al-Thani, however, is that despite both internal and external threats and challenges to their power, Al-Thani and Qatar have remained independent even as other Arabian states, 'Asir, Jabal Shammar, Jawfa and the independent emirates of Dubai, Sharjah and Abu Dhabi that now make up the United Arab Emirates (UAE), for example, were absorbed into larger, state and federal political structures. Qatar's current independence is even more suprising since it was Qatar that proposed to create a greater federation of Arab Emirates under a ruling council after Britian's decision to withdraw from the Gulf in 1968. Instead of welcoming the withdrawal of the British, the Qataris, like the other emirates, feared the domination of neighboring powers. Almost immediately after Qatar called for the creation of the federation and after Sheikh Khalifa Al-Thani, then heir apparent, had been elected the federation's prime minister, Al-Thani grew restless. The parties from Bahrain, the Emirates and Qatar could not agree on the specifics of a federal Constitution. Qatar campaigned for Doha as the capital of the federation but was rejected. It could be said that it was an innate exceptionalism and defense of Qatar's interests that may have so dramatically reversed its enthusiasm to form a federation.[40] Indeed, the exceptionalism of Qatar, in hindsight, could be seen either as a stroke of luck or as a confirmation of the royalist narrative. Even as Qatar's independence and sovereignty was a product of circumstance and the collapse of negotiations that were lead and instigated by Al-Thani themselves, Qatar's somewhat accidental independence is now fully embraced and celebrated as Qatar has developed the economic clout and diplomatic prestige to feel confident on its own. In this narrative it is Al-Thani in particular who have assured the independence and success of Qatar. Another narrative, a narrative that I will emphasize despite the difficulties of finding sources on Qatari, not just Al-Thani history, is that the history of Qatar is also the result of a compromise of power, a constant internal conversation, both subtle and sometimes not so subtle, between Qatari international powers and the royal family.

As modernization and state power has increased, however, this non-Al-Thani history has been steadily sidelined by the creation of a dynastic, Al-Thani centric, narrative. This does not mean, however, that Al-Thani are nearly as vulnerable as they were in the past. In fact, this book argues that Al-Thani have perhaps never been in a more favourable position not only to rewrite the narrative of Qatar's creation but to stay in power in the long term. The only real risk is not that power will diffuse but that power itself becomes too concentrated, too top heavy in the hands of the Emir and his immediate relations. That possibility will be the focus of a later section of the book. For now, the historical reasons for the success of Al-Thani will be outlined.

Dynasties transmit knowledge and experience through family and tribal ties. Modernizing monarchies such as Qatar have some advantages over developing democracies – they are able not only to make long-term decisions but can utilize continuity and historic legitimacy to avoid risk and take rapid advantage of opportunities. It is for this reason most of the same dynasties and tribes that were in power in the Gulf in the nineteenth-century pearl boom and bust – the so-called 'years of hunger' were a result of an over-dependence on pearls – are still in power today for oil boom and possible bust. The survival and prosperity of the small monarchies of the Gulf is not some historical accident, but the result of long historical trends with deep foundations. Most importantly, it is the result of the active, astute, diplomatic approach of the Gulf States towards their neighbours and towards superpowers that balanced one interested party against another. Throughout modern history, Gulf tribes have valued pragmatic independence more than ideology, adopting, for example, a form of 'Wahhabism-lite' more flexible than that found in Saudi Arabia and, since the increase in American dominance in the Gulf, a democracy-lite form that respects tribal traditions and boundaries. Modern commentators are often flummoxed by the blatant contradictions in the foreign policies of the Gulf States: allowing US Central Command to have its base there, while funding the wildly successful and critical Al-Jazeera channel and anti-war conferences. But these contradictions are nothing new to the Gulf or to a country like Qatar where the Ottomans, the British and Saudi Arabia and Iran all contended for influence over the Qatari Peninsula, a peninsula that juts into the shallow waters of the Gulf like a tipping point, the position of strategic balance. Not committing completely to any ideology or power is what the Gulf States are good at, it is what has made Qatar able to pack a punch far beyond its weight.

For the casual visitor or even foreign resident of the Gulf, history seems so easy to ignore. With modern, Western amenities everywhere it may seem, in fact, that the Gulf has no history, or that most of its history has been erased or reinvented by modern development. While Western visitors are used to seeing history in structures and written documents, the Arab residents and citizens of Qatar and the Gulf view their identity through the lens of deep and abiding oral traditions, traditions that have continued to be celebrated in highly advanced technological media, with poetry contests one of the most popular shows on regional television.

Despite Arab citizens' deeply felt appreciation of the richness of their own history and identity, local history seems really irrelevant to the vast majority of non-Gulf residents or expatriates who live in the region and help run most of the Gulf economy. When 80 per cent of the population has arrived after 1980, what use is history to explain social and economic trends? When massive companies and projects are managed, bought and sold by expatriates, who is really in control of a country's assets? What is clear, however, is that the ruling Gulf tribes and their allies still call most of the shots. This is certainly the case in Qatar. A laissez-faire tolerance of economic success reigns, but for local issues often the buck still stops at the tribal *majlis* (traditional semi-democratic councils) and the Diwan of the Emir where almost no Westerner, no matter how connected to global finance, may enter. Inflation may increase beyond 14 per cent, new risks may emerge from Iran or Iraq, and some spending projects may be less successful than others, there may even be some palace coups carefully managed within the ruling tribe, but these weaknesses will not fundamentally alter the historically rooted political and social system of Qatar and the Qataris. Although the individual fate of rulers may be subject to sporadic coup attempts and threats, the basic institutions of the monarchy remain strong. Al-Thani and their closest allies have seen the rise and fall of the British, the Saudis, the Omani and the Ottoman empires.

THE APPEARANCE OF CHANGE

While the emphasis of this book is on social, cultural and historical continuities, the importance of change, especially the dramatic changes of recent decades, will by no means be ignored. Qatar has rapidly changed from a small, highly traditional, tribal society, a society languishing from the collapse of pearl prices in the 1930s and 1940s, into a vibrant, modern nation with a current per capita income higher than Luxembourg.[41] The most stunning changes in Qatar have occurred only in the past decade. It is impossible to drive along the Doha Corniche, a lushly landscaped crescent of land reclaimed from the Gulf, without seeing yet another massive high-rise growing effortlessly on once barren ground. This study will document the transition from the traditional to the modern in Qatar not simply by describing changes in the skyline or in economic growth or numbers, but by describing the less rapid but still profound changes in the mainly tribal arrangements that underlie the outwardly hyper-modern façade that most see when they visit Qatar.

The continuing importance of tribal alliances, the continued internal autonomy of Qatari tribes, and the fascinating, mutually constraining influence they have on the power of the Emir is evidenced most explicitly in the way Doha was first settled strictly according to tribal affiliation. The Khalifa tribe lives in the Madinat al Khalifa 1 and 2, the Hajri in a Hajri village, the Sulati in the Sulati area. Montigny-Kozlowska described these tribal divisions in her foundational anthropological studies of Qatar.[42] In each tribal village within the city, no matter how small, there is a mosque and a *majlis*. *Majlis* is a term meaning both a council and the place a council meets: the local meeting-room where qualified men of the tribe decide on internal matters and the relationship between the tribe and others.

The apparent lack of expressed popular desire for democratic governance in modernized tribal societies in the Middle East like Qatar has often been an enigma for political scientists and non-governmental organizations working in the region. There have been many recent, centralized initiatives to increase democratic participation through the establishment of a Permanent Elections Committee and the formalization of municipal elections. Yet even these reforms may be less a distribution of power than they initially seem: it is possible that this is partially a way of introducing formalized government control over tribal municipalities.[43] There could be no greater contrast than that existing between the *majlis* system with its mix of quiet negotiation and consultation, and what many Qataris imagine as the seemingly bombastic rhetoric found in the parliaments and Congresses of Western democracies.[44] The old alliances and bloodlines of the desert and the fishing (*dhow*), the quid pro quo and the balance of power between the tribes those alliances created, were not destroyed by the sudden replacement of mud huts with concrete and of camels with ubiquitous Toyota Land Cruisers. Mere settlement, even if it is very luxurious settlement indeed, does not instantly a Westernized, modernized, institutionalized society create. *Wasta*, a type of reference system based mainly on one's family and tribal connections, is still as important in eventually landing the coveted position of *mudir*, or director in a company or government office, as education or skills. Although a complete social history of Qatari tribes would be very difficult to create given the secretive way some tribes hold their archives and their information, information that could have serious political consequences, this book provides a survey of the most important issues facing the interaction between traditional and modern trends in Qatari society. One of the main ways Al-Thani have been able to maintain and extended their power in the midst of the limits of this internal tribal system has been to look outward, to develop relationships beyond Qatar through a deft understanding of foreign policy.

A POLICY OF STRATEGIC TOLERANCE
AND MEDIATION

Contrary to popular belief and to the way most histories of the Gulf have been written, the history of Qatar is not simply the story of oil but how oil wealth is used to project influence internally and externally. Oil and natural gas dominate the Qatari economy, and Qataris and especially Qatar's royal family have made particular decisions about what to do with their abundant natural wealth. In many ways, contemporary Qatar could be described as an oil rentier state. There are no real taxes of any kind. The ruler Sheikh Hamad bin Khalifa Al-Thani does not need to depend on the citizens of Qatar for revenue because he has a personal income in the billions, even if Al-Thani do depend on the citizen elite and a shared sense of history for legitimacy. Yet unlike typical rentier states where the ruler uses oil wealth merely to placate and control, Qatar's rulers have instead used oil wealth to encourage, push and prod traditional Qatar's tribes towards globalization and the adaptation of mainly Western institutions. Unlike Saudi Arabia, where reformists in the ruling family are constrained by their alliance with the Wahhabi *ulama*, the rulers of Qatar have been able to experiment with a plethora of open and challenging educational, media and diplomatic initiatives. These include the creation of Education City by the wife of the Emir Sheikha Mozah and attempts to reform Qatar University, sponsorship of the ultra-popular Al-Jazeera network, the funding of the first, massive Catholic church in Doha, and building the Aspire sports village which was intended to train the country's most skilled athletes to compete for Qatar in the 2006 Asian Games and to position Qatar for the 2016 Olympic bid. Qatar's most stunning, recent success was its selection as the host of the 2022 FIFA World Cup. Yet such success often comes at a cost, especially when it is so unexpected by one's competitors. Despite the challenges of 120 °F heat and issues of adequately accomodating fans from around the world, Qatar made a successful case that its wealth and infrastructure plans, including a fully air-conditioned stadium, would offset the disadvantages of hosting a World Cup in the Arabian desert. There have been recent charges of bribery and suggestions that Qatar may have used its significant wealth to influence the decision of FIFA, the World Cup governing board. *The Sunday Times of London* published an exposé and Germany has formally called for investigations despite Qatar's repeated denials of undue influence.[45] Qatar recently cancelled air conditioning plans for the Cup and may move it to the winter. Nevertheless, Qatar's selection as host was a significant coup. Not only will this be the first major, worldwide sporting event for Qatar, it would be the first World Cup hosted in the Arab world. This places Qatar in a position of prominence, especially in the popular Arab imagination. Football is a popular obsession for many in the Arab world and North Africa. Seeing the game take place in Qatar will solidify the feeling that Doha is becoming the center not only of news and diplomacy but also of a wider Arabic-speaking world community. It was certainly a success for Sheikh Mohammed bin Hamad bin Khalifa Al-Thani, son of the Emir, and chair of the Qatar bid committee.

Although there are some setbacks such as the controversy over the 2022 World Cup bid, Qatar is perhaps most astute in diplomacy. When the USA needed a base for its Iraq operations after leaving Saudi Arabia, Saudi Arabia considered itself the holy ground of the two holy mosques. Having American troops on Saudi soil thus angered many Saudis.

However, America still needed a base on the Arabian Peninsula. Qatar provided a way out of the predicament. Sheikh Hamad authorized Qatari land for the enormous Al-Udeid air-force base, headquarters of Central Command (CENTCOM), about 20 miles outside Doha. Its 15,000 ft airstrip is the longest in the region.[46] At the same time, however, Qatar often vehemently opposed sanctions against Iran during its temporary tenure at the UN Security Council. Unlike its neighbours, Qatar allowed for the establishment of an Israeli commercial interest section even as it was a major donor to Lebanese families whose homes were bombed during the Israeli–Lebanese war. Although the interest section was shut down in 2009, these historic overtures to Israel were unique in the region.[47] More recently, Qatari jets have participated in NATO and Arab League bombings against Colonel Muammar Qaddafi in Libya. Qatar has supported anti-Qaddafi rebels perhaps more vigorously than any Arab state and has marketed rebel-supplied oil.[48]

Since the establishment of Al-Jazeera in 1995, the same year as Sheikh Hamad bin Khalifa's succession, Qatar has become a theatre and a stage for the airing of suppressed opinions, the place where the debates and discussions that are outlawed and punished in other Arab and Islamic countries are allowed and often even encouraged. Some American diplomats have criticized Al-Jazeera for its journalistic bias as strongly as they criticize media in dictatorial regimes in the Arab League, especially Saudi Arabia. In fact, as the scholar Ahmed Saif notes, the director of Al-Jazeera and many of its key staff are affiliated with the Muslim Brotherhood, causing some to speculate that 'Al-Jazeera provides an open and accessible platform for the Muslim Brotherhood'.[49] Despite the potential bias of its directors, a bias that may increase its popular appeal among the large number of viewers sympathetic to the Muslim Brotherhood and its opposition to authoritarian regimes and neo-imperialism, Al-Jazeera need not be concerned with profits. Unlike commercial broadcasting organizations such as CNN that rely on private financing and advertising revenue, Al-Jazeera is essentially financed by the state through Qatar Gas, a state-controlled company. Yet Al-Jazeera is just the exposed tip of an iceberg of controversy.

Qatar is host to exiles and renegades from almost all corners of the Arab and Islamic religious and political spectrum. While Sheikh Yusuf al Qaradawi, possibly the most popular and televised Muslim religious scholar, is denied entry into Great Britain, and while Saad Eddin Ibrahim was tortured and imprisoned in Egypt for his highly reformist ideas about democracy, they both flourish in Doha, supported at least indirectly by Qatari government funds. Although the current cacophony of cultural, religious and political views in Qatar may seem incoherent, there is a deliberate method behind this approach to ideas and change. While no news is good news for most countries, almost any news is good news for Qatar as long as the context in which that news is presented points to the outsized influence of Qatar. If the Emir wished, he could instantly close down or closely monitor and manipulate this free forum of ideas with the praise and support of his fellow Arab leaders and even members of the Qatari public who still hold highly conservative views. Yet, with a few revealing exceptions that will be discussed in this book, he does not. What the Emir and his wife, Sheikha Mozah, seem to have grasped is that ideas, creativity and intellectual innovation are the greatest untapped resources in the modern Middle East. This positioning of Qatar as a forum for independent thought in the Middle East, and not simply for material profit as in the Dubai model, is not, of course, simply a selfless act done out of spontaneous benevolence and an idealistic belief in freedom of speech. There is perhaps no better way to subtly tune the ideas that will determine the future of the Arab and Islamic world than to own the stage upon which those ideas are expressed. In this sense and in many others, Qatar, with a population that has just surpassed 1.7 million, and with only about 20 per cent native Qatari, has a voice regionally and internationally much larger than its size. Curiously, the Emir himself has often assumed a rather modest or stand-offish role, preferring not to be personally identified with some projects and aspects of this multifarious national image. The reasons for this are clear. The Emir would rather use his inaccessibility as an asset, providing a buffer between himself and the controversies that inevitability arise.

Despite the motivations and reasons for its success it is clear that Qatar seems heavily tilted towards the present and the future. For many first-time visitors, Qatar seems to be something of a blank slate, a place free of history, a place of possibilities and projects and ideas. On the other, less public, less glitzy and much less understood side, however, Qatar is deeply coloured and textured by its history. The purpose of this book will be to tell the story of both sides of Qatar: the country that seems at the forefront of the most sophisticated changes and developments in the Middle East and the country that is proudly rooted in its tribal past and traditions.

QATAR TODAY

Before supporting the above hypotheses and examining Qatar's past in detail, I will outline some of the complex, extraordinary and diverse characteristics of Qatari society and politics today. By examining Qatar's current state, the historical roots of Qatar's recent successes and challenges can be more easily examined.

First, Qatar is ruled by Al-Thani family. As this book will show, this was not always the case. Bahrain and other powerful neighbours often dominated Qatar before the middle of the nineteenth century. Sheikh Hamad bin Khalifa Al-Thani is currently the head of the family and officially he holds absolute authority. Although there have been recent attempts to establish a law of succession, traditionally succession has not automatically fallen to the eldest or chosen son. Succession and internal family disputes are perhaps the most important checks on the power of the ruler. Another interesting socio-economic check on the power of the rulers is the wealth and influence of merchants such as Al-Darwish, Al-Mannai and Al-Fardan who are not related to the royal family. Al-Darwish and Al-Fardan are Persian in origin.[50]

Despite these checks, Qatar's ruler, Sheikh Hamad, has adopted an independent style of rule and has attempted to raise Qatar's, and Al-Thani's, presence on the international stage. When he came to power in 1995 he was considered the first of a new generation of Sheikhs and rulers in the Gulf. Considered something of a 'Young Turk', Sheikh Hamad has sought an independent and self-sufficient role for Qatar through a flexible foreign policy that has reached out to a wide range of political interests in the region. Realizing the ineffectiveness of the GCC and seeking to relieve Qatar from the suffocating dominance of Saudi Arabia, he has set his own course, often to the consternation of his neighbours.

Second, according to the Qatar Statistics Authority, around seven out of eight workers were non-Qatari in 2007.[51] Most labourers are men in their twenties and thirties from South Asia.[52] The number of women brought to Qatar as expatriate workers is much lower, leading to a potentially volatile, young male population of workers. The issue of expatriate labour seems particularly acute in Qatar where there are even fewer Qataris ready to engage in non-managerial tasks than in other Gulf countries.

Third, most Qataris are Sunni Wahhabis. There is a minority Shi'i population mainly from Bahrain and Iran. Unlike Saudi Arabia where a Shi'a minority has regularly been oppressed, or Bahrain where a Sunni king rules over a Shi'a majority, there is not the same level of overt sectarian hostility between Shi'a and Sunni in Qatar.

Also, oil and gas dominate exports. The redistribution of oil and gas revenues have made Qataris among the richest people in the world. Unlike neighbouring Gulf States such as Bahrain (where unemployment may be as high as 15 per cent) and Saudi Arabia where oil wealth is no longer able to guarantee employment and opportunities for a new booming, young generation, Qatar's resources are so vast and its population so relatively small that it will not face the same creeping problems of its neighbours as quickly. The Gulf specialist Gary Sick outlined seven looming, and potentially existential, problems for Gulf States, almost all associated with oil revenue: budgetary uncertainties, dominance of the public sector, dominance of foreign labour, unemployment, inadequate revenues, absence of popular participation and lack of accountability.[53] It could be argued that Qatar, although facing almost all of these problems in some form or another, is best poised to deal with them. Budgetary uncertainties, lack of revenue and unemployment are not really issues in a country where budgets are calculated well below expected oil and gas prices and where trillions of gallons of gas lie offshore. If Qatar's total population increases at its current rate, revenue may conceivably become a problem, but only decades down the line. Foreign workers do dominate almost every aspect of Qatar's economy.

Nevertheless, Qatar's projected gas revenues are great enough to support such a large expatriate class. Education of Qatari nationals has increased dramatically and huge investments in education may prevent the worst consequences of competition from foreign labour. Finally, accountability and lack of political participation do not seem to be particularly problematic: although there have been some reports of protests and dissatisfaction with the system, the Emir is, it seems, resoundingly popular. A reliance on natural gas and petroleum revenue certainly creates challenges for Qatar but these challenges are not as acute as they are for Qatar's Gulf neighbours. There are a string of reports, including those published by Qatar's own Central Bank, indicating that oil plays an 'excessive role' in Qatar's economy. Even so, these vast petroleum exports have allowed Qatar to begin to surpass Kuwait as the third largest Gulf economy after Saudi Arabia and the UAE.[54]

Another issue is citizenship. Although the Qatari national population is relatively homogenous, Qatari national identity is not necessarily fully established. With so much wealth at stake, citizenship, nationality and national identity are contentious issues. Nevertheless, Qatari society is not so divided as other Gulf States such as Bahrain where a majority are Shi'a while the ruler is Sunni. With only insignificant exceptions the vast majority of Qataris are Sunni Wahhabi Muslim Arabs. This reduces the possibility of open opposition based on religious or ethnically organized opposition. Qatar has been spared the street protests that occur regularly in the streets of Manama, Bahrain.

In foreign policy Qatar faces challenges and successes. Qatar has a complicated relationship with the West and modernity, even if Qatar may wish it to appear otherwise. Officially, Qatar is a major supporter of the USA and even Great Britain, its former colonial protector. Although Arabic is still spoken between Qataris and Arab immigrants, English is the de facto language of business and development. The population and the media (Al-Jazeera) are much less supportive of the governments of the Anglo-Saxon West. Regardless, most Qataris, especially young Qataris, have embraced Western culture and consumerism full throttle. Without any developed or matured sense of postmodernism, environmentalism and other sophisticated antidotes to resist the excesses of the West, Islamic tradition is often the major outlet for the expression of angst at the ill effects of Western consumerism, hyper-development and the sense that new is always better. Although the government flatly denies having a terrorist problem, concluding that the bombing of an English theatre group in 2005 was the work of a madman, certain crucial members of the government have sympathies for Islamic fundamentalism. Unverified revelations by former CIA officers Robert Baer and Melissa Boyle Mahle suggest that high-ranking members of the Qatari government and members of the royal family sheltered key Al-Qaeda operatives including Khalid Sheikh Muhammad, mastermind of the 11 September 2001 attacks on the World Trade Center towers.[55] Although it is impossible to know the full veracity of these reports or the motivations behind the claims, they reveal a certain perception among some observers of potentially deep fissures in Qatar within Al-Thani family, fissures that are difficult, if not impossible to see from the outside. In fact, it is true that a large number of established members of the royal family in government positions have had rocky relationships with the Emir in the past. It may be these differences within the royal family and the government – a government which is in many respects the avenue through which members of the family co-opted – over the relationship between Qatar and the West that represent the most immediate threat to the position of the Emir today and the office of the Emir in the future. Aware that most of his predecessors came to power though coups within the family, some of the sheikhs, members of Al-Thani family, might similarly use a coup to dramatically change Qatar's current, generally pro-Western stance. Such a coup would be much easier if a much more conservative member of the Saudi royal family such as Crown Prince Nayef bin Abdalaziz were to come to power in Riyadh.

Yet the questions and concerns of Qataris are far deeper than the way their reaction to Western-style development may influence policy. Terrorism and fundamentalism are simply the most reported phenomena in the West, but certainly not the most prevalent or intractable issues inside Qatar. Qataris, like Muslims the world over, are encountering what scholar Ali al Allawi calls a spiritual decline, a decline that is 'throwing off their moral equilibrium and clouding their visions of a potentially bright, peaceful tomorrow'.[56]

With its small population, however, Qatar has avoided many of these clouds. Its small population has several advantages. Qataris may not know each other as well as in the 1960s, when it was unnecessary to use passports because airport employees literally knew everybody in the country. It is still common, however, for Qataris to have a strong sense of overarching solidarity. This is especially true when faced with external threats. Qatari society is still largely organized around tribal lineage. Although somewhat less powerful than just a few decades ago, tribes have not disappeared with modern development. They have adapted to modern living. Although slightly less politically important than in the past, the tribal *majlis* is at the centre of social life. Most decisions at the local and even national level are made through the traditional tribal method of discussion and consensus (*shura* in Arabic). Although formal institutions exist and continue to strengthen, mastery of hidden informal networks and *wasta*, often but not always based on tribal lineage, is the currency of success. Also, Qataris are much more flexible in certain family and social norms than neighbouring Saudi Arabia.

Especially when compared with the situation of women in neighbouring Saudi Arabia, women in Qatar have a free and prominent role in society. The most prominent symbol of this is the stature of Sheikha Mozah bint Nasser Al-Misnad, the most public of Sheikh Hamad's wives, whose fame may surpass that of her husband the Emir in some international circles. In many ways it could be said that Sheikha Mozah and Sheikh Hamad act as a dual monarchy – although never overtly questioning the power of the Emir, Sheikha

Mozah has been given a large degree of latitude to implement her own vision of cultural and educational development through the massively endowed Qatar Foundation. Sheikh Hamad can support initiatives such as press freedom through Mozah while distancing himself somewhat from the risks associated with such ventures. Although Mozah is the most outstanding exemplar of the modern Qatari woman, women are prominent at almost all levels of Qatari government and society except the oil and financial sectors. Qatari women are increasingly better educated and trained than their male compatriots.

Using its many advantages, Qatar follows a diplomacy of stealth and wealth and networks. The rulers of Qatar have positioned the country as an impartial broker for various conflicts in the Middle East and the world. Its hefty investment authority and the carrots it can offer, along with the subtle negotiation powers of the Foreign Minister, make Qatar unusually successful. The Qatari elite has created an open environment for debate, social freedom, creativity and religious tolerance as long as those debates are about topics not directly related to Qatar or the decisions of the elite. Many of these initiatives, however, have been challenged by traditional elements in Qatari society, and few of the forums directly address the challenges of Qatari society itself. A society seemingly oriented to diplomacy, Qataris seem to present a unified front to the rest of the world. Yet, although they are sometimes difficult to detect, internal divisions and important differences with Emiri policy do exist under the surface.

Finally, Qatar has exploited potential geographical liabilities and turned them into advantages. Though Qatar sits between Wahhabi Saudi Arabia and Shi'a Iran, it has avoided both assimilation with Saudi Arabia and the possibility of overt threats to its offshore gas and oil supplies from Iran. Border tensions with Saudi Arabia, although there have been flare-ups as recently as the 1992 incident at the border town of Al-Khafus, have largely ceased. The prospects of invasion or disruption from Iran also remain remote with US airpower guaranteeing the destruction of any naval effort. This does not mean that Qataris are naive. A secret cable released by Wikileaks on 28 November 2010 described a meeting between Prime Minister Hamad bin Jassim and the American Deputy Secretary of Energy. The Prime Minister said, 'We might have our own Katrina' when describing the threat from Iran,[57] He described the relationship between Iran and Qatar for his American audience as, 'they lie to us, and we lie to them'.[58] Nevertheless, Qatar is generally seen as an island of stability amid the continuing conflicts of the Middle East, something which, as a possible partner for all major powers, it has exploited.

MAIN ARGUMENTS

In summary, there are three overarching theses in this book; theses that attempt to explain the extraordinary strength and persistence of the Qatari political and social system as well as its potential fault lines.

First, Al-Thani ruling family, especially the inner core close to the Emir and the favoured wife Sheikha Mozah, has used historical myths and heritage to maintain their rule. As the American anthropologist Dale Eickelman observed, Gulf societies have a 'past in search of a public'.[59] An historical unwritten contract exists between Qataris and the ruling family. Although there is always the possibility of a coup, it is unlikely that Al-Thani will lose their grip on power as long as they maintain this unwritten contract with other Qatari tribes and prevent any organized dissent from the non-native population. Nevertheless, tribal affiliation and solidarity is slowly being replaced by national solidarity even as the Emir continues to actively favour his closest family relatives. It used to be the case that an Emir was simply the leader of a major tribe that ruled over an independent territory. There were once many Emirs in Qatar, not simply Al-Thani Emir, as well as many sheikhs, not simply the members of Al-Thani family. Al-Thani have actively bureaucratized traditional tribal leadership roles, putting local leaders and representatives on the government payroll and quieting dissent over the distribution of resources through a slow reformation of Qatari identity and tradition. Heritage and history are mythologized to support Al-Thani rule and the status quo. It is in appearing to preserve Qatari heritage and constructing the myths of Qatari identity that the legitimacy of Al-Thani, especially of the Emir, is assured. The cohesiveness of those deemed true Qataris eligible to vote and their loyalty to Al-Thani can only be more fully explained by a detailed investigation of Qatari history and historical myths. As the scholar, Juan Cole observed, 'tradition' is always a social construct, and that what is 'traditional' in a modern setting is in reality a core of earlier texts or doctrines wrapped in an unacknowledged set of innovations.'[60]

Second, meditation is key to Qatar's success. Qatar and Al-Thani relied on mediation and the balance of external powers, rather than any explicit, internal powers, first to maintain their independence and, more recently, to raise their diplomatic prominence in the region. The *hakam*, the mediator of disputes between tribes, is part of ancient Arab tradition. The Prophet Muhammad himself was famous for his ability to resolve disputes in Medina. Placed in a strategic space between powers, but still small enough to remain nimble, Qatar and Sheikh Hamad have actively sought the power and prestige that comes from mediating disputes not only between foreign powers and voices, but inside Qatari society as well. Qatar has taken advantage of gulfs between major powers in the region to establish itself as a neutral player and base. In fact, the apparent neutrality of Qatar, its courting of different sides of the political, popular and intellectual realm, from Mahmoud Ahmadinejad to George W. Bush, from Sheikh Yusuf al Qaradawi to the poet Adonis and Saad Eddin Ibrahim, is part of how Qatar fosters its own strategic interests and its desire to project influence and weight far beyond its small population. Although such public criticism is rare, it is only when the Qatari regime itself is either criticized or asked to make a specific stand, an increasingly common situation, that the interests of Qatar and the royal family are revealed. During its tenure as a non-permanent member of the UN Security Council, for example, Qatar often went against US initiatives, despite US support for its candidacy. Unaware of Qatar's history or wide-ranging strategic interests, many were surprised by Qatar's stance on the Security Council. During the Cold War, Qatar abruptly changed allegiances, allowed Moscow to open an embassy, and obtained Stinger missiles when it became clear that the USA would only supply Stingers to Qatar's neighbour Bahrain, with which Qatar had a border dispute. Clearly, Qatar did not completely trust US promises of protection. Sheikh Hamad's role as *hakam* within Qatari society is, of course, deliberately much more subtle and less public. Nevertheless, the Emir, like his father Sheikh Khalifa, has positioned himself as the ultimate *hakam*, somewhat subverting the traditional role of local chiefs and tribal councils.

Sheikh Hamad has recently faced new challenges in his role as a mediator, since the Facebook and Twitter generation have targeted the Emir and Al-Thani family. Part of the wider 'Arab Spring', this group has accused the Emir and his wife of being too close to Israel and the USA. It is not clear, however, how many followers are actually Qatari and how many are, perhaps, dejected loyalists of regimes that Qatar has helped overthrow in Egypt and Qaddafi. The Facebook page entitled 'The Qatar Revolution 2011 Against Hamad bin Khalifa', for example, promised major protests. It also includes some YouTube vidoes proporting to show violent clashes between protestors and Qatari security forces. In addition, there are images of Sheikh Hamad meeting with Israeli officials. The website asks 'Why did Al Jazeera not publish these photos?'[61] There are currently some 5,000 fans of the page.[62] Most of these protest pages on Facebook have a religiously conservative bent. In addition, the web has been swirling with somewhat dubious reports and rumors of attempted coups by army officers against the Emir and conspiracies to bring Abdalaziz bin Khalifa, the brother of the Emir, back from exile in France to take the place of the Emir. One of the main reasons for the coup, according to these reports, is the behavior and dress of Sheikha Mozah, behavior deemed to be too open and public for the wife of a ruler.[63] It should be noted, however, that even as there are large numbers supporting Facebook pages against the Emir and Sheikha Mozah, there are even larger numbers supporting Sheikha Mozah. Her Facebook page lists some 51,000 fans.[64]

Yet, even as the Facebook generation has created ties across traditional identities either to support or protest the Emir, the third main argument of this book is that tribes and lineage still matter within Qatar's internal political scene. Almost all accounts of Qatar have focussed on the personal rule of Al-Thani or the economic development of the country, or, to a limited extent on recent centrally controlled attempts at 'democratization'. In classic anthropological terms, Qatar has been transformed from a segmentary state dominated by traditional tribal, segmentary means of control, to a unitary state, a state where power is centralized. Yet the transition to a unitary state is not absolute or complete. In fact, it is not only Al-Thani but also Al-Sudan, Al-Naim, Bani Hajr, Al-Attiyah, and several other prominent families and tribes who exert influence in Qatar at various levels. The transition to democratization has closely followed established tribal boundaries and identities. The tribal *majlis* still often decides not only personal matters but also internal matters of justice and the Emir still personally receives complaints from Qatari citizens and tribal leaders. Recent municipal election districts were drawn almost exactly according to old tribal districts in Doha and Qatar. Also, research has shown that an overwhelming majority of Qataris will vote for their own tribe's candidate over any other.[65] Despite the temptation to concentrate power, it is only by maintaining the support of all Qataris, including the many, sometimes contentious branches of Al-Thani family, that the Emir can rule effectively. In addition to the internal manoeuvring and politics of Al-Thani family, evidence of dissent from non-ruling tribes and the internal politics of these tribes must be understood and taken into account.

The reader might be surprised that there is almost no mention of oil wealth and economy in the three theses above. This is intentional. Qatari society is not simply an empty container into which oil and progress are poured. Rather, a complex and real set of historical and social influences make up the particular circumstances of Qatari society today. This is not to say that oil does not matter; rather, it should be seen as a characteristic and a catalyst, not a primary and independent cause. Oil, natural gas and its impact will be discussed and analysed within the particular cultural and historical context of Qatar. First, however, a discussion of Qatar's geography reveals its somewhat precarious situation before the discovery of oil.

2

Qatar – Geography of a Near Frontier

iplomacy was never simply an option for Qatar. It was always a necessity. Qatar's vulnerable geography has demanded diplomacy and negotiation. Positioned at the midpoint of a triangle of potential empires and powers with Oman to the south, Iran to the east and Greater Arabia to the west, and with richer and more populous Bahrain always attempting to play puppet master from the north, Qatar and Qataris have always had to make strategic decisions to protect their fragile but viable independence. Before the full consolidation of state power and national sovereignty under Al-Thani, a process that continued throughout the twentieth century, the Qatari Peninsula served as a near frontier: a place where the conflicts and designs and ambitions of much more powerful, populated and influential neighbours could be played out. A potential spur into Bahrain and a potential bridge between Arabia and the central Gulf, Qatar was the strategic base of ambitious rulers, colonists and neighbours who largely neglected the actual residents of the Peninsula until the Qataris defied meddling by outsiders and forced themselves onto the historical scene, creating an independent political geography.

The earliest historical records indicate that Qataris have had a great deal of practice at playing regional superpowers off against each other. The country's vulnerable geographic position and the stubborn sense of independence it inspired meant Qataris abhorred the adoption of radical, absolute political and religious ideologies that might draw them completely within the sphere of one of their neighbours. One of the most remarkable questions of Gulf history must be why the miniscule and, even by pre-modern Gulf standards, poor community of pearl fishermen in Qatar was never fully absorbed into neighbouring, much more powerful states, empires and federations. Qatar was often threatened with disappearance. In 1916, with Abdul al Aziz of Al Saud in possession of Al-Hasa and ready to engulf Qatar, the British Political Resident in Bahrain remarked nonchalantly, 'I think it would be a pity if Qatar disappeared as a separate entity.'[1] Defying all expectations, however, Qatar did not disappear but survived extreme challenges, tests and challenges at times even greater than the harshness of its physical environment. Beginning with this discussion of Qatar's geography, this book will demonstrate how Qatar was able to maintain its remarkable, if somewhat improbable, autonomy.

QATAR'S GEOGRAPHY

The land of Qatar is shaped by constant geographical extremes. Satellite images of Qatar reveal a barren and dry landscape scarred with diagonal lines from the south-east to the north-west – bands of sand and dust and ground etched by the *shamal*, the powerful northerly winds that come in late summer to fill the oppressively hot summer skies with dust. Although there is a small amount of cultivated land in the north of the country and there have been many attempts at desert agriculture, only some 5 per cent of Qatar's land can be used for herding and grazing. Arable land is estimated at around 3 per cent of Qatar's land area. Although there were some nineteenth-century reports that Qatar received a 'greater fall of rain' than surrounding territories, the rain was not enough to support large-scale agriculture.[2] Over 13,000 acres of Qatari land were under production in 1988, providing only 20 per cent self-subsistence even before the recent, and explosive population boom. The uncultivated and unsettled land is by no means worthless. There are large quantities of gypsum, limestone and clay loam used for cement production and export. Some 63,000 tonnes of celestite, used in electronics, were found on the Peninsula's scorched landscape.[3]

The sweltering heat is a continuous and unrelenting concern and the daily rhythms and cultural practices of much of traditional Qatari society and the style of its architecture, including the famous, crenellated wind-tunnel tower that is an emblem of the region, revolve around avoiding the heat. Temperature is so much a part of life in Qatar that determining the amount of heat in a given day is a significant political and economic act, closely regulated by the government. The Ministry of Labour in Qatar has attempted, often unsuccessfully, to enforce the use of breaks and the provision of shade for expatriate labourers.[4]

There is a brief two- to three-month respite from the 35–50°C temperatures in the winter months from December to February. Rain does fall in Qatar but often leads to more problems with flooding and a peak in car accidents. Qatar's cities are not built for rain and road drainage systems are virtually non-existent. In fact, it is often only in the much awaited rain or in the extreme wind that nature seems to make herself felt, returning with a vengeance temporarily to remind the modern, air-conditioned, comfortable residents of Doha of her fierce presence. Dust turns to mud, mud turns to slicks and windshields are caked with an opaque film. After a downpour, however, the landscape seems to breathe in relief; desert grasses and desert hyacinth appear after even a smattering of rain. The only significant inland body of water in Qatar is salty, the Khor Al-Udeid, a sand-covered estuary from a river that flowed across the Arabian Peninsula millennia ago.

The mangrove forests and marshes in the north provided much-needed wood for traditional home construction, and they continue to be a natural sanctuary. Occasional desert brush provides nourishment for the hearty oryx, a type of white antelope with long horns sharp enough to pierce a hardwood door, and the reem, a small delicate antelope that can survive on very little water. The endangered oryx with its remarkable ability to migrate across hundreds of miles of desert in pursuit of rainwater is the national symbol of Qatar. Attempts to preserve the animal have become a national obsession.

Much of the Gulf around Qatar is extremely shallow and filled with a cornucopia of sea snakes, coral and colourful sea slugs. These species are specially adapted to withstand dramatic changes in water temperature from around 11°C in the winter to as high as 40°C in the summer months due to the shallowness of the water. There are also large herds of dugong or manatee that feed on the sea grass and some sea turtles that nest on shore. The environmental diversity of Qatar's shallow, warm waters is surprisingly rich and several species of marine life have yet to be discovered or identified.[5] In 2008 there were around 1,955 known species, of which 955 were marine animals. It is the shallow, hyper-saline waters of the Gulf that provide prime habitat for the oysters and pearls of the fishing fleets, one of the only reasons for the existence of a permanent population in Qatar before the oil boom. Although Qatar is some 4,247 square miles in area, it is the 559 miles of coastline that provide the setting for much of Qatar's history.

Centered around a broad bay halfway down the east coast, Doha and the outlying suburbs of Al-Rayyan, Lusail and Wakra form the largest population area in Qatar. Proximity to the brilliant turquoise-coloured Gulf is a significant determinant of land prices near the capital. The poorest areas of Doha, the so-called 'industrial city' where row upon row of tightly packed bunk houses shelter Qatar's growing south Asian migrant population, is furthest from the Corniche and the well-heeled waterfront where five-star hotels compete to illuminate the night sky. Al-Khor, a shipping and oil centre, is Qatar's second city. Ras Laffan Industrial City, some 50 miles north of Doha, hosts one of the largest liquid natural gas (LNG) facilities in the world. It is also the starting point for the The Dolphin project gas pipeline. The aim of the Dolphin project built the gas pipeline from Ras Laffan to Taweelah in the UAE, providing natural gas to the Emirates while bypassing the Saudis. This was done despite Saudi objections. The Saudis claimed that the underwater pipleline crossed through Saudi territory even as the pipline was already being laid.[6] The city of Dukhan, although important for oil and industry, is the only major population centre on the west coast, a region of Qatar that has been neglected since the foundation of Al-Thani power in Doha and the assertion of an independent Qatari identity. By facing east, Doha has avoided interference both from Arabia to the west and Bahrain to the north. Although there is a smattering of farms and wells and Qataris enjoy regular falconry forays into the desert, the only significant inland population area is Al-Udeid air base, headquarters of US Central Command.[7]

The discovery of oil has not significantly changed the outward, maritime character of Qatar's populated areas. Until the very recent past, the interior of Qatar had no significant settlement. Immediately outside populated and irrigated areas the land returns to desert. Stunted brushwood and desert grass may push through the dry surface. There are only a few small date groves and gardens, once fiercely contested by the small number of nomadic tribes that traversed the Peninsula.

AN INLAND GEOGRAPHY OF SOCIAL DIVISIONS?

No longer confined to the obvious limits of its natural geography, Qatar today is entering a post-geographic era. Pumped from below the sea, oil and gas has transformed the geography of Qatar, creating an artificial, human geography and climate. Because of its nearly unbearable climate on land, Qatari society used to be almost completely oriented towards the sea. Unlike the United Arab Emirates, Oman or Saudi Arabia, Gulf countries with significant inland populations, oases and settlements, the vast majority of Qataris have always lived along the coast and there are no permanent settlements at all in the interior of the country.[8] This does not mean, however, that the Bedouin are not an important factor in the social history of Qatar. The social divisions between Bedouin, (*bedu*), and *hadar* (descendants of settled villagers), remain strong and some Qataris, maintaining a sense of pride, will refuse to buy products in parts of Doha they consider '*hadar*'. Although it is true that many hadar often engaged in semi-nomadic grazing activities and even some *bedu* would at times go pearling, the distinction remained in the self-identification of the Qatari tribes. Regardless of their daily activities, the Bedouin still considered themselves proudly independent of the village chiefs, not as clients but as noble rulers of grazing land whose loyalty could be purchased only if their honour was maintained. According to John Gordon Lorimer, a political agent for the Viceroy Curzon of India who accompanied the Viceroy on a tour of the Gulf in the early twentieth century and wrote the secret *Gazetteer of the Persian Gulf*:

> Some of these northern Na'im have become pearl divers, but the majority are still pastoral and depend for their subsistence upon their livestock. The Bedouins of the northern Na'im are retained as mercenaries both by the Sheikh of Bahrain and by Al-Thani Sheikhs of Doha, and the protection of these Sheikhdoms is considered to devolve principally upon them during the absence from home of the pearl fleet ...[9]

For centuries there have been seasonal migrations by inland Arab Bedouin to take advantage of grazing in Qatar after the rains. In fact the word 'Qatar' has been translated as 'grazing ground'.[10] These movements, although in lesser numbers than elsewhere, should not be underestimated.[11]

Two major Bedouin groups roamed through their Qatari *dirab*, or the area where they had a right to graze: Al-Naim and their cousins, Al-Murrah. Al-Naim and Al-Murrah each fall into two major dialect and cultural groups: the Murrah-Ajman and the Manasir-Hawajer (Bani Hajr) Khalid-Naim. The Murrah-Ajman, it is assumed, come to the Gulf only recently from Central Arabia, about 150 years ago.[12] Al-Naim, but not necessarily their cousins, have consistently remained aligned with Bahrain and Al-Khalifa dynasty. The Naim, in fact, engaged in an almost unique form of seasonal, maritime migration between Qatar and Bahrain, an extraordinary anthropological phenomenon since it is often assumed that Arab Bedouin only migrated on land. Both groups of Bedouin in Qatar often capitalized on the pearl market by demanding protection money while the fishing boats were out to sea. They were a constant source both of worry for village chiefs but also of mercenary protection. Several Al-Thani Emirs relied on the Bedouin to maintain power and authority over family rivals. There was even fierce competition between Gulf States for Bedouin citizens after independence from Britain in the 1970s. An indication of their lasting historical impact in Qatar is the fact that Bedouin heritage and culture is still celebrated by urban Qataris today. As the anthropologist Roger Webster noted in his 1987 dissertation on Qatar's *bedu*:

> The *bedu* act as a reservoir of indigenous Arabian culture and skills which is drawn upon by the wealthy families of the coastal cities where Arabian traditions are diluted by the influx of foreigners and the rapid pace of development.... Ironically, as the traditional life of the desert becomes more irrelevant to the needs of a growing industrial society so it becomes more highly valued for its symbolic and sentimental significance, at least in the eyes of the traditional elites. Therefore the cash value placed on camels, falcons, poetry and hunting skills is elevated to levels quite out of proportion to any practical economic usefulness.[13]

Thus, the potential usefulness, but also potential threats of the Bedouin to the urban elite remain. Just as Al-Thani used Bedouin mercenaries in the pre-oil past to secure their political hold over rival families and tribes, they now use the Bedouin and pearl-fishing lifestyle (see Chapter 7) to shore up 'heritage' identity. Even so, the Bedouin remain somewhat fickle in their loyalties; their fluid links to Qatar's neighbours, including the ever-threatening Saudi Arabia, are troubling despite the existence of the new, modern geographic realities created by oil.

Desalination, development and dredging have created a new geographic reality, completely separating most modern residents in Qatar from the geographical challenges of the past. With summer days reaching upward of 50°C and extremely sparse rainfall, Qatar could not support its present exponential growth in population without massive investments in infrastructure and planning, without the creation of new geographic realities. As Qataris dramatically transform their surroundings and create new geographies that connect them irreversibly with the rest of the world, new questions arise and will arise. Of course it is possible that these new geographic realities, created to strengthen Qatar, will ironically threaten the Qatari's proud, historic sense of independence. It is possible that the geography of globalization, which has allowed Doha to sprout decadent tropical gardens overnight, could lead to a geography that also overwhelms the minority of Qataris and sprouts those very uncompromising, universalistic, religious or imperialistic ideologies that have been the ruin of many a small, independent state. Nevertheless, it appears so far that Qataris, especially in the ruling class, have lost none of their historic character of diplomatic flexibility, pragmatism and tolerance mixed with a steadfast sense of independence.

The barren interior of Qatar, basically a dry, elevated part of the Gulf, has had an obvious impact on its destiny as a nation. So little was known about Qatar's geography before the twentieth century that mapmakers as late as the nineteenth century would often depict it as an island rather than as a Peninsula, or would reduce it to a small stub on the eastern Arabian shore. It was common for Western geographers to consider Qatar, wrongly, a part of Bahrain, calling it, for instance, 'Bahran'. Bedouin tribes eked out a living from the few natural springs and occasional rains and scrub. Yet Qatar always had hidden riches, first from the sea as buckets of pearls were harvested, and then from underground and offshore as petroleum was discovered. Qatar's geopolitical situation, jutting into perhaps the most politically volatile waters on Earth, also makes it extremely important as a strategic ally.

THE BENEFITS AND RISKS
OF AMBIGUOUS GEOGRAPHY

Not quite an island, Qatar's geography is ambiguous. With its 559-mile coastline, it has most of the advantages of an island without the risks of isolation. Throughout history Qatar and Qataris have been isolated enough by their geography to hide away from authority and escape notice when needed, but not so isolated as to be forgotten. Although early mapmakers were wrong to describe Qatar as an island, the short and defensible strip of land connecting Qatar to Saudi Arabia and then to Abu Dhabi has often allowed Qataris to act like islanders. It is this narrow strip of land attaching Qatar to Arabia that has naturally been the focus of border disputes. Although Qatar currently claims it has no border with the UAE, for example, the UAE has made claims to 20 miles of its southern border. Saudi Arabia has frequently attempted to assert its claims to land on Qatar's southern border.

Before the modern period, the few people who inhabited the Qatari Peninsula would have probably been happy enough to continue their quiet village lifestyle of fishing and pearling on the Gulf. Qatar was not a place to start empires or even establish a regional state. There were many points in history when most native Qataris (meaning the oldest settled tribes of Sudan, Ma'adhid and Bani Khalid) would have enjoyed being left alone Nevertheless, the geography of Qatar has made the country paradoxically not only both separate and independent from its neighbours physically, but also with the potential to be intimately connected to major events in the region and the world.

Before the discovery of oil and natural gas, Qatar was not particularly strategically important in its own right, except for the simple fact of its location. Jutting into the Gulf, the location of Qatar has placed it in the centre of disputes and power struggles between the most significant Gulf powers: the Saudis, the Omani, the Persians and Bahrain. In the nineteenth century the mild geographical isolation of Qatar, not so far from events but also an almost perfect place of escape, made it a magnet for exiles from various nations and tribes, exiles who have used Qatar repeatedly as a base for what the British called 'piracy' or for angry power-plays between surrounding sheikhs and Emirs. Qatar today continues to leverage its geographic location – it is both an asset and a risk.

3

The Origins of Qatar – between 'Emergence' and 'Creation'

Qatar is one of the world's most unlikely political entities. Surrounded by powerful and expansionist neighbours and projecting into Gulf waters, waters rocked by centuries of conflict, Qatar has one of the more extraordinary stories of state formation in the Gulf. Unlike the long-established ruling families of other Gulf States such as Al-Sabah of Kuwait or the Zayed family of Abu Dhabi who had a coherent, if admittedly local, political presence in the region long before the British dominated it, the power of Al-Thani of Qatar is relatively young. The treaty of 1868 between Muhammad bin Thani and Britain, discussed in detail later in this chapter, was the first formal recognition of a Sheikh of Qatar. Until the central prominence of Al-Thani had been established by the treaty the Qatari Peninsula lacked a cohesive independent centre. This centre only came with the growth of Doha (Bidaa), the chosen, if small, headquarters for Al-Thani in the middle of the nineteenth century. Zubara on the north was the main city on the Peninsula for much of the eighteenth and early nineteenth century – but it was seen as an appendage of Bahrain. Local Qatari villagers established Zubara as early as 1638, but it was the migration of Kuwaiti Utubi tribesmen of the Khalifa and Jalahima clans in 1765 that led to the establishment of the Murair fort and a significant trading zone. In 1783 Bahrain captured Zubara, subsequently controlling it directly and largely ignoring the surrounding inhabitants of Qatar.[1] Villagers and chiefs of tiny settlements outside Zubara would sometimes coordinate their resistance to Bahrain's expansion in the Peninsula, but not under the leadership of any particular family or 'Sheikh of Qatar'. It would be inaccurate, however, to label Qatar a completely artificial creation of the British or to credit only the British and the Ottomans for the establishment of Al-Thani power, even if Al-Thani and the Qataris did use British recognition to their advantage. Britain's role can easily be overstated. As a scholar of Middle East anthropology observed:

... [R]ecognition of the power and cultural hegemony of the West does not require as a correlate the rejection of the possibility of constructing general comparative arguments about Middle Eastern culture, nor does it require negating the real historical and cultural patterns of Middle Eastern society simply because that society has been viewed through western eyes.[2]

Although Qatar's political coherence was important to Britain, the British did not single-handedly create Qatar. Simply because they emerged later than other ruling families of the region, however, does not diminish the fact that Al-Thani themselves were a major factor in their own success at securing Qatar and in convincing external powers, through force or through diplomacy, of Qatar's need for political independence and of the need for them to rule. As the expert in the British protectorate James Onley has argued, British protection, 'was not imposed coercively ... Britain largely conformed to local expectations of a protector's duties and rights'.[3] The Qataris, like many smaller populations in the Gulf living beyond the periphery of major urban centres, had long paid protection money, or *khuwa*, to powerful neighbours such as Bahrain and Abdalaziz bin Saud, ruler of Al-Saud to the west, while maintaining its effective independent status. Britain was just the latest power in a region prone to imperial expansion. Thus, instead of seeing Qatar as either a creation of the British or as a state that emerged largely through the efforts of Al-Thani and the Qatari people, both external and internal elements shaped Qatar's extraordinary rise from a largely empty, barren land to a coherent political entity, culminating with the formal Anglo-Qatari Treaty of 1916 that recognized formal British protection of Qatar. This 'protection' has continued in a defacto fashion under the unofficial US imperium. As with Britain, Qatar and Al-Thani have certainly maintained tight relations with the USA as a necessity, looking to the USA as the most powerful players in the region even as they steadily increase their own independent political, diplomatic and economic capital. Such economic versatility has deep-seated cultural roots, and it can even be seen in Qatar's ancient history.

ANCIENT HISTORY

Although concrete evidence of palaeolithic settlements in Qatar have yet to be discovered, the earliest evidence of human habitation on the Peninsula are still ancient. In the 1950s Danish archaeologists claimed to have discovered stone tools dating back more than 50,000 years. A French team beginning in 1976, however, disputed these results. Using carbon dating they found tools and artefacts dating no earlier than 6000 BC.[4] A recent, major discovery of arrowheads by Danish and Qatari archaeologists in 2007, however, has been dated back an extraordinary 700,000 years. According to one Danish archaeologist, 'not only are these tools the oldest traces of man in South Arabia, they are among the oldest in the whole world'.[5] Despite these debates over Qatar's ancient past, it appears that Qatar has been fairly continuously inhabited, if in small numbers. With few land resources Qataris have relied since ancient times on the sea and on trade.

Qatar and the Gulf region in general have an ancient and continuing role as an entrepôt and trading link between Mesopotamia and the Indian subcontinent. Qatar was connected to the ancient Dilmun civilization centred on Bahrain from 2450–1700 BC. Indeed, recent archaeological excavations at Al-Khor Shaqiq by the Qatar Archaeology Project have yielded Dilmun Barbar pottery. Dilmun provided an essential trading link between the ancient Indus Valley civilizations and ancient Babylonia. Plying the gulf and the waters of the Indian Ocean, Dilmun merchants traded in oil, silver, resins and copper.

Further evidence of Qatar's ancient links with the Indus came from the work of Beatrice de Cardi, the world's oldest working archaeologist. Beatrice de Cardi worked not only in Qatar but in Baluchistan, Pakistan where she found grey pottery incised with various patterns similar to those found in Qatar by the Danish expedition. In Ras Abrouq she and a Danish team discovered fifth-millennium BC Ubaid pottery from Mesopotamia. The work of the indomitable Beatrice de Cardi has confirmed the place of Qatar as a stepping-stone between the world's first civilizations with her discovery of red-stripped Barbar ware from the Bronze Age at Ras Abrouq.[6] Although it may be difficult today to imagine Qatar as a green landscape, there was once a time when grass could come up to the knees. Tools discovered in prehistoric sites show evidence of a large freshwater lake. Between 8000 and 4000 BC there was a significant increase in the rainfall in Arabia, allowing the desert to bloom. Some scholars even claim that rivers flowed throughout the Arabian Peninsula including the Pishon River mentioned in Genesis. Limestone vessels for the preparation of wild grains have been discovered in Qatar. Although the social history of the pearl-fishing Qataris must have remained fairly consistent, there were important, historic breaches such as the coming of Islam.

According to Qatari tradition, the Prophet Muhammad's envoy Al Ala Al-Hadrami was sent to Qatar and Bahrain in 628 AD. Impressed by Islam and sensing the valuable benefits to commerce and conquest the new faith would bring, the Arab tribes quickly converted. There were several Arabs, however, who may have remained Nestorian Christians, or may have adhered to Zoroastrianism or local religious beliefs for some centuries. Although information on this period is obscure, it is likely that some settled populations in Qatar did not instantaneously convert to Islam. An important seventh-century saint and mystic, named Isaac of Qatar, became a leader in the Syrian Church.[7]

Despite the return of progressively drier conditions in the last couple of millennia, vibrant trade in pearls continued for centuries. The recent discovery of an Arab *dhow* off the coast of Belitung in Indonesia laden with some 60,000 pieces of gold, silver, precious cobalt and white ninth-century Tang ceramics confirms the existence of a busy maritime trade route between Baghdad and Xian, capital of Tang China. Ships filled with aromatic woods from Africa and fine textiles and goods from Abbasid Baghdad would leave Basra and pass through the Gulf, stopping at ports in Bahrain, Qatar, Iran and Oman en route, and then catch the seasonal monsoon winds to India and China. To this day the Arab *dhow*, crafted from African hardwood and Indian teak and fastened together with coconut-husk fibre, not nails, has continued to ply the Gulf and the Indian Ocean. Chinese porcelain, West African coins and even pieces from Thailand discovered in Qatar, now on display at Zubara museum in the north of Qatar, indicate that *dhow*s would make regular stops at Qatar ports on their voyage to the Indian Ocean. Al-Huwailah on the Qatari coast was one of the principal pearling ports of the eighteenth century. Recent excavations in the north-east of Qatar by Dr Andrew Peterson near the site of the new causeway built to encourage trade with Bahrain has revealed the surprising extent of trade in Qatar itself before the twentieth century. The bustling settlement here was organized according to tribal household. There are cannonballs in the extensive remains of the settlement – evidence of retaliation against these Qatari villagers for their capture of dates and food supplies from passing ships. Indeed, lack of food supply was often the cause of raids on passing ships, not simply the desire to acquire material wealth. Qatar continues to fret over its 'food safety' despite the reliability of modern shipping networks.[8]

The rise of the British East India Company and the expulsion of the Portuguese from the Strait of Hormuz in 1622 was the beginning of British commercial, if not overtly political, involvement in the region. A new trading route through the Syrian Desert, linking the Mediterranean to the Gulf and India increased the Gulf's importance as a commercial zone in the eighteenth century. Although the Dutch briefly made claims on the Gulf, their interests were quickly focussed on the Far East Asia market. Napoleon's invasion of Egypt in 1798 caused the British to refocus their attention on the Gulf. As a colonial rival to the French, the British wanted to ensure a secure passage to India where the French also had claims. In 1798 the British successfully gained the exclusive support of the Imam of Muscat, Oman who had influence throughout the region, including Qatar. While the fall of Napoleon allowed the British to relax their hold over the Gulf, occasionally the French would still harass the British and attempt to win over local sheikhs. Such efforts were easily suppressed by British naval dominance. The only real threat to British operation of its trade corridors after the fall of Napoleon was 'piracy' and maritime warfare between rival sheikhs. This caused Britain to establish the trucial system – a system of treaties, including the General Treaty of Peace of 1820 and the 1853 Perpetual Maritime Truce, that essentially attempted to regiment and organize the fluid social patterns of the Gulf, recognizing particular Emirs as responsible for designated parts of the territory, even if such responsibility was as much paper fiction as a reality. The Ottoman Emperor Sultan Abdul Hamid's attempts in the 1870s to centralize authority and increase Turkish land presence in the Gulf complicated matters. The attempted stabilization of the Gulf region around designated sheikhs with a sense of independent sovereignty, however, was an ongoing process and was not truly formalized until almost a century after the first trucial agreements were signed in 1820. It has only been in the past 20 years that final, legal, recognized borders have begun to stabilize.

THE RISE OF AL-THANI

The establishment of Qatar as an independent sheikhdom separate from Bahrain was by no means inevitable. In his report on the Persian Gulf issued shortly after the signing of the General Treaty of Peace with the Arab tribes of the Persian Gulf in 1820, Lieutenant Macleod described Bidaa (the town that would become Doha) as simply 'subject to Bahrain'. Although it was 'governed by a Sheikh named Buhur bin Jubran of the tribe of the Abu-o-ainee [Al-Ainain] all of the other sheikhs having quitted the place', he simply assumed that Bahrain was in charge, despite the fact that communication between Qatar and Bahrain did not seem to be especially clear. For example, 'The people seemed to know very little of the conditions of the treaty [of 1820 with the British], and had neither flag nor register, excepting one boat, which had been procured through the Sheikh of Bahrain ...'. In a final blow to British awareness of any notion of independence in Bidaa before the rise of Al-Thani, Macleod assumed that 'as they are entirely subject to Bahrain, I did not think it necessary to enter very minutely on the subject [of Qatar]'.[9] Nevertheless, Lieutenant Macleod could have simply misread the loyalties of the Bidaa residents or even what being 'entirely subject' to Bahraini authority could have meant to them. Indeed, only two years earlier in 1821 British ships had bombarded Bidaa for alleged piratical activity despite the fact that the town's residents were apparently ignorant of the treaty.

Whatever the case, Buhur bin Jubran was no doubt aware of the advantages to be gained by being an independent outpost of the more closely monitored Bahrain. Several times Qatar would serve as the place where quarrels between rivals for the sheikhdom of Bahrain could be conducted, often with the interference of the Wahhabis from the realm of Al-Saud, who had a vested interest in maintaining Bahrain in a subject state – Bahrain would pay the Wahhabi ruler a regular tribute. Muhammad bin Khalifa, brother of Abdallah bin Khalifa of Bahrain, for instance, used the Qatar coast 'in order to have at his disposal the naval resources of its inhabitants, and to keep an open communication with his colleagues [Al-Saud clan]'. The Qataris took advantage of this quarrel between the Bahraini brothers to advance their own cause: they 'favoured decidedly the cause of Mohamed bin Khaleefa, and established him in Fowarah [Fuwayrat: a Qatari village]'.[10] The Qatari chief Isa bin Tarif was particularly good at rallying and organizing Qataris. The rise of Al-Thani, on the other hand, seems to be something of a surprise as they are hardly mentioned, if at all, in accounts of Qatari involvement in Bahraini and Al-Saud politics until the 1850s.

In fact, before the rise of Al-Thani, Isa bin Tarif was the chief favoured by the British. His move to Bidaa in 1843, was seen as:

> an arrangement considered in every respect highly satisfactory, as bringing with him within the limits of the restrictive line, and placing that port (exceedingly difficult of access) in possession of a chief in whose sincere wish to put down irregularities at sea, of a piratical nature, every confidence was placed – inclinations very different to those entertained by Salmin bin Nassir Sooedan [Chief of Al-Sudan], the former sheikh of Biddah ...[11]

It was Al-Sudan, perhaps amongst the very oldest of residents in Doha, who would have risen to a position of ultimate leadership in Qatar were it not for the timing of British intervention. Indeed, the exceptional rights and privileges exercised by Al-Sudan, their exemption from taxation in the pearl industry for instance, have only recently been somewhat overshadowed by the overwhelming wealth and power of Al-Thani in modern Qatar.

Despite the existence of successive chiefs from families not remotely related to Al-Thani, it was not until the recognition of Sheikh Muhammad bin Thani by the British in the middle of the nineteenth century that Qatar began to emerge as separate political entity. While the British were inclined at various points to recognize and support previous sheikhs such as Isa bin Tarif, Muhammad bin Thani was much more aware of the need to submit to British demands and to respect their punitive measures against 'piracy' even if such acts were not under his direct control. At the same time, he learned not to give in to the British entirely. If it were not for Muhammad bin Thani's leadership and his deft, diplomatic manipulation of intervention by outside powers, Qatar could have easily become a part of the Kingdom of Bahrain or even Kuwait. Furthermore, even Bahrain was not always Qatar's most powerful threat. There were several occasions when it appeared that all of the small Gulf Emirates would be swallowed up either by the tribes of Al-Saud to the west or by Persia to the east. Several, much larger powers could have easily engulfed both Qatar and Bahrain. Lieutenant Kemball noted in his report to the British government of Bombay in 1844:

> The small but fruitful island of Bahrein [sic] appears at different seasons to have excited in an extraordinary degree the ambitious desires of divers nations. His majesty the Shah ... had on two separate occasions manifested an inclination to assert a right of supremacy over it; the Imam of Muscat [Oman] has from time immemorial longed and craved to possess the fertile spot; and now we find that Turkish authorities [are] intriguing and seeking to induce Sheikh Mohamed bin Khalifa [leader of Al-Khalifa in Bahrain] to renounce his state of independence and own his allegiance to the Ottoman Porte.[12]

Although there were both settled and fishing village tribes in the Qatari Peninsula such as Al-Sudan and the Bani Khalid, a powerful Arab tribe that had asserted its independence from the Ottomans in 1680, it was exiles of Al-Khalifa who happened to dominate when the first detailed British records of the Qatari Peninsula were compiled by officials in the Gulf and agents of the British Government of Bombay. Lieutenant Kemball for example, who compiled his study of the 'Uttoobee tribe of Arabs' in 1844, emphasized the dominance of Al-Khalifa in the northern half of the Gulf, but made little mention of the inhabitants of Zubara and Qatar who had been living there at least since the sixteenth century, such as the Naim tribes, the Hawajer (Bani Hajr) Bedouin and the Ma'adha. Al-Khalifa were an especially adventuresome and opportunistic segment of the Utubi branch of Arabs, a large confederation of tribes from Central Arabia. They had migrated from Arabia to Kuwait in the 1760s. From Kuwait they expanded their trading, fishing and piracy operations, conquering the Island of Bahrain in 1783 and developing the small village of Zubara in the north of Qatar as a commercial and trading settlement. Only the later Al-Thani domination of Qatar as an independent sheikhdom in the second half of the nineteenth century would rebalance Qatari trade and contacts towards Doha and the south.

Al-Khalifa and their large settlement at Zubara were oriented towards the north, towards Al-Khalifa home settlement in Kuwait and towards the wealthier and more populated Island of Bahrain. Bahrain could be easily reached from Zubara across a relatively short waterway – the shallow Gulf of Bahrain. As many as 5,000 merchants, pearl-fishers and traders populated the settlement of Zubara, a truly significant population for the region and the time. Yet the fact that Zubara, once the only truly urban settlement in the Peninsula, is today little more than a ruin, while Doha, previously a small village compared to Zubara, is a gleaming metropolis testifies to the ultimate success of Al-Thani in asserting their independence from Bahrain and Al-Khalifa. By the end of the nineteenth century Al-Thani had established their authority on the Peninsula and Doha's population was 12,000. By 1908 Zubara and Bahraini villages on the west coast of Doha were practically abandoned. In the late eighteenth and early nineteenth century, however, the independence of Al-Thani from Bahrain was by no means assured. Even in the present century rivalry between Al-Khalifa in Bahrain and Al-Thani in Qatar has not completely subsided. The dispute between Bahrain and Qatar over the largely uninhabited but gas- and oil-rich Hawar islands on the west coast of Qatar, a dispute which nearly turned into a serious military conflict until being resolved in the 1990s in Bahrain's favour in the international courts, is one major example of the continued tension between Bahrain and Qatar.

Although Qatar eventually asserted its status as a soverign territory independent of Bahrain with population and power moving from Zubara to Doha, the influence of Bahrain was lasting and significant. Through intermarriage with Al-Thani line, Al-Khalifa remain perhaps the second most powerful and influential tribe in Qatar. Bahrainis, both Shi'a and Sunni, have moved to Qatar since the decline in oil revenue and development. Zubara under Al-Khalifa was a free trade zone, leading to the creation of a large business community because no customs duties were levied. The historic example of Zubara was closely followed by Al-Thani as they have attempted to create and encourage trade in Doha. Emblematic of their common cultural and historical ties, the flags of Bahrain, bright red and white grounds divided by a saw-edge – and Qatar, dark maroon and white with the same pattern dividing the two colours – both based on the British requirement to fly a red and white flag to designate a 'friendly' ship – are almost indistinguishable. Not all the sheikhs of the trucial coast submitted willingly to the British treaty clause requiring the display of flags. One sheikh, Rahmah bin Jabir, who operated from the Qatari shore was particularly sceptical of the meaning of the flags. In his 1823 report on the 'Affairs of the Persian Gulf', the British Lieutenant Macleod commented rather slyly:

> Observing that the Sheikh seemed to consider the adoption of the pacified flag as implying a nearer and more dependent relation with our Government than it really does, I took occasion to explain to him that it was the Arab, not the British flag; but those tribes who were parties to the treaty with us had agreed to distinguish themselves by wearing round the red flag a border of white, which is alone emblematic of peace, in token of their relinquishment of piracy.[13]

In Lieutenant Macleod's view, all the sheikhs of the trucial coast were potentially piratical and needed to be 'pacified'. In the view of Rahmah bin Jabir, British interference and the adoption of the British Treaty meant not only pacification but effectively subordination.

RAHMAH BIN JABIR

The last of a generation of proud, independent adventurers, Rahmah bin Jabir was the most famous of nineteenth-century rebels to use Qatar as an outpost. In many ways Zubara was close to the centre of Al-Khalifa power, but not close enough to avoid Zubara and Qatar being used as an ideal base for rebellion by brothers and cousins of ruling Al-Khalifa sheikh. Substantially larger and more difficult to control than the contained and relatively isolated island of Bahrain, Qatar was also used by adventurers and pirates such as Rahmah bin Jabir who skilfully took advantage of Al-Khalifa divisions. In these respects, the swashbuckling Rahmah bin Jabir was a forerunner of Muhammad bin Thani, founder of Al-Thani dominance of the Peninsula. Unlike, Muhammad, however, who was at least as interested in establishing a long-term power base on land, Rahmah relied on piracy in an era before increased British patrols of the Gulf made the practice less tenable. Had Britain been a land-based empire, and had there not been a strategic need for the British to secure shipping between Basra and Bombay, it could have been Rahmah and his descendants who were recognized as rulers of the Peninsula and its waters. Rahmah, a member of Al-Jalahimah branch of the Utubi, warred against Bahrain and Bahraini shipping from his bases in Qatar.

Although the attacks were never directed against the British, the Crown could not tolerate disruptions and disturbances on its vital route to India. Rahmah was compelled to sign the 1820 General Treaty of Peace, to reconcile with Abdallah bin Ahmad Al-Khalifa, the ruler of Bahrain in 1824, and to cease all piracy, his main source of revenue. As Article 1 of the Treaty stated, 'there shall be a cessation of plunder and piracy by land and sea on the part of the Arabs, who are party to this contract, for ever.' Furthermore, Article 4 stated rather paternalistically that 'the pacificated [*sic*] tribes ... shall not fight with each other.'[14] The signing of this treaty effectively placed Bahrain and, by extension, Qatar under the trucial system, a system that left local sheikhs to their own affairs as long as they could be held responsible for maintaining maritime peace.

Although hailed as a successful 'example' the treaty was broken before the ink had a chance to dry. War broke out again the next year between Bahrain and Rahmah. The reign of the pirate Rahmah, a name remembered in legend to this day in Qatar, ended in one last spectacular display of the culture of honour and defiance. In 1826 he was defeated by the combined forces of the Bani Khalid – residents of Qatari fishing villages who had not gained much from the booty of Rahmah and had tired of the depredations of war against Bahrain (Al-Thani, in contrast, would form a close alliance with the Bani Khalid) – and the Bani Khalifa. Mindful of his legacy, Rahmah, the last wildly successful sheikh of the Gulf seas, decided on death before surrender. The British Resident in Bahrain, Colonel Stannus, described the dramatic scene of the final moments of the life of blind and elderly Rahmah and his son:

> ... but Rahmah perceiving that his people were rapidly falling around him, mustered the remainder of the crew, issued orders to grapple with his opponents, and after embracing his young son was led with a lighted torch to the magazine which immediately exploded, blowing his Baglow [ship] to atoms and setting fire at the same to the Bahrine [Bahraini] boat which soon afterwards shared a similar fate.

Although he rejects as 'mythical' the presence of piracy in the Gulf, identifying raids as local forms of resistance to British control, even Sultan Muhammad Al-Jassimi, the ruler of Sharjah and writer of *The Myth of Arab Piracy*, recognized Rahmah bin Jabir as a 'pirate'.[15] Nevertheless, isolated from any effective political control, and simply empty of any significant number of inhabitants, Qatar was a very effective base for piracy and seemed to be open to any sheikh or strong man who wished to use it as a base.

Although sea raids did not completely cease, the explosive death of Rahmah was the end of an era. No longer would large-scale and organized sea piracy be a serious threat and raiding was becoming a much less viable option for rebellious and charismatic leaders. Qataris who lived on the Peninsula but who did not necessarily participate in the piracy were often blamed and even punished with retaliatory bombings from British ships for the actions of pirates. Throughout the early history of Qatar Al-Thani Emir would also occasionally be called upon to pay restitution for raids by those using Qatari territory even though he had almost no effective control outside Doha, let alone over the Qawasim and other tribes that occasionally used empty stretches of the Qatari coastline to launch profitable attacks on trade. Nevertheless, it would no longer be as feasible as it was under Rahmah to use Qatar as a convenient base for continuous raiding. The death of Rahmah and the domination of the British Navy turned Qatar inward and inland. No longer could 'rulers' of Qatar effectively exploit its strategic position as a beachhead.

The new political reality of British Naval domination made the barren and lightly populated land more important than it ever had been. With Britain patrolling the seas, it was those sheikhs who maintained their authority inland who would prosper – a reversal of the previous power system that had favoured the tribe and the leader most willing and most able to extract resources from the seas. Until World War I almost all British agents in Bombay saw much of the Gulf coast as a chaotic region to be passed over as quickly as possible en route to India. Bombay almost always over-ruled British agents in Cairo who often had a more subtle understanding of the importance of internal Arab affairs but who may not have appreciated as fully the economic importance and weight of British interests in the subcontinent. It was this control of Gulf affairs from Bombay and the easy dismissal of the importance of the land and tribes of the Gulf that gave Al-Thani the space to assert a tenuous independence not only from the British but from their rapacious neighbours.

DID BRITAIN CREATE AL-THANI DYNASTY?

The British do not seem to have plunged into Gulf affairs with great alacrity. British agents frankly professed a disinterest in the 'internal affairs' of the 'piratical Arabian Chieftains'. In fact, this doctrine of non-interference was 'wisely enjoined as the first principle of government policy ...'.[16] In 1871, just three years after the important 1868 agreement establishing the rudiments of Al-Thani authority in Qatar, the British Foreign Secretary himself declared a policy of official disinterest in the Gulf:

It should never be forgotten that, in all its main features, our position in the Persian Gulf is one which we have taken up on grounds of policy. Its foundation in Treaty is of the most meagre and narrow kind.[17]

In fact, although they put heavy demands on and made threats towards those sheikhs who signed their treaties, the British generally conceded that the social and political structures and the internal boundaries of the Gulf region were characterized by a dizzying variability. 'To fix the limits, therefore, of the lands actually belonging to, or claimed by, each tribes respectively, would, without present information be impossible ...'. Many British agents had come to view the residents of the 'piratical coast' with a high degree of contempt. Only 'the conviction of the irresistible power of the British Government ... have alone reduced them to succumb to its will, and restrained them from acts of piracy ...'.[18] The British soon learned that one of the main causes for the existence of so-called 'piracy' was the tendency for clans to break away from tribes.

It is by no means uncommon for one of the branches of a tribe, to the number sometimes of several hundred individuals, in order to escape excessive taxation and oppression, or with a view to secure themselves greater immunities and advantages, to secede from the authority and territory of their lawful and acknowledged chief into that of another, or to establish themselves and build a fort on some other spot, and assert and maintain independence ...

Indeed, it was precisely this mutability and constantly changing dynamic of early nineteenth-century Gulf society that the British ultimately found unbearable. In their desire to 'organize' the 'lawful' chiefs of the Gulf, Britain sought specific chiefs with whom it could do business and from whom guarantees of security for shipping and trade could be wrested. Although some Qatari sheikhs attempted to defy the authority of the British (such as Isa bin Tarif who refused to pay a penalty to the British), relying on internal allies and codes of honour, they were all ultimately vanquished by both the strength of British Naval supremacy and the willingness of the British simply to support those chiefs whose actions seemed to be most aligned with British interests. The Qatar monarchy emerged as an expression of the general needs of British imperial policy even if the British did not create the specific conditions that led to the ascendancy of Al-Thani.

In many respects, early and mid-nineteenth-century Qatar was an extreme manifestation of the variability of tribal territories and affiliations in the Gulf. While sheikhs in other parts of the Gulf were fairly well established and known, the monarchy in Qatar germinated, as it were, in virgin territory. The new Qatari monarchy was unlike other, more traditional Islamic monarchies such as that of Morocco, where the monarchy had ruled for centuries, or much of the Ottoman Middle East, governed by often-hereditary beys, or Ottoman governors. There was simply no known tradition of monarchy or dynastic succession in Qatar before the treaty of 1868 between Muhammad bin Thani and the British Colonel Pelly.

Though Al-Thani were still just 'first among equals' in the 1860s, even the idea of 'first among equals' or the elevation of one particular tribal chief and one particular tribe above the others on the Peninsula had not been the practice just decades earlier. Qatar then was mainly a territory where disaffected clans or branches of tribes could settle and find an independent base from which to carry on pearling, or, in the case of Rahmah, to engage in piracy. There was no tribe that could claim to dominate the Qatari Peninsula, no overall chief who could reasonably claim to represent Qatar. Even as late as the twentieth century, Al-Thani Sheikh only collected revenue from the pearl-fishers in Doha and its immediate surroundings; other sheikhs controlled revenue in Al-Wakra, and the revenue from villages in the north was only enough to pay the Bedouin tribes for protection. Indeed, the ability of Al-Thani Sheikh to prevent raids on shipping from his territory was very limited, even as the British made him responsible for 'piratical' activity.[19] Certainly there were chiefs of villages, but these men had very little control over the tribes in their settlements. Discontented tribes could simply pack up, leave and settle elsewhere, as did the residents of Al-Wakra, an entirely new settlement in the 1840s that emerged after Al-Ainain's honour had been challenged. According to one survey, the entire:

> town of Wakra did not exist ... [it has] since [been] erected by the present Chief, Ali bin Nasir, who, with his tribe (the Boo Ejman) formerly resided in Biddah, but having offended the Uttoobee Sheikh [Bahrain], the dwellings of imself [*sic*] and followers were destroyed by that chief, who contemplated their forcible transfer to Bahrain. To avoid this offensive arrangement, Ali bin Nasir and his tribe took possession of the site of their present residence, at the foot of the Jubbul Wukra [Jabal Wakra].[20]

Indeed, the very architecture of nineteenth-century Qatari houses reflected this impermanence. Made out of reeds, palm fronds and mud, houses were easily replicated elsewhere. Almost no stone structures existed. Most supplies and basic foods had to be imported. Water was often brackish, limited or difficult to access, forcing women to walk sometimes miles to reach good wells. One mystery of early nineteenth-century Qatar is not the lack of population, but why there were any substantial settlements at all. The commercial opportunities in Bahrain, Lingeh, Oman and the UAE were much greater than in Doha or Qatar. Yet, Qatar, lacking any real, overall claimant to its territory, and able to serve as a market for free trade, attracted merchants willing to brave the reefs of the Peninsula to avoid tax duties. The main reason people stayed, as in ancient times, was the excellent pearling off Qatar's shore. In fact, almost uniquely in the Gulf, most pearl divers in Qatar were free born. At least 50 per cent of the Qatari population engaged directly in pearling, the highest proportion in the Gulf.[21] Dependence on one resource was risky. Declines and variations in the pearl market could decimate a village, or easily bring it to ruin. Almost all supplies had to be imported, leading to expensive, inflated prices for basic food and essentials.

Before Muhammad bin Thani consolidated his position in the 1850s, several other tribes and prominent men were the leaders of Bidaa (Doha). As even the British acknowledged in several reports, Al-Thani were not always considered the representatives of Qatar. In his secret *Gazetteer of the Persian Gulf*, J. Lorimer, observant assistant to the Indian Viceroy Lord Curzon during his travels through the Gulf, revealed that Her Majesty's government was fully aware that Al-Thani were not always in charge.[22] According to him, 'Nothing is known of the manner in which Al-Thani had attained by 1868, predominant influence in Qatar …'.[23] Unlike the authority of other Emirs around the Gulf, including Al-Sabah of Kuwait who are described as having been predominant for generations, as were the tribes of the Emirates, Al-Thani did not, according to Lorimer, have a deep historic claim to power. Although Lorimer's account cannot always be completely trusted and it was obviously influenced by his own interpretation of British imperial interests in the region, there is plenty of evidence pointing to the lack of any real exercise of authority by Al-Thani, or even any significant role at all for Al-Thani Sheikh before the early 1800s. Instead, the politics of Qatar seemed highly variable. Before 1868 and British recognition, of Al-Thani authority in Qatar and in Bidaa (future Doha), rule was highly fluid and loosely organized around different native tribes and it would shift between different sheikhs and different families. The internal reasons for one tribe to become more prominent than another does not seem to have been based on religious affiliation or descent from the Prophet – Al-Thani, for instance, are Tamimi and not from the family of the Prophet – but rather on ability and, often, the charisma of a particular chief. Nor did authority seem to stem from the length of a tribe's tenure on the Peninsula.

Indeed, if authority in Qatar were determined simply by which tribe had been there the longest continuously, power would legitimately not be vested in Al-Thani but in Al-Musallam. One of the earliest records of a fairly powerful 'Sheikh of Qatar' comes from Ottoman sources. According to Zekeriya Kursun, 'In 1555, one Mohammad bin Sultan beni Muslim [Al-Musallam] was the Sheikh of Qatar with its headquarters at Al-Huwailah' and he resided in Qatar. Al-Musallam were in control of Zubara before the arrival of the Utubis. They were even in Qatar before the Bani Khalid.[24] The town of Al-Huwailah, now a dusty, abandoned ruin, was more significant than Bidaa by the turn of the nineteenth century. According to the family history of Al-Thani recounted by the second Al-Thani Emir of Qatar, Sheikh Jassim bin Thani, the ancestors of the current

Emir did not arrive in Qatar from the Jabrin Oasis, and subsequently from Kuwait, until the 1750s.[25] They did not seem to have anything more than a very local prominence on the Peninsula and do not feature in the historical record or the survey logs of British captains. By the 1820s, Al-Musallam were outnumbered. The Peninsula was inhabited primarily by the Al bu Kuwara tribe (a tribe that affiliated itself with Al-Thani). However, 'In the absence of any central authority these coastal towns and villages were governed by local Sheikhs'.[26] Before 1850 Bidaa (Doha), the future capital and central focus of Al-Thani power, had only about 400 residents, although nomadic tribes such as the Munasir frequented it. During the pearling season the population would swell to 1,200.[27]

Lieutenant Macleod, British Resident of the Persian Gulf, visited Bidaa in 1823 to find it under the administration of the Sheikh of Al-Ainain, not Al-Thani. It was the Qatari Al-Ainain chief, not Al-Thani chief whose whereabouts were largely unknown, who was considered Doha's representative. It was also Al-Ainain who assisted the British in their survey of the Qatari coast and who could have achieved British recognition had they been in a position to demand separation from Bahrain or convince the British of their independence. The raider Rahmah bin Jabir, not any member of Al-Thani family, was one the most powerful men on the Qatari Peninsula until his capture. The rest of Qatar outside Bidaa was ruled by whoever could make the most effective claim to the land. In 1835 the people of the small fishing village of Al-Huwailah, led by Isa bin Tarif, rebelled against the authority of Bahrain and 'opened a correspondence with the Wahhabis' of Al-Saud.[28]

It was only by 1862 that Bidaa, Doha and Doha al Saghir (the three separate, neighbouring settlements that would become modern Doha), had been united under the nominal authority of Muhammad bin Thani and a Bahraini governor. The population of this group of villages had expanded from a few dozen to some 5,000.[29] The Bahraini governor was a member of Al-Khalifa who had married the daughter of Muhammad bin Thani. By 1867, however, relations between Muhammad bin Thani and the Bahraini governor had broken down. After the prominent son of Muhammad, Jassim, was imprisoned in Bahrain, a Bahraini fleet destroyed much of Doha in 1867. Although it appeared that Wakra and Doha had been 'blotted out of existence' by Bahrain and its Abu Dhabi allies, Al-Thani and several prominent Qataris finally resolved to confront Bahrain directly.[30]

THE 1868 AGREEMENT

Disturbed by the disruption caused by the conflict between Bahrain and Qatar, Colonel Pelly formally reprimanded the Bahraini chief for breaking his promise not to engage in unauthorized warfare. All disputes were to be submitted for settlement by the British Resident in Bushire. Colonel Pelly also negotiated an agreement, if not a formal 'treaty' with Muhammad bin Thani in 1868, the first formal recognition of Qatari independent sovereignty by the British. Although the agreement was more a list than a treaty, a list designating Muhammad bin Thani's responsibilities and limiting his options, a list of promises by Muhammad bin Thani with no real obligations on the part of the British, it was a formal recognition of his ability and his authority to control and bear responsibility for the tribes of Qatar. In fact, as recently as 2001, Bahrain claimed the agreement did not do much to support the formal independent claims of Qatar as it required that Muhammad bin Thani maintain the same relations with Bahrain as it had before, but that he direct any disagreements through the Resident.[31] Nevertheless, the 1868 agreement is highly significant. Although it was not absolutely the 'first time a British official had any dealings with Qatar' – the British had attempted to negotiate with the Suwaidi chief on the issue of piracy years earlier – it 'represented a milestone in the political evolution of Qatar.' It 'implicitly' recognized Qatar as independent from Bahrain.[32] Although various attempts were made to strengthen the weight of the 1868 agreement, it would not be until World War I that Britain would enter into more formal treaty arrangements with Qatar. The following is the content of the declarations made by Muhammad bin Thani and sealed by him and Colonel Lewis Pelly on 18 September 1868:

I, Muhammad bin Sanee [Muhammad bin Thani], of Gutter [Qatar], do hereby solemnly bind myself, in the presence of the Lord, to carry into effect the under mentioned terms agreed upon between me and Lieutenant-Colonel Pelly, Her Britannic Majesty's Political Resident, Persian Gulf.

1st – *I promise to return to Dawka [Doha] and reside peaceably in that port. [Muhammad bin Thani had previously removed himself from Doha to Khor Hassan in the north of Qatar to coordinate operations against the Bahraini governor.]*

2nd – *I promise that on no pretense whatsoever will I at any time put to sea with hostile intentions, and, in the event of a dispute or misunderstanding arising, will invariably refer to the Resident.*

3rd – *I promise on no account to aid Mahomed bin Khalifa, or in any way connect myself with him.*

4th – *If Mohamed bin Khalifa fall into my hands, I propose to hand him over to the Resident.*

5th – *I promise to maintain towards Sheikh Ali bin Khalifa, Chief of Bahrain, all the relations which heretofore subsisted between me and the Sheikh of Bahrain [who had prevailed in the dispute with Mohammad bin Khalifa for the rulership of Bahrain] and in the event of a difference of opinion arising as to any question, whether of money payment or other matter, the same is to be referred to the Resident.[33]*

An indication of the extraordinary importance of this somewhat simple declaration as a founding document of Qatar, the last promise of Muhammad bin Thani to uphold relations with Bahrain, is that it was cited as late as 2001 in an International Court of Justice Report on disputes between Bahrain and Qatar over various territories.[34] As the court finally concluded in paragraph 133 of its ruling on the Qatar-Bahrain border dispute:

> The agreement [of 1868] recognized the Chief of Qatar as being on an equal footing with the Chief of Bahrain, and not as a subordinate in any hierarchical relationship to himself or any part of the territory of Qatar. The contrary proposition of Bahrain in the current proceedings is not upheld in the text of either of the two main 1868 Agreements [an agreement was signed establishing the need for the Qatari sheikhs to pay tribute through Bahrain; see appendices of Colonel Pelly's report to Bombay cited in Note 32] or by the documentation and circumstances relating to their conclusion ...

Nevertheless, the fact that it took an international ruling in 2001 to determine the full meaning of the 1868 declaration is indicative of its vague implications for the actual sovereignty of Qatar.

Perhaps even more important than these specific promises declared by Muhammad bin Thani and their implications for Qatar's sovereignty was what they meant for Qatar's internal political development and the seemingly inevitable ascendancy of Al-Thani after 1868. The fact is that Colonel Pelly did not ask any other Qatar sheikhs to agree individually to the arrangement but rather 'addressed a letter to all the chiefs of Gutter, informing them of the arrangements arrived at, and warning them of the consequences of any future breach of maritime peace'. Colonel Pelly declared that 'it is expected that all the Sheikhs and tribes of Gutter [Qatar] should not molest him [Muhammad bin Thani] and his tribesmen.' Furthermore, he expressly assured the authority and stability of Al-Thani supremacy, stating, 'If any one is found acting otherwise, or in any way breaking the peace at sea, he will be treated in the same manner as Sheikh Mohammed bin Khalifa, of Bahrain, has been.'[35]

Although most of the principal chiefs of Qatar were on board the mother ship of Colonel Pelly's fleet, the *Vigilant*, it was Sheikh Muhammad bin Thani who was selected to make the proclamation. The scene must have been highly symbolic. Rather than disembark onto Qatari land, Colonel Pelly was able to control and stage the entire affair, so impressing the sheikhs into submission with the finery and power of a British war vessel in full display.[36] While Colonel Pelly thought this action made Muhammad bin Thani the true representative of all Qatar, the other Qatari sheikhs on board, 'Sheikh Jebran ibn Bahar, Sheikh Mahomed ibn Saeed, Sheikh Abdoolla ibn Mahomed, Sheikh Fudhel Ibn Mohanna, and Sheikh Ranshid ibn Jabar', did not see Muhammad bin Thani's authority in such absolute terms.[37] In fact, ironically, while the general agreement of 18 September was made between Colonel Pelly and Sheikh Muhammad bin Thani, an agreement of 11 September to pay the Sheikh of Bahrain damages and tribute was made by individual tribal chiefs.[38] Certainly, in the artificial confines of the *Vigilant*, Muhammad bin Thani could command a certain supremacy, but never was that supremacy historically pre-ordained. Although they agreed to his status as the most powerful of the sheikhs, the sheikhs had selected him as their spokesman, not as their monarch. While it would give too much weight to the actual power and influence of the British inside Qatar to suggest that Britain essentially created the social and political conditions of Qatari society, the British did create an element of categorical friction, a stickiness of identity, in a society that had once had a fluid and dynamic tradition of legitimacy and power.

The meeting on the *Vigilant* not only established Qatar as a more independent entity, it changed the social dynamic of Qatar. No longer did the most respected man in Doha need to base his power ultimately on the Islamic *baya*, the oath of allegiance and obliga-tion between ruler and ruled, or the *shura* and *majlis*, the council of respected sheikhs in Arabic tribal and Islamic religious tradition, that power was now based on the full weight of the British Navy. As Lisa Anderson has aptly observed, before imperial inter-ests created European-style monarchy in the Middle East, 'Political authority has been exercised and justified not as an aspect of family or property but on religious grounds.'[39] Legitimate rule, according to centuries of tradition, was based on Islamic principles and on local conditions. Qatar was small enough that its constituent tribes, most of them from the Najd region of what is now Saudi Arabia, and many of them related, knew the members of all other tribes personally. Britain did not establish its treaty with Qatar in order to rule it, or even to dominate it but rather to try and understand it according to European categories and assumptions about rule, monarchy and succession. By throwing its support and power behind Muhammad bin Thani, Britain found a predictable and stable, if not always loyal, representative of Qatar. To put it simply, Britain needed to find somebody to deal with in Qatar. Whether intentionally or unintentionally, this desire spawned a whole range of consequences for Qatari society. Al-Thani power was 'created' by British interference even as it 'emerged' from Qatari society and the country's internal history. Yet the British were not the only imperial power with an interest in Qatar. The Ottomans also saw the Peninsula as a strategic part of their land-based, as opposed to Britain's sea-based, empire.

QATAR AND THE OTTOMANS

Although it was both the British desire to identify a leader and the Qatari desire for that leadership that supported Al-Thani claim to rule, the power of Al-Thani would not have been nearly as solidified by the end of the nineteenth century had it not been for Ottoman interference in the Peninsula. The 1868 accord was an agreement, not a formal treaty with Britain. Unlike other Gulf States, therefore, Qatar was formally not in the same treaty relations with Britain and had less leverage to protect itself from the rise of Ottoman power in Al-Hasa, on the western shore of the Gulf. By conquering the land, not simply controlling the seas as was the wish of Britain, the Ottomans provided the 'official' frontiers of power and bestowed the authority needed to elevate mere tribal strongmen to dynastic Emirs. Yet even on land the Ottomans were certainly not without dedicated rivals. Al-Saud of Riyadh, following the radically charged 'Wahhabi' doctrine of Muhammad ibn 'Abd al Wahhab, were often a major enemy of the Ottomans. In fact, the Sunni Ottomans and the Wahhabis had both denounced each other as 'unbelievers', against whom *jihad*, or holy war should be fought. Although Al-Saud of Riyadh repeatedly lost ground to the Ottomans and sometimes came under their suzerainty, they continued to return, often with a vengeance, and lay renewed claims to Ottoman territory. From 1795 to 1818, from 1830 to 1838 and from 1843 to 1871, Al-Saud controlled Al-Hasa on the eastern shore of Arabia and made regular incursions into Bahrain and Qatar. Yet the greatest threat to the Ottomans on a strategic level came not from the Wahhabis but the British. Typical of the power politics and balance of power game of nineteenth-century Europe, the Ottomans, though 'the sick man of Europe', were determined to defend their remaining possessions against British incursions. Not knowing British intentions for the Gulf, which before the discovery of oil were limited to securing the seas, the Ottomans overestimated the desire of the British to conquer the Gulf. As Frederick Anscombe observed in *The Ottoman Gulf*, 'Overblown suspicion [of the British] often diverted scarce resources to meet unlikely outside threats instead of to fix problems caused by maladministration.'[40]

The presence of the Ottomans was important for the history of Qatar, however, primarily because it provided Al-Thani, especially Muhammad bin Thani's son Jassim, with the opportunity to use the rivalry between Britain and the Ottomans to their advantage. Although many designate 1868 and the recognition of Muhammad bin Thani as the beginning of Al-Thani rule, it was not until 1871 and the incursion of the Ottomans that Al-Thani truly emerged as the titular representative of Qatar. With the Ottomans began a long history of successful Al-Thani manipulation of external powers to shield and support their authority on the peninsula, a strategic manipulation, often subtle, sometimes more explicit, that has continued into the present period.

The impetus for Ottoman involvement in Qatar began shortly after Muhammad bin Thani signed the 1868 treaty with the British. In 1869 the new Ottoman governor of Baghdad Ahmed Sefik Pasha established a new foreign policy to consolidate Ottoman land power over the Gulf. Even though the Ottomans had no hope of competing with the British for naval domination, they could squeeze the British from the shore by establishing an Ottoman hold over the Arabian shore. The Ottomans used a split between father and son, a split that would become a familiar feature of Al-Thani family politics and the interference of outsiders in that politics, to find an opening into Qatar. Muhammad bin Thani refused to recognize Ottoman authority and kept his contacts with the British and traditional tribal base. He must have correctly sensed the potential for the expansion of Ottoman ambitions in Qatar. His son Jassim, however, accepted the Ottoman presence and in 1872 Qatar was designated a Kaza, or small district, under the Sanjak of the Najd. The son Sheikh Jassim, not Muhammad, was designated as the Qaim Maqam, regional governor, without pay, but Qatar was exempted from paying Ottoman taxes, excepting the religious *zakat*. Soon Ottoman flags were hoisted above the house of Jassim; Abdalaziz of Khor Shaqiq and the chief of Khor Udeid similarly put up flags. Sheikh Muhammad, whose house was not far from that of his son, refused to raise an Ottoman standard. This did not lead to an all-out conflict between father and son, however. In many ways the arrangement suited Al-Thani. With Muhammad bin Thani favouring British protection and Jassim allowing the Ottomans into Qatar both imperial powers could be kept from making outsized demands. Ironically, it would only be after the death of Muhammad bin Thani in 1878 that the Ottomans would start to demand more explicit use of Qatar to balance British power.

A ZUBARA PROBLEM

In 1878, however, it was not the Ottomans but Al-Naim and their split loyalties between Qatar and Bahrain that allowed Jassim the opportunity to assert his authority, just as his father had done ten years earlier. Despite Jassim's alliance with the Ottomans, they refused to help him deal with factionalism within Qatar or with Bahrain's claims on Zubara. Although Jassim had consolidated much of his power by the time of Muhammad bin Thani's death in 1878, he still needed to assume control over his father's direct followers, especially those opposed to Ottoman intervention. An opportunity arose for Sheikh Jassim to do so after the Naim attacked ships from Bidaa at sea and after the Sheikh of Bahrain dispatched troops to Zubara to reinforce the Naim against Al-Thani. Indeed, the Sheikh of Bahrain had maintained extensive contacts with the Naim, an indication of the fluidity of borders, across maritime boundaries. It was this fluidity that Britain wished to suppress to avoid confusing conflict and disorder in the seas. The locking down of the Naim did much to benefit Al-Thani and the emergence of Qatar as a cohesive geographic expression. According to British officials:

The Chief of Bahrein [sic] should not have been encouraged to dispatch troops to the mainland for the reinforcements of his allies, the Naim tribe. On the contrary he should be advised to rely for support on the assistance of the British government, which will, if necessary, be given him either to repel attacks by sea or to frustrate a threatening movement from the mainland.[41]

Although the British denounced the Bahrainis and effectively delegitimized the long-established maritime nomadism discussed in Chapter 2, the Bahrainis and the Naim did not simply give up their alliance, even after Jassim destroyed Zubara in 1878. The Sheikh of Bahrain continued to provide allowances to the Naim in Qatar and the Naim would send tribute to Bahrain. The Sheikh of Bahrain also regularly used 100 Naim in his army and personal bodyguard.[42] The problem of Zubara, the Naim and Bahrain would not simply go away even if the advantage was clearly on the side of Qatar and Al-Thani. If anything, the threat from Zubara, Bahrain and the Naim, unsustainable because of British prohibitions, gave Al-Thani another source of legitimacy with the tribes of southern Qatar.

The Ottomans proved useful to Al-Thani. Indeed, Jassim conspired several times with the Ottoman governor Nasir bin Mubarak to overthrow Sheikh Isa of Bahrain.[43] Relations with the Ottomans would only break down when it became clear to Jassim that the Ottomans were more interested in restricting British control of the Gulf than in securing benefits for Al-Thani. Although given the title of deputy governor and officially a vassal of the Sublime Porte, the Ottoman Sultan, Sheikh Jassim was never willing to allow the Ottomans to establish a truly effective presence in Qatar or anything close to direct rulership.

THE BATTLE OF WAJBAH

If Qatar's conflict with Bahrain helped to consolidate Al-Thani power, Qatar's assertion of independence from its major inland colonial protector – the Ottomans – provided Jassim Al-Thani with an aura of authority. In October 1892 the Ottoman Wali, or governor, Mehmed Hafiz Pasha took some 200 Ottoman soldiers to Bidaa to assert Ottoman rights to establish larger, more permanent bases at Zubara and Khor Al-Udeid with administrators and government representations. These bases would be in addition to the Ottoman contingent already stationed in Bidaa. Sheikh Jassim refused to meet the Wali and kept himself and a garrison of fighters locked away at the fortress of Wajbah. The Ottoman Wali captured and kidnapped Sheikh Jassim's brother Sheikh Ahmad bin Muhammad bin Thani and 13 prominent Qatari chiefs, keeping them on the Ottoman ship, the *Merrikh*. Knowing his country well and taking advantage of his position as the defender, Sheikh Jassim acted quickly. The capture of the chiefs of some Qatari tribes only solidified the resolve of Al-Thani and non-Al-Thani alike. Jassim used nomadic fighters, mainly the Bani Hajr, and couriers to intercept Ottoman messengers and stop Ottoman reinforcements from Al-Hasa. When the Wali arrived at Wajbah, Jassim and his small contingent of Qatari tribes, taking advantage of the water wells at Wajbah and strategically stored food supplies, repelled the large, thirsty Ottoman force. In the end some 400 Qataris, women, men and children were killed, but Sheikh Jassim and the Qataris had effectively asserted Qatari independence from direct, Ottoman interference and had shown the Ottomans that they were not simply a dispersed group of tribes that happened to inhabit a strategic peninsula in the power games between Ottomans and the British. The Qataris, under Jassim's leadership, had asserted themselves as a force and a presence to be respected. Although the Ottomans would continue to use Qatar and Al-Thani as part of their wider strategic initiatives, the Qataris themselves would now be seen more as allies than simply as imperial pawns. Jassim's extraordinary letter directly to the Sublime Porte in Istanbul shortly after the Wajbah incident shows how this pugnacious, local governor of an out of the way Arabian province had increased his diplomatic stature. Sultan Abdul Hamid II personally appointed and approved an investigation of the incident and approved a plan to remove Mehmed Hafiz Pasha from his post.[44]

The Battle of Wajbah, Sheikh Jassim's defeat of the Turks through the collaborative effort of Qatari tribes, has recently been used to elevate Sheikh Jassim to the status of 'founder of the country'. National Day, which I witnessed when it was first celebrated in 2007, is occasioned by military parades, conspicuous displays of the Qatari flag and other 'national' symbols. There are even instances where the traditionally white, Qatari male *thob* is adorned with vests coloured like the national flag. Sheikh Hamad established a State National Day Celebrations Organization Committee (SNDCOC) to organize elaborate events connecting Qatari heritage and history to the notion of 'unity' under Al-Thani leadership. Jassim was, according to the SNDCOC website, the 'ruler who led the country toward unity'.[45] Instead of focusing on the role of the tribes in supporting Sheikh Jassim, the focus is clearly centred on the necessity of Al-Thani leadership over tribal division. Interestingly, National Day has somewhat surpassed Independence Day in the size and importance of the celebrations, despite beginning only in 2007. After all, as will be explored later, independence from Britain was not occasioned by any systematic struggle but rather a desire, in some instances, to maintain British protection. The Ottoman Empire, soon to disappear as mere artefact, was a much easier mythical enemy.

There may a more subtle reason for the choice of Jassim over Muhammad bin Thani, as it further marginalized the branch of Al-Thani descended from Ahmad, the brother of Jassim. By making Jassim, not Muhammad the 'national' hero and founder, the descendants of Jassim have a much more explicit claim to rule.

THE END OF OTTOMAN INFLUENCE

Jassim's defeat of the Ottomans was part of a larger pattern of revolt and demands for independence by Arab subjects of the Sublime Porte. By 1902 the Ottomans had weakened substantially and Jassim focussed his energies on protecting Qatar from the ambitions of the young Abdalaziz Ibn Saud who had taken Riyadh back to Wahhabism. It was in this year, in fact, that Jassim formally became a Wahhabi – although Wahhabism had existed in Qatar decades before, this 'conversion' was much more of a political, symbolic act, a pre-emptive recognition of influence by Al-Saud. By 1913, however, Wahhabi expansion under Ibn Saud began to threaten Qatar's viability directly. It would be in this context that Sheikh Abdallah bin Jassim, the new ruler of Qatar would sign a formal treaty with Britain, heralding a new era of intense British involvement in Qatar and Qatari history – the Protectorate.

CONCLUSIONS – REASONS FOR AL-THANI SUCCESS BEFORE OIL

In summary, there are several reasons for the successful establishment of Al-Thani dynasty in Qatar, some are the result of British intervention, others of particular factors within Qatar and Al-Thani family.

1. Length of reign. The first two Al-Thani sheikhs, the founding sheikh Muhammad bin Thani, his successor Jassim bin Muhammad, and even Abdallah, the grandson, lived to a remarkably old age. This continuity of rule over time created a precedent for a rarely broken reliability.

2. Continuity of succession and power. Rule remained within Al-Thani line. Except for the *baya* or oath of allegiance of leading members of the family and leading tribes, there was no pre-existing principle, institution or precedent for succession. This allowed Al-Thani to define the realities of power after each succession.

3. Persistence of settlement. Al-Thani, unlike other prominent tribes on the peninsula that regularly moved in search of better markets or opportunities, maintained a persistent presence in the region of Bidaa and Doha. This established their authority and created the conditions for constructing a traditional, ancestral precedent for their rights over the land.

4. Vacuum of authority. The benefits of authority in Qatar, although significant, were not nearly as great as they were after the discovery of oil. The relative lack of competition for authority gave Al-Thani the space to establish a powerful status quo.

5. British and Ottoman intervention. As explained earlier, Al-Thani sheikhs effectively played British and Ottoman interests off against each other for the benefit

of their own power and position in Qatar. Paying tribute to more powerful outsiders to protect their position was part of a long historical tradition in the Gulf.

6. Traditional forms of allegiance. Al-Thani relied on the allegiance, not the obedience or subjection, of other Qatari tribes. This allegiance was given not only because of the command of the British to the other Qatari tribes to respect the authority of Al-Thani. Al-Thani required this reciprocal allegiance to maintain their power.

7. A unifying symbol for the diverse peoples of Qatar. As the dramatic victory at the Battle of Wajbah demonstrates, Al-Thani Emir could be a rallying point for unified Qatari action against the overstepping of outsiders. Qataris are actively reminded of this symbolism today with National Day celebrations of Sheikh Jassim's leadership.

All the above reasons explain the persistence of Al-Thani rule. They are reasons that existed before oil. Oil only served to deepen the entrenchment of Al-Thani power in Qatar.

4

Creating Social Realities – Qatar and the British in the Twentieth Century

In his popular book *Guns, Germs and Steel*, Jared Diamond argues that Europeans were able to colonize and dominate Asian societies because of superior technology.[1] There was, according to Diamond, almost no successful resistance to European domination until well into the twentieth century. Qatar, however, avoided outright colonization. The Ottomans were only able to claim tenuous control over Qatari land, ceding real power to Muhammad bin Thani. Both external powers were kept at bay by the resourcefulness of the Qataris under Muhammad bin Thani and his successors, especially Sheikh Jassim Al-Thani. Qatar, led by a successful line of tenacious and usually astute Al-Thani Emirs, successfully resisted full external domination. They accomplished this not through technological superiority but through the deft use of diplomacy and negotiation. Only at the last resort, as at Wajbah against the Ottomans in 1892, would the Qataris use force to protect their position. The Qataris continually searched for rivals who would be partners. When the First World War eliminated the Ottomans as a balance against the British, the sheikhs appealed to American oil contractors to compete with the British, thereby gaining much greater concessions. It could be argued that this practice of balancing rival interests, neighbors and powers continues to this day as Qatar reaches out to both Iran and the United States. Although there were, as now, external powers that had an interest in Qatar, the Qataris avoided 'colonization' in the fashion of India or Africa or even the Mandate of Egypt. Unlike the jubilation and liberating experience of other post-colonial states, many Qataris and the Qatar royal family were shocked to see British military protection and guarantees evaporate in the late 1960s. Less of a colonial power than an advisory service, the British were providing consultancy and bureaucratic services, as well as free military protection to the state and Al-Thani family. After all, it was the British Empire that had first recognized Muhammad bin Thani as the leader of Qatar.

THE GROWTH OF BRITISH INTEREST IN QATAR

Although Muhammad bin Thani announced his obligations to Britain in the Treaty of 1868, the Ottomans still heavily influenced Qatar's inland territory until the First World War. A formal protection treaty with Britain was not signed until 1916, but even then there was little direct political interference by the British until 1949 when the first large ship filled with crude oil left Qatar's shores. Before 1949, Qataris experienced severe economic distress from the collapse of the pearl market and the stoppage of oil exploration and drilling during the Second World War. There were even accounts of Qataris dying of hunger, something completely unimaginable today. The presence of the British and the initial establishment of Western institutions under the Protectorate helped solidify the status quo tribal arrangements. Al-Thani family gained especial power as the favoured ruling tribe through which the British dealt with most of their affairs. Other, powerful commercial and political interests, however, also existed in Qatar. The merchant shi'a Al-Fardan family, for example, possessed far more wealth than Al-Thani. Although important, British involvement in Qatar was fairly relaxed even in the 1960s as Qatar began to take control over much of its foreign affairs, joining organizations such as OPEC, WHO and UNESCO.

The impact of British rule on the social hierarchy and structure of much larger protectorates and colonies such as Egypt and India has been well documented. Similarly, this chapter will argue that the British Protectorate with the cooperation of Al-Thani elite planted the seeds of institutional development in a way that favoured certain entrenched tribal interests and placed Al-Thani firmly in a position to dominate governance and state building.

THE ANGLO-QATARI TREATY

Just as his grandfather had done before him when he signed the treaty of 1868, on 3 November 1916 Sheikh Abdallah bin Jassim Al-Thani came on board a British ship, the *Lawrence*, surrounded as his grandfather had been by the trappings of British imperial might, to negotiate a new treaty with Britain's representative Lieutenant-Colonel Sir Percy Cox. The writers of the treaty, written for Sheikh Abdallah in the first person, did not lose the parallels between Muhammad bin Thani and Sheikh Abdallah's agreements with Britain. The opening paragraph states:

> Whereas my grandfather, the late Sheikh Mohammed bin Thani, signed an agreement on the 12th of September 1868 engaging not to commit any breach of the maritime peace, and whereas these obligations to the British Government have devolved on me his successor in Qatar.[2]

The historic link between the interests of the British and the institution of the Sheikh of Qatar are clearly established. Yet the Anglo-Qatari Treaty went much further than the comparatively brief 1868 agreement.

Although it fails to mention the many informal agreements and understandings between Britain and Qatar, the Anglo-Qatari Treaty of November 1916 became the explicit, legal foundation of Qatar's protectorate status. Unlike the treaty of 1868, much shorter and more of a statement of will than a complex legal document, the Anglo-Qatari Treaty of 1916 reflects as much the maturation of Al-Thani rulership and of Qatar as an independent political entity, as the increased necessity of closer, more involved relations between Qatar and Britain. Sheikh Abdallah was somewhat more subtle, and is often not credited with the same bold leadership skills of his storied predecessors, Muhammad bin Thani and Sheikh Jassim. Although not always the most deft of rulers, the son of Jassim, Abdallah bin Jassim (r. 1913–49) sharpened Qatar's separate legal identity not simply through bold confrontation and traditional, regional negotiation but through perseverance and even a subtle manipulation of British interests, using a mixture of collaboration and obstinacy that kept the British content enough to serve his interests but not secure enough to take him, or Qatar, for granted. Yet from the beginning Abdallah had far more than British demands to worry about. Like Prince Tamim, the current Crown Prince of Qatar, Abdallah, the fourth son of Jassim, was his father's favourite. Jassim made him governor of Doha in 1905 and groomed him for power. After Jassim's death, however, major internal threats emerged.

Perhaps the most important threat on the mind of Sheikh Abdallah was his father's difficult relations with Abdalaziz, future king of Saudi Arabia (Saudi Arabia did not come into formal existence until the unification of the kingdoms of the Nejd and the Hijaz in 1932). Abdalaziz opposed Sheikh Jassim's sponsorship of the Turkish garrison on Qatari soil. Major Trevor, Political Agent in Bahrain in 1913, even suggested that 'possibly Bin Saud may attempt to take over Katar altogether'.[3] Indeed, between the Turks, Al-Saud and the British the situation grew quite difficult to balance after the death of Jassim. Yet, in fact, the internal situation in Qatar appeared to be even more perilous. There were erroneous reports and rumours that members of his own family had killed Sheikh Abdallah. Qatar seemed yet again to be on the brink of being consumed by Al-Saud after Sheikh Abdallah's brother and rival Sheikh Khalifa bin Jassim Al-Thani intrigued with Bin Saud to overthrow Abdallah. Later, this posed a serious problem to Britain since:

> if Qatar should fall into the hands of Bin Saud, the consequences for the Trucial Chiefs, commencing with Abu Dhabi[,] are bound to be most serious. They have been severely scourged this year by the ravages of plague and, on top of that, comes financial ruin, caused by this most disastrous War now raging in Europe.[4]

The British were determined not to be drawn into an inevitable conflict with Bin Saud should he decide to advance into the Trucial States. Doing so would draw Bin Saud onto the side of the Ottomans. Indeed, Abdalaziz bin Saud, who did not participate in the Arab revolt against the Ottomans, would acknowledge Ottoman suzreignity in 1914 to focus his efforts at defeating the rival al-Rashid to the North. In any case, the British did not want Qatar to fall into the hands of a potential Ottoman ally. The British, sensing the serious danger posed by the death of Jassim and the instability in Qatar, decided to put their full weight behind Sheikh Abdallah. It was in this context that the Anglo-Qatari Treaty was formulated.

Article 1 of the Anglo-Qatari Treaty reiterated many of the principles of previous agreements between the Gulf States and Britain, mandating cooperation with 'the High British government in the suppression of the slave trade and piracy and generally in the maintenance of the Maritime Peace'. The Article declared that Qatar would be included in the same 'treaties and engagements' entered into between Britain and the Arab sheikhs of 'Abu Dhabi, Dibai [Dubai], Shargah [Sharjah], Ajman, Ras-ul-Khaima and Umm-al-Qawain'.

As this list of previous agreements indicated, it was notable that compared with the other emirates of the Gulf, Qatar was relatively late in receiving such formal recognition. Bahrain's treaty was negotiated 26 years earlier in 1880 and again in 1893. Kuwait's was finalized in 1899. The sheikhs of the UAE and Qatar were last. Indeed, several attempts had been made at the highest levels, including by Lord Curzon, the Viceroy of India, who had visited the Gulf in 1903, to formalize Qatar's protectorate status. It had been during this visit that Lord Curzon made his famous address to the Trucial sheikhs declaring his interpretation of British interests in the region. 'Why should Great Britain continue to exercise these powers?' Curzon replied to his own question with the following triumphalist summation of British interests:

> The history of your States and of your families, and the present condition of the Gulf, are the answer. We were here before any other power in modern times had shown its face in these waters. [Note the avoidance of any mention of the French or Portugal.] We found strife and we have created order. It was our commerce as well as your security that was threatened and called for protection. At every port along these coasts the subjects of the King of England still reside and trade. The great Empire of India, which it is our duty to defend, lies almost at your gates ...

In a claim of unselfish virtue that reflected some of the rhetoric of recent US intervention in the region, Curzon continued:

> We are not going to throw away this century of costly and triumphant enterprise: we will not wipe out the most unselfish page of history. The peace of these waters must be maintained [and] your independence will continue to be upheld; and the influence of the British Government will remain supreme.[5]

Although his ambitions for the Gulf were strong, not everyone in the British imperial establishment shared his philosophy. Curzon's attempts to formalize relations with Qatar were thwarted by Britain's ambassador to the Sultan's Sublime Porte in Istanbul who feared that any further British intervention in Qatar would unnecessarily upset the Ottomans who had established a presence on the Peninsula. The outbreak of the First World War and the increased importance of communication between Britain and its empire during the war, however, immediately sharpened the need for formalized relations with Al-Thani, as with other, major Arab sheikhs and leaders including Ibn Saud and the Sharif of Mecca. According to Britain's strategic plan, the Arabs would cooperate with Britain against the Ottomans in exchange for promised, greater freedoms. By maintaining relations and treaties with individual sheikhs, the British established the sheikhs' internal power and continued dynastic authority.[6]

Much of what made the Anglo-Qatari Treaty important was not simply in what it said but in what it implied. It is important to note, for instance, that once again the Anglo-Qatari Treaty, like the 1868 treaty, was meant to bolster Abdallah's power and did not take into consideration the diverse and complex power structures of local Qatari politics. As the first sentence, indeed the first word 'I' makes clear, the treaty is not made between Britain and Qatar but between Britain and Al-Thani ruler Sheikh Abdallah: 'I, Sheikh Abdallah bin Jassim bin Thani, undertake that I ...' The British elite's understanding of the sheikhdoms as authoritarian, desert aristocracies created the legal foundations of present-day authoritarianism. This authoritarianism was based as much on British assumptions and desires as on the negotiated, complex of Qatari or Arab social realities. Practically no distinction was made between Sheikh Abdallah and Qatar: they are implicitly assumed to be, legally speaking, almost one and the same. Only Sheikh Abdallah's signature and seal is mentioned, not the signatures and seals of Al bin Ali, Al-Sudan or the Kuwari, or of Abdallah's rival family members.

Sir Percy Cox was the British representative whose name was affixed to the Anglo-Qatari Treaty. Known as Sir 'Kookus' in Arabic, Sir Percy was, with those semi-legendary civil servants Gertrude Bell and William H.I. Shakespear (d. 1915), a member of that club of imperial diplomats and adventurers that would, seemingly single-handedly, transform the Arab world and usurp the power of local actors.[7] When Lord Curzon visited Sir Percy Cox in Muscat, for instance, he judged that Cox had not only managed to oust the pesky French who supported the slave trade but credited him with running the place.[8] From his perspective as a senior civil servant, rising rapidly through the ranks, Sir Percy saw Qatar as another protectorate fit into British imperial needs and objectives. One of the most important ways of limiting the internal power of rival Qatari clans was through control of the internal distribution of arms. The British effectively made Al-Thani the sole legal distributor of arms, thereby giving them sole authority over the weapons and means of warfare.

In fact, the British were very aware of the weakness of Abdallah's position *vis-à-vis* his family. In a discussion with Lieutenant-Colonel Grey, the Political Agent in Kuwait, Sheikh Abdallah indicated,

> his cousins and older brother, Khalifa, were envious of his position, and always ready to intrigue against him with Abu Dhabi, an ancient enemy, or others, whenever opportunity offered. I suggested that a treaty between him and His Majesty's Government would bring them to see the necessity of abandoning this course; and he admitted their fear of reprisals by us in the event of an attack upon him ...[9]

Clearly, the British were not ignorant of the domestic dissent against Abdallah. Also, they indicated that the British treaty recently created with Abu Dhabi would prevent any intervention in the internal affairs of Qatar. Grey even agreed to provide Abdallah with a 'field piece' or gun superior to his brother's gun located 4 miles north of Doha.[10] Percy Cox offered to 'send for Khalifa [to come on board the *Lawrence*] and give him a homily and a warning, or to write one to him ...'.[11] The tightening of British interests around a singular 'stable' ruler is clearly evident – British might made an immediate impression on the traditional, social power dynamic of Qatar. No longer would the British be a distant partner that nominally supported an Al-Thani Emir as long as he kept trouble at bay. More than any humiliating 'homily', Percy Cox's plan to allow only Sheikh Abdallah to control the import and export of weapons was one of the most effective ways to increase the Sheikh's authority.

The third Article of the treaty established limits to Qatar's arms exports and important trade but also gave Sheikh Abdallah sole authority to make 'personal' purchases from the Muscat arms warehouse in Oman. These weapons were for the Sheikh's own use or for the arming of his 'dependents'. In fact, he was forbidden from arming other tribes or selling arms to 'the public' – the non-Al-Thani tribes. Far from a limitation on his power, this clause effectively established his monopoly over arms while the Anglo-Qatari Treaty also gave him an excuse to confront any dissent by other tribes.

> I undertake absolutely that arms and ammunition thus supplied to me shall under no circumstances be re-exported from my territories or sold to the public, but shall be reserved solely for supplying the needs of my tribesmen and dependents whom I have to arm for the maintenance of order in my territories and the protection of my Frontiers. In my opinion the amount of yearly requirements will be up to five hundred weapons.

In the original draft of the treaty the British were going to allow Abdallah 1,000 weapons and more latitude in distributing the arms. However, the final draft was changed so that, according to Percy Cox, it would 'provide reasonable safeguards against the sale to the public of rifles obtained by the Sheikh through our auspices'.[12] Although there was some evidence that the arms trade had died down slightly, Lieutenant-Colonel Grey on the *Lawrence* reported Sheikh Abdallah mentioning that 'some Afghans had visited the port with a view to the purchase of rifles, and had returned to their country empty-handed'.[13] Nevertheless, the consolidation in the hands of the Sheikh of the right to purchase weapons substantially bolstered his position. Abdallah almost immediately asked for rifles from Muscat after the treaty was signed. He was particularly fond of . 303 carbide short rifles with Martini action to be used by camel warriors.[14]

Sheikh Abdallah expressed 'uneasiness' about the sixth Article, which allowed the British to impose customs taxes.[15] At the same time the Article also implicitly allowed Sheikh Abdallah to maintain control over the customs house, an important source of pre-oil revenue.

British interest in propping up the power of Al-Thani, however, effectively ended when it came to external affairs. The fourth Article virtually hands over all of Qatar's foreign policy to the British government, even forbidding correspondence with 'any other power' without the consent of the 'High British Government'. Nor was Abdallah permitted to 'cede to any other Power or its subjects, land either on lease, sale, transfer, gift, or in any other way whatsoever'. A prohibition on selling land to non-Qataris, originally part of a British strategy to control Qatar's foreign commitments, continues to this day, with the exception of the artificial-island pearl development. Abdallah also committed the Qataris to making no 'pearl-fishery concessions, or any other monopolies, concessions, or cable landing rights, to anyone whomsoever'. The main reason for this clause was that there had been previous instances when the French had attempted to establish a pearl trade with Qatar – little did Percy Cox know that Qatar was sitting on huge natural reserves of gas and oil.

Articles 7 to 9 outline further details of the British protectorate in Qatar. Article 7 urges Abdallah to 'undertake to allow British subjects to reside in Qatar for trade and to protect their lives and property'. These 'British subjects' were not simply from Britain but included imperial subjects from the entire British Empire, including British India – a source of some tension between Abdallah and the British. The Qatari pearl merchants and divers seemed to resent the special rights accorded south Asians. According to Lieutenant-Colonel Grey, Abdallah:

> said that the people of Qatar were still strongly anti-foreign, and would not consent to the reception of foreign traders, and that he would be in constant fear of trouble resulting to himself from the bad treatment of such persons by his people.

Abdallah, in fact, wanted to preserve the commercial privileges of Arab traders in Qatar. Sir Percy Cox allowed some leniency and delay in the enforcement of the Article, indicating in a separate addendum that the Article only applied to British merchandise, not British or British-Indian traders, for a period of at least ten years.[16]

Slavery was another issue where Abdallah demanded concessions. Although the treaty was to ban the trade in slaves, Sir Percy Cox admitted the following in a secret telegram that accompanied the treaty:

> As regards the question of slaves already existing in Qatar the Government of India will realize that if the Political Officers were to take any ill-considered line of action in the direction of manumission of Qatar slaves pursuant to the conclusion of this Treaty Sheikh Abdallah's position among his dependents would straightway become extremely difficult.

Percy Cox justified his position, indicating that:

> the trade in new slaves at all events by sea has practically ceased to exist in the Gulf of late years; a few, no doubt, continue to be brought over [by land] from the Mecca side, but very few; and among those already here it is found that ... cases of serious maltreatment are by no means common, nor are the Sheikhs concerned unamenable to advice. I am of opinion therefore that both our requirements and the interests of the negroes will be adequately safeguarded by our making our abstention from interference contingent on the hypothesis that the Sheikh and his dependents treat their slaves fairly.[17]

Perhaps Sir Percy was unaware that Sheikh Abdallah had a tendency to physically punish slaves from his brother's retinue, causing outrage even among his own people.[18] Although they heard of occasional abuses, it was apparently in the interest of the British to ignore the treatment of slaves as an unnecessary distraction from immediate strategic needs.

Article 8 allows Britain to establish a Political Agent in Qatar. Article 9 allows for a British Post Office and a Telegraph installation 'anywhere in my territory whenever the British government should desire them'.

Although he was given implicit advantages in previous Articles in the treaty, only the last two Articles explicitly state Britain's obligations. The tenth article restates British guarantees to 'protect me and my territory from all aggression by sea and to do their utmost to exact reparation for all injuries that I, or my subjects, may suffer when proceeding to sea upon our lawful occasions.' Article 11 goes much further, however, in that it explicitly suggests that Britain will also 'provide good offices' (but not necessarily guarantee the same protection as it would at sea) to Abdallah, Al-Thani and Qatar on the land, lending the possible weight of the British Empire to the guaranteed independence of Qatar and the continuation of Al-Thani power internally. 'They also undertake to grant me good offices should I or my subjects be assailed by land within the territories of Qatar.' Sir Percy Cox was careful to limit the applicability of this clause. The Article continues that it is 'thoroughly understood that this obligation rests upon the British Government only in the event of such aggression whether by land or sea, being unprovoked by any act of aggression on the part of myself or my subjects against others'. In later correspondence, the British refused to provide anything other than 'diplomatic assistance to the Sheikh of El Qatar ...'.[19] Sheikh Abdallah continually attempted to demand British assurances against internal aggression by recalcitrant subjects.

In some respects the lack of British meddling actually hampered Abdallah's plans. He attempted to rely on the British to legitimize Ali, his son as his choice of successor. The British, however, were relucatant to be involved in internal Al-Thani family matters and preferred to deal with whatever Emir who would eventually emerge. As a British government officer pronounced in secret correspondence:

> If the son is the strongest man he will succeed without the necessity of any prior recognition by Government, if he is not the strongest man then any recognition given now might mean incurring possibly very inconvenient obligations later on.[20]

EFFECTIVENESS OF THE TREATY

In many respects the treaty was nominally successful in defending mutual British/Al-Thani interests. Abdallah was recognized as the independent ruler of Qatar by the world's foremost naval power. He was given the title of Companion of the Most Eminent Order of the British Empire and a 'seven-gun salute'.[21] This formality was not without importance, as Zahlan has remarked:

> British support for a ruler was conveyed in many different ways, even in the number of gun salutes he was accorded. In 1929, for example, the rulers of Kuwait, Bahrain and Qatar were the recipients of seven-gun salutes; the ruler of Abu Dhabi received a five-gun salute; and the ruler of Dubai, only a humble three. That year, an attempt was made by the family of Sheikh Said of Dubai to depose him. The Political Resident stepped in to uphold the ruler: he warned that any move to depose Sheikh Said would incur the strong disapproval of the British government. To reconfirm his support, a public and audible gesture to Sheikh Said followed: he was granted a five-gun salute ... the salutes of Kuwait and Bahrain were raised (to 11) as a mark of approbation after they signed oil concessions a few years later.[22]

More substantively, the treaty not only further assured the stability of Abdallah's position, it also prevented a takeover of Qatar, or at least caused Al-Saud to think twice about such a move. Nevertheless, the threat of action by Abdalaziz bin Saud was constantly on the mind of Abdallah and seemed a very real prospect. In 1923, Lieutenant-Colonel Trevor, Political Resident of the Persian Gulf, went so far as to suggest that:

> I think it would be a pity if Qatar disappeared as a separate entity; from our point of view it is convenient to have rulers of the coastal districts on the coast, but I do not see any practicable means of preventing peaceful penetration of the country by Akhwan and Bin Saud's adherants ...[23]

The Akhwan, or Ikhwan, were the proselytizing, radical 'brothers' of the Wahhabi move-ment who had been making forays into Gulf territories to enforce a strict interpretation of doctrine. Bin Saud would eventually repress the Ikhwan when they rebelled against his authority. In Qatar, however, there was genuine fear of radical influences disguising the intentions of Al-Saud to absorb Qatar, a concern that has continued to the present. In fact, a perpetual and continuing problem for the Qatar ruling family has been the tendency for certain Qatari tribes to defect to Saudi Arabia when they grew disaffected with the Emir. This was recently a concern with Al-Murrah Bedouin, many of whom recently had their Qatari nationality revoked, and then reinstated, by Sheikh Hamad bin Khalifa Al-Thani.

For Abdallah, the threat of defection seemed even more dire, constant and existential. Many of Al-Ainain of Wakra, a tribe that had once been more prominent than Al-Thani before the treaty of 1868, emigrated to what was the small fishing village of Jubail in Al-Hasa with promises of gifts and money.[24] By 1930, Sheikh Abdallah had established good relations with Abdalaziz bin Saud but feared Abdalaziz's successors. One of Bin Saud's sons had come to Qatar and 'interrupted' evening prayer, presumably to correct the Qataris and instruct them in a purer version of Wahhabi Islam.[25] During oil option negotiations in 1926, Sir Percy Cox had conversations with Abdalaziz bin Saud about the grant of a concession for oil in Al-Hasa district. Abdalaziz 'proposed to include the whole of Qatar and [Cox] took him to task for it'. It was only at this point that Ibn Saud accepted an eastern boundary along the Salwah Bay.[26]

Sheikh Abdallah's constant requests for more arms and support from the British often only elicited a muted and half-hearted response. In fact, in one of his repeatedly used negotiating tools, he repeatedly threatened to 'resign' and 'hand the country over to you [the British] to do what you like with'.[27] Although his negotiating skills may seem blunt, he was, in this way, effective. For example, Abdallah only agreed to an 'emergency landing ground' in Qatar after further assurances of British protection.[28] It is unclear, in fact, if what saved Qatar were the guarantees of the British or the fundamentalist Ikhwan rebellion and shifting political climate in Arabia, distracting Bin Saud from his expan-sionist plans. The perpetual 'problem' of Abdalaziz's imperial ambitions remains a very relevant fear for Al-Thani today, who hope as much for American support as they did for earlier British support in the defense of their territory and in upholding the viability of their rule. British and American interests in the stability of the Gulf and of Qatar only increased with the discovery and exploitation of oil.

THE OIL CONCESSIONS

In one of the greatest upsets in the history of geological science, most geologists erro-neously assumed the Gulf region was empty of petroleum. This belief was shattered after William Knox D'Arcy signed an oil concession with the Shah of Persia in 1901.

The Anglo-Persian Oil Company (APOC) was formed shortly afterwards in 1908 and APOC became the primary supplier of oil to the British Navy. APOC's strategic importance increased rapidly after the outbreak of the First World War, causing the British government to acquire a 51 per cent stake in APOC.[29] The 1916 treaty with Abdallah allowed APOC and the British government to make exclusive claims to potential oil deposits in Qatar. As the pearl industry declined in the 1920s Sheikh Abdallah, who typically faced opposition from both relatives and Abdalaziz bin Saud, was eager to sign an oil agreement with APOC that would allow him to consolidate his position. Frank Holmes, representing APOC, began to explore the possibility of concessions with the Sheikh and the first option was awarded to APOC in 1926.[30] The Sheikh, as concerned about foreign interference as he had been during negotiation of the 1916 treaty, did not however agree any formal concessions and nor did he demand any substantial expansion of company activities in Qatar.

The Sheikh's position was suddenly improved with the advent of big American oil interests and their competition with the British. After 1932 the Standard Oil Company of California secured a major concession from Abdalaziz bin Saud. Qatar seemed to be well within the sights of the Americans. In fact, Saudi Arabia, formed as a united kingdom in 1932, regularly threatened Qatar – Bin Saud indicated to Abdallah that he had no right to make oil concessions to APOC nor to any British company and that oil in the hinterlands of Qatar belonged to the Saudis.[31] The British were determined to stop this interference. Sheikh Abdallah, however, was not immediately impressed by British attempts to help secure Qatari oil. Instead, he deftly managed to encourage competition between APOC and other oil companies, even receiving offers from the Standard Oil Company. The British government quickly intervened, forcing Abdallah either to choose APOC or risk withdrawal of British protection. Besides, the Anglo-Qatari Treaty of 1916 prevented the involvement of non-British subjects in Qatar, or even their entry into the Peninsula. APOC swiftly established a presence in Qatar, building a headquarters for their operations and beginning serious geological surveys.

By 1935 Sheikh Abdallah's staying power had eroded significantly, and he had to take out a mortgage on his own house for 'a debt of 17,000 [Indian] rupees'.[32] That year he finally signed the oil concession with APOC, having been backed into a corner. Abdallah received a large payment of 400,000 Indian rupees upon signature of the agreement, with a further 150,000 to be paid to him personally each year. This amount was increased to 300,000 Indian rupees after the sixth year. The agreement also recognized Abdallah's son Hamad bin Abdallah Al-Thani (d. 1948) as the legitimate heir to Qatar. The Sheikh's only significant objection to the concession was a clause that exempted British subjects from Qatari law. Out of this disagreement developed the concept of a dual legal system, with non-Muslims being tried in Bahrain, Muslim Qataris tried in Qatar and a Joint Court headed by the Sheikh and the Political Agent in Bahrain to resolve disputes between British subjects and Qataris. A political arrangement was also signed, securing British control over oil operations in Qatar and increasing British interference in Qatar's internal affairs. Shortly after the concession was signed by APOC, the company was transformed into an affiliate of the Iraq Petroleum Company, similarly controlled by the British, and renamed Petroleum Development Qatar Ltd, the predecessor to Qatar Petroleum.[33]

The 1935 agreement also helped Abdallah consolidate power and prevent rivalry within his family. One of its most important elements for the future of Al-Thani was that the British had recognized Hamad bin Abdallah, Abdallah's favourite son, as heir apparent. Although Hamad died in May 1948, his recognition by the British allowed Abdallah to prevent and contain rivalry and rebellion from hopeful heirs until just before the beginning of major oil shipments from the Peninsula. Oil prices were fixed at a mere four Indian rupees a tonne,[34] but rebellion soon broke out again as Abdallah's family demanded a share of the profits and a stake in the succession. Finally, Abdallah abdicated and put his other son, Sheikh Ali bin Abdallah (1949–60), in power. Ali agreed reluctantly, however, that Hamad's son Khalifa, rather than his own heir, should succeed his son Ahmad. Had Khalifa been a weak or disinterested personality Ali could have easily pushed his own line of succession and Ali's grandsons would be ruling today. Unfortunately for Ali's branch of the family, Khalifa turned out to be a formidable character. Ali's reign was dominated by rivalry with Khalifa and Khalifa's attempts to consolidate his power. Although Ali's son Ahmad bin Ali took power in 1960, Khalifa was recognized as deputy ruler and was heir apparent and named Crown Prince. Qatar at the time was just emerging as a fabulously wealthy place. In the 1960s Qataris were somewhat adrift, even if British Agents managed many of their affairs. There were only about 30,000 Qataris in the early 1960's and many Qataris were even lured into buying 'gold plated' cars by unscrupulous foreign merchants.[35] The ruler, Ahmad took little interest in government and spent much of his reign in Europe. The large Al-Thani family was restless with many family members making demands for a larger share of the oil wealth and stirring up trouble. As promulgator of decrees and official arbiter in Ahmad's absence, Sheikh Khalifa eventually took on more and more substantial formal powers and began a process of stabilization and development.

5

Sheikh Khalifa and the Enigma of Independence

It did not take long for Sheikh Khalifa to oust the disengaged ruler Ahmad from power in a bloodless coup in February 1972. Sheikh Khalifa's accession occurred while Ahmad bin Ali was on a hunting trip in Iran. The coup was well planned and the Saudis sent troops to the border to ensure Ahmad would not attempt to restore his power. There were few objections to the coup as Ahmad had been largely absent from the country and had not fulfilled his constitutional obligations to form an Advisory Council and remain engaged in foreign affairs. In a pattern of promised reform that would be repeated in 1995 with Khalifa's own overthrow by Sheikh Hamad, Khalifa promised change and even agreed to a mere $250,000 personal salary. Khalifa could still draw on treasury funds as much as he wished but he still seemed to separate the state from his personal possession. Ahmad, in contrast, blatantly benefitted from a full quarter of Qatar's increasingly massive oil wealth.[1]

Although he did not live up to all of his promises of 1972, the reign of Sheikh Khalifa saw the solidification of Qatari national identity and the construction of a modernized traditionalism that reflected profound ironies in the national psyche. Gaps of wealth and experience meant older and younger generations became increasingly estranged from one another. While by no means as polarized as Saudi society, during this period Qatari society began to split apart not simply along tribal lines but as a result of an often ambivalent reaction among some sectors to the perceived threat of rapid change, especially to Wahhabi Islamic identity. Qatar's economy was almost completely dependent on oil during the reign of Sheikh Khalifa. Falling oil prices in the 1980s moderated the growth of the Qatari economy and led to government deficits and a severe reduction in per capita income. The consequences of Qatar's involvement in the Persian Gulf War will also be outlined in this chapter. Although directly hit only once by a unlucky Iraqi scud missile, the example of Kuwait and the hundreds of widowed Kuwaiti refugees who entered Qatar, did much to clarify Qatar's need for guarantees of strategic protection from the USA in exchange for Qatar's cooperation and adherence to the dominant unipolar, world power.

In 1978 the press and publications department of the Qatari Ministry of Information distributed a collection of speeches by Sheikh Khalifa. The rule of Sheikh Khalifa, according to this official source, had singlehandedly brought about 'a renaissance of modern Qatar.' According to the Ministry of Information, the official mouthpiece of the Emir, Sheikh Khalifa was almost exclusively responsible for Qatar's rise and rapid transformation. It was hoped that 'our future generations can turn to this booklet [of speeches] to review the features of this phase of enlightened rule …'.[2] Future generations have not been as unambiguous in their praise of Sheikh Khalifa as he may have hoped in the 1970s. In fact the history of Sheikh Khalifa's reign was much more complex and problematic than the Ministry of Information was willing to dilvuge in 1978. By the end of the next year, 1979, Qatar had taken complete control of the profits of Qatar Petroleum, founded in 1974.

Sheikh Khalifa's place in Qatar's history has recently been questioned by Qataris, especially since the Emir Sheikh Hamad bin Khalifa Al-Thani deposed Sheikh Khalifa, his father, in 1995. Although Sheikh Khalifa's administration created the foundations of the modern state of Qatar, he claimed ownership over those changes, making the building of Qatar an almost exclusively personal project, rather than a project that would benefit the state and Qataris as a whole. In fact, Sheikh Khalifa's reluctance to hand over state monies after the coup in 1995 indicated that he still felt as if the success and development of Qatar was largely a personal accomplishment for which he should be personally rewarded.

Although Sheikh Khalifa's claim to have singlehandedly created modern Qatar is dubious, since he was supported by his family and wealthy merchants and his ideas were influenced by outside contractors, there is no doubt that he kept a close watch over Qatar's development. During the first 12 years of his reign, Sheikh Khalifa involved himself in almost every aspect of government, micro-managing and controlling decision-making almost to a default. Although it could be argued that Sheikh Khalifa's nearly dictatorial, personal involvement was necessary, that rapid development in a conservative and cautious society such as Qatar needed a strong-minded visionary, not all sources agree. Even Westerners who supported the Emir's modernization plans and who viewed Qatar's development mainly as a means of increasing investment were critical of the Emir's absolute control over funds and projects. In its 1978 quarterly review of the Gulf States, the Economist Intelligence Unit commented:

> For several years there has been some criticism of the efficiency with which business at the highest level is conducted. It has been pointed out that the ruler, while working hard and

conscientiously, had tended to allow the administration to get over-centralized. Most paper-work is expected to pass through his hand, and it has even been said that when he is away cheques for contractors and oil companies are not signed.[3]

Sheikh Khalifa's personal, vigorous involvement in the development of Qatar as well as his stronghold on power, can be explained, to some degree, by his childhood and young adulthood. Denied his right to rule as a young man, and nearly denied again when his uncle wanted to bypass him, Sheikh Khalifa was thrust into the intimacies of family politics at a young age.

Born in Doha in 1932, Sheikh Khalifa is the son of Sheikh Hamad bin Abdallah Al-Thani, who had effectively been ruler designate under his own father, Abdallah. Deemed too young to rule when his father died in 1948, it was Sheikh Khalifa's uncle, Sheikh Ali bin Abdallah Al-Thani, who was made ruler the following year. By 1960, however, with Ali's son Ahmad on the throne, Khalifa was officially recognized as Vice-Emir and Crown Prince despite the fact that Sheikh Ahmad seemed to want his own son, rather than his Khalifa, to be next in line for the throne (see Table of Al-Thani Rulers and Princes, p. ix). The lack of any clear law of primogeniture or succession in Article 22 of the provisional Constitution of 2 April 1970 would only encourage Sheikh Khalifa to solidfy his position and mount a coup. Yet Sheikh Khalifa's shaky legal position *vis-à-vis* the provisional Con-sitution was certainly not the only reason for his coup. Sheikh Ahmad, who preferred his villa in Switzerland over the scorching heat of Qatar, had been effectively missing in action as Emir. It was Sheikh Khalifa, not Sheikh Ahmad, who announced Qatar's independence on Qatar Television on 3 September 1971. On 22 February 1972 Sheikh Khalifa took complete control from Sheikh Ahmad while Ahmad was on a hunting expedition in Iran. The ultimate breaking point was Sheikh Ahmad's plan to make his son Abdalaziz the Heir Apparent, breaking the agreement of 1949 that had specifed Sheikh Khalifa's succession.

Sheikh Khalifa would later claim that it was his declaration of Qatar's independence in 1971, not any negotiations under the authority of Sheikh Ahmad, that launched the modern state of Qatar and that indelibly linked his image with independence in the popular mind. In the speech announcing the kingdom's independence, Sheikh Khalifa boldly terminated the treaty of 1916 and all other special treaties linking Qatar to the UK as a protectorate. He did not reveal, of course, secret negotiations with the USA to replace the UK as the special military protector of Qatar and the ruling family.

Sheikh Ahmad and Sheikh Khalifa had contrasting visions about the future of Qatar, with Sheikh Ahmad advocating union with the United Arab Emirates and Sheikh Khalifa sabotaging these proposals.[4] Another reason for Sheikh Khalifa's coup may have been Sheikh Ahmad's dramatic exit from the 1969 Supreme Council of Rulers (the Gulf Cooperation Council would not be formed until 1981) meeting. Sheikh Khalifa had been elected prime minister of the Gulf federation. Perhaps sensing Sheikh Khalifa's ambitious attempts to increase his personal power and ally with Saudi Arabia, Sheikh Ahmad decided to renounce the planned intensive meddling in Qatar's internal affairs by any international body.

Following the coup, Sheikh Khalifa quickly went to work expanding the reach and the authority of the state, increasing the armed forces, and establishing public housing benefits, old age pensions, housing units and food cooperatives. The founding of Qatar University produced Qatari graduates who were automatically placed in high government positions. In 1977 he named Hamad, the present Emir, as his successor. This caused a rift within Al-Thani as the family of Ahmad claimed a deal had been struck to make one of their own the successor. According to the deal, Qatar's succession was to alternate between the descendants of Ali and Hamad much as power swung between clans in Kuwait. The Emir's brother Suhaym also objected to the succession of Hamad. Even as Hamad was clearly the choice of the Emir, the most important checks on the Emir still came from his son and they gradually increased as Hamad matured. Appointed heir in 1977, Major-General Hamad slowly and effectively developed internal and external loyalties, especially the powerful Hamad Al-Attiyah, maternal uncle of Hamad. Hamad's appointment as successor sidelined Suhaym bin Hamad (d. 1985), the brother of the ruler and Abdalaziz bin Hamad, minister of finance and oil, who contested Hamad's right to the succession. A suspicious plot to blow up the Doha Sheraton in 1983, that icon of the Doha skyline, was linked to coup plots to assassinate all the Gulf leaders gathering for the Gulf Cooperation Council meeting.[5] Some seventy Qatari officers were arrested, including relatives of the ruling family. A series of public investigations revealed supposed 'Libyan' connections to the incident. Doha promptly broke ties with Tripoli. There was a strong suggestion, however, that the Libyans, if involved at all, were simply supporting a rival group of Al-Thani and other Qataris who resented the coup of 1972. Qatar did not forget the supposed Libyan connection to coup attempts. Indeed, Qatar's full-throttled, vigorous participation in the most recent campaigns to oust Colonel Qaddafi in 2011 can be at least partially explained by the memory of this plot. Other coup attempts were linked to Suhaym, the brother of the Emir, who resented not being chosen heir. After Suhaym's death in 1985 his sons reportedly attacked Isa Ghanim Al-Kuwari, the Information Minister whom they suspected to be behind a plot to kill their father. Nasir bin Hamad al Thani, the brother of the ruler, was admitted to a hospital with a bullet wound in 1986. The exact nature and veracity of these internal palace disputes are difficult to verify.[6]

Most of Khalifa's efforts to promote economic growth focussed on traditional industrial sectors. Qatar became the third Arab country to enter the steel industry after Egypt and Algeria, and the Qatar Steel Company was the first integrated factory of its kind in the Middle East. Throughout Sheikh Khalifa's reign its production was well above nor-mal production rates.[7] There was also the Qatar National Cement Company, founded in 1965 and the first national industry, which exploits local gypsum and limestone deposits. The entire production is sold in Qatar, as is much of the steel. The Qatar Flour Mills Company in Umm Said produces bread in European and Arab styles and distributes prod-ucts at subsidized prices. However, as the 1988 UN Development Organization report on Qatar lamented, 'The overall performance of the maufacturing sector in Qatar does not seem to have matched the rate at which the country's industrial base expanded …'.[8] Qatar's exports other than crude oil consisted mainly of natural gas liquids, fertilizers, petrochemicals, steel and refined petroleum products. 'The share of non-oil exports in the country's total export earnings is around 10 per cent.'[9] Many of Sheikh Khalifa's attempts to diversify into other industrial sectors ended without substantial success. In 1988, with oil prices in decline, the Qatar Steel Company and the Qatar Petroleum Company were running at a loss.[10] Soon Qatar would run into deficit and would face several years of relatively tight budgets. It was in this context that Sheikh Hamad, the successor and Heir Apparent, would gain support for a successful coup against his father in 1995. The coup would itself cause some serious economic consequences for Qatar.

Qatari citizens have not been threatened with serious economic hardship since the 'years of hunger' before the Second World War. Nevertheless, Qataris and the new Emir are clearly aware of the cycles of the market despite the current illusion of unmiti-gated prosperity. Qatar's economy seems especially vulnerable to changes in leadership. A decline in oil prices and the mismanagement of revenues by Sheikh Khalifa, who left with much of the country's cash reserves ($2.5–7.5 billion) after he was deposed in 1995, caused a serious tightening of government spending in the mid-1990s. In 1994–5 government spending, main driver of the Qatari economy, fell by at least 19 per cent.[11]

As economic development faltered in the 1980s, political reform also stagnated. After dramatically promising reform when he came to power in 1972, Sheikh Khalifa effectively centralized power. While the constitution called for 'a proper basis for the establishment of a true democracy' there was little movement in development of power-ful, internal political institutions. The advisory council, mandated by the Constitution, was filled with close followers of the Emir and members of Al-Thani family. The ruler simply informed the council of the desired policies.[12] The Persian Gulf War and the dra-matic fall and recovery of the Kuwaiti state sent shockwaves through the region. Citizens demanded greater accountabiliy and stability within their own societies. A 1991 petition by 54 prominent Qataris calling for a true legislative body and demands for improve-ment in the health and education systems revealed the tensions bubbling beneath the surface, tensions and aspirations for greater openness and change that Hamad bin Khalifa would himself promise after his coup in 1995.

6

Sheikh Hamad
and the Future of Qatar

More rapid development has occurred in Qatar since Sheikh Hamad's bloodless coup in 1995 than in all the decades since the first major export of oil in 1949. Even while oil was in a slump in the 1990s Sheikh Hamad and his government found innovative ways of magnifying their impact on the world stage. Immediately after gaining power Hamad was able to sponsor and host Al-Jazeera, with broadcasts that soon reached over 35 million Arabic speakers. He started a process of slow democratization and electoral reform with the creation of Doha Municipal Council in 1999. His wife Sheikha Mozah has been at the forefront of cultural and educational development with jaw-dropping educational and institutional initiatives such as Education City. With its wise investment in liquefied natural gas (LNG), Qatar became the world's fifth largest exporter of all forms of natural gas and the largest exporter of LNG at 31 million tonnes a year.[1] In January 2011 Qatar's proven natural gas reserves stood at 896 trillion cubic feet, 14 per cent of all world proven reserves and third only to Russia and Iran. In 2009, Qatar's natural gas exports were 18 per cent of total global trade in natural gas.[2] In contrast, Qatar is only sixteenth in the world in terms of crude oil exports – although this is still a very substantial amount of crude oil for a small country.[3] Natural gas, however, is the main driver of Qatar's economic success.

While the crude oil reserves of Qatar will probably be depleted by 2020, the North Field natural gas deposit is expected to provide some 200 years of production.[4] In fact, there is so much natural gas seeping out in the Persian Gulf waters near Qatar that previously unknown species of bacteria have evolved to use the hydrocarbons from gas and oil.[5] With natural gas seen as a green alternative fuel for future energy consumption, and with billions of already known reserves in the massive North Field whose exploitation will seemingly run far into the future, an era of apparently unlimited spending budgets began. Architects and planners from the West experienced something they may have never experienced before: development projects and proposals that were often scraped not because they were too far-reaching but because they were not ambitious enough.

Much of the economy and many sectors of education and government are dominated by an expat community that outnumbers Qataris by almost ten to one. Uncontrolled population growth, hyper-inflation linked to a declining dollar and scarcity in real estate, gridlock, not only on the congested roads but in Doha, a capital city that can barely contain its ballooning numbers, are all challenges facing the Emir and the current Heir Apparent Sheikh Tamim bin Hamad Al-Thani.

While the Emir maintains a somewhat low profile, he portrays himself as an advocate of women's equality and involvement in government, innovation, major educational reform and modernization at all levels of society. Born in 1952, Sheikh Hamad's career in politics began long before his eventual rise to power. As early as 1977 he was proclaimed Heir Apparent. As the head of the Supreme Planning Council in the 1980s, he was already intimately involved in laying the foundations of rapid, future growth. Traditional housing was destroyed from the foundations, and the social arrangements on which they rested were transformed, as Hamad sought to sweep away social and economic barriers to development, even barriers that supported the legitimacy of his father's reign. He focussed assiduously on the development of Qatar's petrochemical industry as the main engine of growth. Hamad was also supreme military commander. His experience at the Royal Military Academy at Sandhurst (graduating in 1971) and his command of the Hamad Mobile Battalion in Qatar provided Hamad with intimate contacts in the Qatari armed forces, contacts that would be useful as the eventual showdown with his father came to a head. He deftly directed funding towards the modernization of Qatar's military infrastructure. He was hailed as a military hero for his command of the Qatari forces that liberated the Saudi town of Khafji during the Persian Gulf War (1990–1). In fact, the official biography of Hamad provided by the Qatari embassy in Washington DC continues to hail Sheikh Hamad and his leadership at Khafji.[6] He rapidly gained prestige not only within Qatar but within the international community.

THE COUP

The coup of 1995 really began almost six years earlier in 1989.[7] When Hamad instigated a Cabinet reshuffle and put his allies into positions of authority. In 1992, another change in the Cabinet further consolidated his position and made it difficult for the allies of Khalifa and Abdalaziz, Khalifa's other potential successor, to gain traction. Indeed, by 1992, after the end of the Persian Gulf War, Hamad was virtually already in control. He successfully deposed Sheikh Abdalaziz from his position as Finance Minister. Although Abdalaziz probably left Qatar with a good deal of cash, he was effectively exiled to Paris and New York, where he currently enjoys some noteriety as a wealthy player in the real estate markets. The USA, the major Gulf protector, recognized the importance of maintaining a strong ally in Qatar and implicitly supported Hamad's increased grasp on power. Hamad's Sandhurst experience and keen interest in the military only added further strength to his position. As supreme military commander and a newly decorated war hero, he had more control over the armed forces than his father.

Khalifa had lost most of the energy of his youth and, according to some reports, had descended into alcoholism. It was only when he attempted on several occassions to bring back Abdalaziz from exile that Hamad decided to act. Having carefully assembled the necessary support both within Al-Thani and from other prominent Qataris, Hamad took advantage of his military training. Khalifa had left the country for Geneva where he was allegedly undergoing medical treatment. Shortly after he left, Hamad ordered tanks and military personnel to surround the Emiri Diwan. In a matter of days Al-Thani and the chiefs of prominent Qatari tribes gave Hamad their *baya*, or oath of allegiance. Only a few Sheikhs delayed doing so, perhaps out of allegiance to Khalifa or concern about the the stability of the coup. Even as neighbouring Gulf governments met the news of the coup with trepidation and even supported attempts by Khalifa to mount counter-coups, however, recognition by the USA and other, major foreign powers came quickly. Although there is some speculation that the USA was heavily involved in supporting Hamad's accession, most of the reasons for Hamad's success were internal – Sheikh Khalifa's allies had slowly and steadily been converted to Hamad's camp in an accelerating, self-perpetuating game of alliances until the balance had shifted irretrievably in his favour. Few sheikhs or family members wanted to be found on the wrong side of the power game. Those who continued to support Sheikh Khalifa were faced with dire sentences, including a 2001 appellate court death sentence for members of Al-Thani conspiring for the overthrow of Sheikh Hamad.[8] A countercoup in 1996 involved Sheikh Hamad bin Jassim bin Hamad, the former chief of police, who attempted to seize a tank a border post along with the support of border bedu.[9] Indeed, the involvement of the bedu in this failed countercoup may shed further light upon Hamad's continued weariness about Al-Murrah bedu and their citizenship in Qatar. Khalifa would return almost a decade after the coup in 1994 to attend the funeral of his wife Shaikha Mozah bint Ali. He was called 'Father of the Emir' and a gradual rapproachment and public reconciliation between father and son allowed something of a settlement of lingering acrimonies after the 1995 coup.

THE HAMAD ERA

Hamad acted immediately to secure the inevitability of his rule and that of his chosen successor well into the future. A February 1996 counter-coup attempt quickly fizzled out and the perpetrators, arrested on the border with Saudi Arabia, were put on trial. Several enemies of the current regime remain in exile but have almost no chance of returning to power. Again, the animosity of Qataris towards Saudi Arabia coupled with Saudi support of almost every coup attempt against Hamad has done much to rally the general Qatari populace around the rule of Hamad. In 1996 Hamad announced his third son Jassim son of favoured wife Sheikha Mozah, as Crown Prince and changed the Constitution to increase further his control over the succession. His younger brother, Abdallah, was made Prime Minister. Both of these early appointees, however, would lose their positions in the next decade as Abdallah resigned and Hamad formed new alliances with Hamad bin Jassim bin Jabor Al-Thani, 'HBJ', the Foreign Minister, who became Prime Minister in 2003 and who has continued to gain influence and world prominence second only to the Emir himself. In 2003 Tamim, the Emir's fourth son, replaced his brother as Heir Apparent. Prince Tamim, born in 1980 and much more in tune with the current generation was seen as a much more appropriate successor. Tamim is also the son of Sheikha Mozah.

Although he was praised for his liberalizing agenda in the early 2000s, Sheikh Hamad has recently slowed down the pace of constitutional, democratic reform, consolidating his power and concentrating influence within a select group of family allies. A 2002 constitutional commission produced drafts that would create a legislature and guaranteed the right to vote. Although approved in 2003, many aspects of the Constitution can still be interpreted in a way that supports the central power of the Emir. The ruler still appointed 15 of the 45 members and a two thirds majority was needed to pass measures. The Emir could veto any decision. A 2005 Constitution also guaranteed religious liberty (Article 50), privacy and presumption of innocence. His vigorous leadership and support for development and investment within Qatar has led to a major boost in the economy and the population of Qatar. Resting his influence on Qatar's vast gas fields and using the tools of international mediation, Hamad has increased his power not only within Qatar but within the international arena. As the following chapters will now examine, Qatar's future under Hamad and his successor Tamim will likely remain both secure and prosperous even as potential social divisions and ills remain unresolved.

HAMAD'S QATAR AND THE WORLD – A DIPLOMACY OF STEALTH AND WEALTH

Although written some 1,400 years ago, the stories in Ibn al Ishaq's biography of the Prophet Muhammad are still a living and active part of the mindset and the values of Muslims in Qatar. Some of the most famous stories from the life of the Prophet describe the value of mediation and peacemaking. According to Ibn al Ishaq, the elders of Mecca were engaged in a vicious quarrel over who should be selected to move the sacred black cornerstone of the Kaaba in place after its rebuilding around 600 AD. The Prophet Muhammad was a young man, an orphan from a clan of the Quraysh elite that had become economically marginalized. As he observed the quarrel between these powerful older men, the young Muhammad had a sudden revelation – he would suggest that the black stone be placed on a carpet. Each elder could then hold a corner or edge of the carpet and carry the black stone safely to the Kaaba. Praising Muhammad for finding an equitable and diplomatic solution, the Meccan elders suggested that he be chosen for the great honour of lifting the stone out of the carpet and into its niche in the Kaaba.[10] Although among the weakest and the youngest of Meccans, Muhammad was able to use mediation to gain the position of highest prestige. It was his mediation skills that led the warring clans of Medina to invite him to rule their city. Eventually, Muhammad would use his mediation skills to establish the political bedrock of an empire.

Inspired by Muhammad's example, the power and respect given to the mediator became an entrenched tradition. Of course, a respect for mediation is not confined to Arab culture; many Western editorials have praised the Qatari Foreign Minister Hamad bin Jassim as a 'modern-day Metternich'.[11] Through its media and increasingly prominent profile in Western markets, Qatar has, in fact, become as much a negotiator of relations between the wider Western and Islamic worlds as between Arab states.

Contrary to most orientalist representations of the Arabian Peninsula, representations that often depict the Arab male sheikh as a proto-tyrant and absolutist, Arab society has historically been much more egalitarian than the stratified class structure of Western nations. With a constantly shifting social landscape of Bedouin kin groups and migrants, no one group could easily overpower another. Tribesmen within the tribe were considered equal and a sheikh could be abandoned by a tribe if he consistently made wrong turns in the search for pasture and water. Nevertheless, blood feuds and conflicts, though often imaginary and based on underlying economic and social factors, were frequent and could consume a large proportion of scarce resources. In this context, successful mediation and persuasion has been a source of power and prestige. The successful resolution of disputes could mean an increase in profit, trade and livelihood for all involved.

Unsurprisingly, mediation had a long and storied history in the Arabian Peninsula after the example of the Prophet. Even in the modern context of nation-states, many of the same rules of mediation and diplomacy apply. Rulers in the Gulf and in the Middle East region address one another as 'brother': a greater sign of respect and affiliation than any cold, official title. A successful mediator must hide his interests and must provide specific incentives to all parties. He must expect his reward from providence and await gratitude only at the end of negotiations. He must control the space and separate each interest group, but also bring them together at strategic points. Qatar's tactics during the Lebanon negotiations in 2008 have become legendary. Housing all groups in the conflict at the Sheraton Hotel, Qatar literally had control over the keys when the purse strings were not convincing enough. While the USA had no chance of negotiating with Hezbollah, officially a terrorist group, Sheikh Hamad bin Jassim brought together Lebanon's Prime Minister Siniora and Parliament Speaker Nabih Berri, a senior opposition leader, for the first time in months and brokered an historic peace deal. Celebrations broke out in Lebanon with signs saying 'We all say: We thank you Qatar'.[12]

Qatar, although weak in military clout and small in size, has used mediation to advance its prestige and position in the region and, increasingly, in the world. Ostensibly distant from most international disputes, its size prevents it from being perceived as overtly biased or as having any major interests. While superpowers and regional powers such as the USA, Egypt and Saudi Arabia are hampered by their history and more complex constituencies, the Emir of Qatar and the Foreign Minister Sheikh Hamad bin Jassim, blessed with the overwhelming support of the small Qatari population and trillions of gallons of natural gas reserves, have made Qatar into a fast and nimble wonder ship of international diplomacy.[13] Also, millions of dollars spent in aid and Qatar's many charity organizations in high conflict regions such as Lebanon have provided Qatar with a channel to enter negotiations. Shortly after the historic Lebanon peace agreement, Hamad bin Jassim lost no time in jetting off around the Middle East, further securing Qatar's reputation as *hakam* and mediator.

Although a complete list of Qatar's recent mediation activities would be nearly impossible, especially since a great deal of negotiation can occur outside public, media knowledge, a representative list of Qatar's far-flung diplomatic ventures indicates that Qatar must now be taken seriously as a *hakam,* a respected mediator:

1. Libya – Qatar mediated between Libya, the USA and Britain, a mediation that helped lead to the dismantling of Libya's nuclear program in 2003.[14] Qatar also negotiated the successful release of Bulgarian nurses in Libya accused of spreading AIDS in 2007, probably by agreeing large compensation payments to their Libyans accusers. There are also news reports that Qatar was instrumental in convincing the British government and the Scottish Parliament to release the ailing high-profile Abdelbaset al-Megrahi accused of the Lockerbie bombing over Scotland.[15] Qatar has recently played a very active role in supporting and training the anti-Qaddafi fighters. Qatar has been rewarded with lucrative oil contracts and access to Libyan markets. Qatar's unusual interest and involvement in Libyan affairs can be linked to the alleged involvement of Libyan spies in the potentially devastating assassination attempt of all Gulf Cooperation Council leaders in Doha in 1983.[16] Qatar even set up a television station for the Libyan opposition to Qaddafi and Sheikha Mozah lived and worked in Libya in her youth.

2. Chad – Qatar and Libya sponsored peace talks between Sudan and Chad after an attack on the Chadian capital by Darfuris in May 2008.[17]

3. Iraq – Shortly before the US invasion, Sheikh Hamad bin Jassim told Iraqi President Saddam Hussein that he was sent 'to ask him to give up authority and that

war will eventually take place, and that the US is serious'. Saddam pointedly asked the Qatari Emir why he was allowing his country to host US bases, especially since it was Kuwait, not Qatar, that had been invaded by Saddam more than a decade earlier. The Foreign Minister simply stated that Qatar was obligated to honour security agreements.[18]

4. Hamas, Fatah and Israel – Doha is the only Arab capital that is regularly visited by all major Palestinian factions. In October 2006 Qatar began sponsoring mediation efforts between Hamas, the Palestinian group controlling Gaza, and Fatah in the West Bank, seeking to achieve reconciliation. The Palestinians recognized the importance of Qatar's involvement, and the country was acknowledged by both sides as a state of strategic weight in the region.[19] Travelling to Gaza City, Sheikh Jassim shuttled between Mahmoud Abbas of Fatah and Ismail Haniya of Hamas. The groundwork for negotiations may have started in Qatar, where Khaled Meshal, titular leader of Hamas, and Mahmoud Abbas reportedly met. Qatar's involvement did not go unnoticed by Egypt, the traditional mediator between the Palestinian factions. Upset that it had been replaced by an upstart wealthy emirate, Egypt accused Qatar of 'exploiting the blood of the Palestinians to score political gains'.[20] Qatar's plan calls for a two-state solution and an implicit recognition of Israel. The failure of Qatar's immediate efforts, however, led some to conclude that Qatar was a 'well-meaning but lightweight player seeking a role too great for its actual level of influence'. This impression was largely negated after Qatar's breakthrough for Lebanon. In a secret diplomatic cable, the Foreign Minister of Egypt Aboul Gheit, is described as seeing the Qataris in the same category as Syria – as 'sychophants' of Iran.[21]

5. Lebanon – Qatar's now famous mediation in May 2008 has propelled Qatar's credibility as a negotiator. While the Saudis had generally failed in their efforts, Sheikh Jassim and Qatari negotiators were able to strike an agreement, having established longstanding relations with both Hezbollah and other parties in Lebanon.

6. Iran and the UAE – After Iran refused to refer its case to the International Court of Justice in 2001, Qatar was involved in attempting to negotiate an agreement between Iran and the UAE over the sovereignty of the greater and lesser Thumbs and the Island of Abu Musa.

7. Yemen and Al-Houthi rebellion – Although attempts to negotiate between Al-Houthi and the Yemeni government were frustrated and the 2007 peace agreement broke down, Qatar was still seen as 'the only player that seems to be able to make any difference', according to Professor Gerd Nonneman of Chatham House in London.[22] Qatar offered to host the leaders of Al-Houthi rebellion in Doha if they made a peaceful agreement or wished to leave Yemen and find refuge in Qatar.

8. Sudan – Qatar hosted representatives of both the government of Sudan and the Justice and Equality Movement in February 2009. Qatar has been actively involved in attempting to resolve conflicts in Sudan often at the further expense of its relations with Egypt. As with Gaza, Egypt sees itself as the natural negotiator for this conflict.

9. Morocco and Algeria – Qatar was involved in negotiations between Morocco and the Western Sahara. In 2004 the Polisario Front released 100 Moroccan prisoners after Qatar brokered a deal.[23] Also, Qatar has hosted Algerian opposition figures.

10. The Opposition – Qatar hosts exiled opposition figures from a number of Arab and Islamic countries. Muawiya Weld Taya, the Mauritanian ex-president, Sajida Khayrallah, wife of Saddam Hussein, Naji Sabri, the Iraqi ex-minister, Sheikh Abbas Madani, founder of the Islamic Salvation Front in Algeria, Saleem Yanderbaiv, the Chechnyan ex-president, and several other prominent figures have found refuge in Qatar. The prospect of settling down in the wealthy emirate, often with a pension and support, provides opposition figures with an exit strategy, but also gives Qatar leverage with current regimes. Yet residence in Qatar does not necessarily guarantee security for all political exiles. In 2004 Russian secret agents killed Chechen leader Zelimkhan Yandarbiyev, blowing up his car after he left a mosque in Doha. Recently, Qatar has supported the rebellion against Bashar al Assad of Syria and the expelling of Syria from the Arab League.

Despite this impressive list of Qatar's mediation activities, Qatar's international affairs are not only defined by mediation prestige. Qatar has its own interests to preserve and promote. Although these interests may seem obscured by its apparently 'disinterested' status as a negotiator, they have a very real impact on its relations with the international community. This chapter will discuss the origins, the consequences and the sustainability of Qatar's highly adaptive international and foreign policy. Qatar has successfully made itself into a world stage of opinion and controversy. In many respects it was a successful foreign policy of balancing powers that created Qatar and it will be foreign policy and Qatar's international commitments that secure both its incredible wealth and its independence for the future. Although nimble and effective at international diplomacy, major regional challenges that directly impact Qatar, such as the future of Iran and the US military presence in the region, or the threat of terrorism, may require it to take a more overt, and hence less powerful, role in the region's international affairs. Despite its past international successes Qatar must encounter deep foreign policy dilemmas: What is the nature of Qatar's special relationship with the USA? How has Qatar positioned itself between two very different and, in many ways, very antagonistic neighbours: Saudi Arabia and Iran? Will Qatar be willing to relinquish its powerful and unique diplomatic capital as commitments to the regional union or Gulf Cooperation Council (GCC) increase? What will become of Qatar in the event of serious destabilization in the Gulf region, especially with the threat of an insurgent and nuclear-weapon armed Iran or possible Al-Qaeda attacks?

This chapter will address these questions by discussing the history and current state of Qatar's international relations with key players in the region and the world. Qatar's strategy has been to keep a very straight face, not to reveal its precise views on divisive international issues, excepting the Israeli–Palestinian conflict, and to deal with each of its strategic partnerships individually. By doing so, Qatar has become a mutual friend between enemies. Unlike lumbering major powers or even regional powers with complex diplomatic establishments and interests that are often stated or easily implied at the outset, Qatar's diplomacy is not only more nimble, it is also a tighter ship. The only thing that is implied by Qatar's involvement is that substantial amounts of money can be made available should cash become necessary to resolve an issue or increase Qatar's prestige and opportunities. Since Qatar seems to follow a country by country, or organization by organization, approach to its diplomacy, it makes sense to follow this in outlining below the nature of its relationship with key countries and key players both regionally and internationally.

Saudi Arabia

One of Qatar's most important and longstanding international relationships is with Saudi Arabia. It was Muhammad bin Thani's deft use of Saudi support against Bahrain in the 1850s that helped raise Al-Thani from obscurity to prominence in Qatar. Indeed, Al-Thani trace their ancestry to Saudi Arabia and most Qataris practice a lighter form of Saudi Wahhabism. Nevertheless, Qatar's relations with Saudi Arabia have remained strained and complicated throughout the history of Al-Thani rule in Qatar. Basing his argument on the claim that all Bedouins of Arabia are his, the Saudi monarch has continuously claimed that the Saudi border line should be extended wherever the Bedouin would have trod: 'Bin Saud tells them that all the Bedouin of Arabia are his, and his neighbors only hold the towns.'[24] This and related claims explains the constantly troubled and complicated relations between Al-Thani in the pearl-fishing towns along the coast and the Bedouin and other tribes who affirmed their allegiance with Saudi Arabia when they found themselves opposed to Al-Thani, or simply wished to avoid taxation. A political, economic and religious giant that not only neighbours but appears to swallow Qatar in its shadow, Saudi Arabia currently shares Qatar's only land border. That border has predictably been the scene of conflict between the two, especially as every square mile of land on the Peninsula has been transformed in recent years from barren desert into the site of lucrative oil deposits. Although the Qatari government officially professes good relations with Saudi Arabia, the Qatari people, especially the youth, seem to see the situation differently. At a BBC Doha debate on 15 February, 2009 a majority of attendees concluded that Qatar was in a 'cold war' with Saudi Arabia.[25] My male students at Qatar University often brought up Saudi Arabia and the brave efforts of Qataris from specific tribes such as Al-Kuwari to defend the border against Saudi aggression.

The beginning of Qatar's current border conflict with Saudi Arabia was a 1965 agreement for the boundary to run from Al-Salwa to the west to Khor on the Gulf in the east. Qatari independence in 1971 led to complications, especially since many new states in the Gulf refused to recognize agreements made under the British Protectorate. The UAE and Britain maintained that the UAE border extended to the southern Qatari border region, a sandy inlet and remnant of a prehistoric river called Khwar Udaid. The Saudis disputed this claim and assumed that all the territory around Khwar Udaid was Saudi, effectively requiring all traffic between Qatar and the UAE to pass through Saudi Arabia. In 1992 a clash between Qatar and Saudi Arabia at the border outpost of Al-Khafus, an outpost that used to border the UAE but that now borders Saudi Arabia, led to the death of three. Qatar claimed Saudi Arabia attacked the border post while Saudi Arabia claimed the conflict occurred between Bedouin within Saudi territory. Allegedly, the conflict was sparked after 'a leading sheikh of Al-Murrah tribe, Emir Mohammed bin Shraim, and a party of his followers, armed as usual in the desert tradition, had gone to the area to investigate a [alleged] Qatari camp.'[26] Although it was claimed that there was 'no evidence' whether this expedition by Al-Murrah was private or sanctioned by the Saudis, Al-Murrah were the official border guards of Saudi territory. It had only been in 1990 that the UAE had conceded its border with Qatar to Saudi Arabia, cutting Qatar off from its southern, Gulf neighbour. Prince Hamad, the future Emir, immediately called for a suspension of the longstanding 1965 border accord with Saudi Arabia, calling the incident 'a grave precedent in Saudi-Qatari relations'.[27] Saudi Arabia proceeded to invade and occupy the border post at Al-Khafus. This immediately provided an opportunity for regional powers to claim new ties with Qatar and hedge themselves against Saudi Arabia. Iran and Iraq openly supported Qatar against Saudi Arabia, calling the incident an act of aggression. Iran even indicated a willingness to sign a joint defence agreement with Qatar. In fact, some of Qatar's recent attempts to firm up relations with Iran may be traced to Qatar's less than friendly relationship with Saudi Arabia.

It was only in 1999 that Qatar and Saudi Arabia signed a clearer demarcation agreement. Nevertheless, tensions remain and conflicting interpretations of events on the border have led to hostile reactions against Saudi Arabia by the Qatari population. The recent temporary revoking of the Qatari passports of some 5,000 members of Al-Ghafran clan of Al-Murrah Bedouin was related to their historic role as a border patrol for Saudi Arabia in 2004. Qatar also claimed that members of the clan still held Saudi citizenship and were thus ineligible to maintain their Qatari citizenship as well. Under the Qatari law of 1961 a person can lose their citizenship and even become 'bidoun,' or 'without' any citizenship if they commit a 'serious crime.' According to some of these exiled tribesmen, the law has been expanded to include those who forcefully criticize the Qatari media or royal family.[28] That said, the Qatari government claimed Al-Murrah received 'monthy payments ... from government sources in either Saudi Arabia or Qatar or both.'[29] Jill Crystal identified 6,000 members of the clan who lost their passports after a 1996 coup attempt.[30] In both 1996 and 2005 Saudi Arabia supported coup attempts against the Emir, further straining ties with Qatar and supporting the perception of a covert 'cold war' between Saudi Arabia and Qatar. Indeed, the Saudis are not particularly fond of the Emir's tolerance of open criticism of Saudi Arabia by the media in Qatar. They have also increasingly seen Qatar as a rival, especially as it has gained prominence in international negotiation and as the site of US CENTCOM after US military withdrawal from Saudi territory. As the scholar Ahmed Saif noted:

> In spite of its small geographic size, Qatar is emerging as a relatively major player in the Gulf, to some extent at the expense of Saudi Arabia. Much of Qatar's policy can be understood as an attempt to remove or decrease the perceived overbearing Saudi dominance.[31]

The fall of Saddam Hussein has removed the strategic need for Saudi protection from Iraqi aggression and has refocused Qatar on mitigating Saudi Arabia's efforts to extend its influence and its borders into small Gulf countries. Even though Qatar also follows Saudi Wahhabism, Qataris distinguish between their more open 'Wahhabism of the sea' and Saudi 'Wahhabism of the desert'. The Shi'as are allowed their own religious legal system for family law. Catholic churches have been built on Qatari soil. Hindu merchants even celebrated a hindu gold festival.[32] These activities would not be tolerated by the strong clerical class in Saudi Arabia. Admittedly, the power of the Qatari Emir over the religious establishment is much greater than that of the King of Saudi Arabia over Wahhabi clerics. The Saudi monarchy would perhaps prefer to be less hard line, but the pull of the religious clerics is great and their ability to incite dissent is much greater than in Qatar. That said, the difference in the way Wahhabism is enforced is also largely explained by the way of life of Qataris who, unlike the Bedouin nomads who struggled against each other over wells and oasis agriculture, were exposed to trade and a more complex form of village life. They also had to develop ways of effectively farming the sea as a collective community. A paragraph from the British Admiralty files of 1916–17 sums up the situation for most Qataris before oil:

The chief occupation in El-Qatar is pearl fishing, supplemented in some places by the breeding of camels. The interests of the peninsula are essentially maritime; the men live by the sea, and for much of the year upon it; the towns and villages turn their backs, as it were, on the barren land ... Little live stock is owned by the settled inhabitants ...[33]

In addition to these basic differences in the maritime trading culture of Qatar and the largely Bedouin culture of the Saudi elite, analysts have viewed Qatar's political reform agenda as a way in which the Emir has attempted to distinguish Qatar from Saudi Arabia in Western eyes. It could even be argued that Saudi Arabia provides some indirect, unintended benefits to Al-Thani. Like the threat of any good, potential enemy, Saudi Arabia's alleged interference in Qatar only solidifies support around Al-Thani and the current Emir. While the coups of 1996 and 2005 as well as alleged later coups, for instance, were mainly centered around domestic clans or those loyal to the former Emir, Sheikh Hamad and his allies could blame Saudi interference as the primary cause of coups. This allows the Sheikh to deflect and delegitimize any serious, internal opposition as simply another attempt by Saudi Arabia to destabilize Qatar.

There have been some recent signs of limited, public rapproachment between Saudi Arabia and Qatar. In September 2007 the chairman of the board of Al-Jazeera, Sheikh Hamad bin Thamer Al-Thani, travelled to Saudi Arabia to seek ways in which Al-Jazeera could be allowed to report from Saudi Arabia after it had prohibited all Al-Jazeera operations and withdrawn its ambassador to Qatar in 2002. Al-Jazeera appears to have moderated some of its reporting of Saudi affairs.[34] These disputes over Al-Jazeera, however, do not resolve the fundamentally tenuous relationship between the Saudis, who see Qatar as an upstart, and the Qataris who view their larger neighbour with trepedation, especially in the context of a region that has seen constant changes in national borders and claims on natural resources. Saudi Arabia objected, for example, to Qatar's Dolphin energy initiative, a plan to pipe gas from Qatar to the UAE, Bahrain and Oman, bypassing Saudi Arabia.

More than resources, however, there is a dispute over what it means to be a true Arab and Muslim in the modern world. Saudi sponsorship of the rival Al-Arabiyya station based in Dubai confirms this split. The Saudis have also allowed extensive criticism of Qatar in international London-based Arabic newspapers financed by Saudi Arabia such as *Sharq al Awsat*. In 2006 Qatar retaliated in the newspaper media war, annoucing plans for its own Arabic newspaper based in London. Qatar-Saudi relations may become even more contentious as Saudi Arabia transitions from the current, liberalizing leadership of King Abdallah.

Bahrain and the Gulf

At first seen as a 'Young Turk' who potentially threatened the entrenched interests the old guard, Sheikh Hamad's relationship with other Gulf monarchs started off badly after ousting his father in 1995. Bahrain and the UAE, for example, continued to acknowledge the claims of Hamad's father. They allowed him to stay in their territory to plot counter-coups. As Hamad swiftly and decisively avoided these counter-coups and his power became greater, and as his influence and deft diplomatic skills became increasingly respected, he has cautiously supported greater contact with the leaderships of Kuwait, Bahrain, the UAE and Oman.

The Qatar and Bahrain flags – one with vertical bands of white and dark maroon, divided by a serrated edge made up of triangles, the other (Bahrain) white and bright red, but with an otherwise identical pattern – are not only relics of a common past under the British Protectorate, they are a potential nightmare for diplomatic protocol experts. Yet Qatar and Bahrain share not only the patterns of their flags. Historically, politically and geographically Qatar and Bahrain have the deepest of ties. Nevertheless, border disputes, disputes whose origins lie deep in the history of both countries, have, in the past, hampered relations between them. It was not until December 1999 that Qatar and Bahrain agreed to open full diplomatic relations with each other.

Realizing that unimaginable riches could lie beneath their shallow shores and marine territories, Qatar and Bahrain recently exchanged fire over the disputed Hawar Islands, a group of largely barren rocky islets off the western shore of Qatar occasionally occupied by the Dawasir tribe. Zubara, clearly a part of the contiguous Peninsula of Qatar but historically an outpost of Bahrain, was also claimed by Bahrain as late as the 1990s despite the reality of effective Qatari sovereignty. The International Court of Justice finally ruled in May 2001 that Bahrain could claim the Hawar Islands although it was required to give up all claims on shoals or land on the Peninsula of Qatar. Since the 2001 decision, relations between Bahrain and Qatar have radically improved. Bahrain, although historically more established in the oil economy than Qatar, has begun to run out of oil supplies and an increasing number of Bahrainis are coming to Qatar for employment. A planned causeway bridge between Bahrain and Qatar is expected to lead to even further links between the two Gulf monarchies. The 28-mile causeway, to be called the Friendship Bridge, was expected to take at least five years to complete.[35] Nevertheless, there has been little progress on the project despite many announcements, recent promises hold out the possibility that the bridge will be completed by 2015.[36]

Qatar's relations with Abu Dhabi, the UAE and Oman have also improved markedly since Hamad's coup in 1995 when the UAE allowed the deposed sheikh to maintain a Shadow Cabinet there and supported attempts to restore Khalifa. A primary reason for improved ties with Qatar is the common threat of Saudi domination of the region. The Dolphin energy pipeline, planned to bypass Saudi Arabia and connect the Gulf States to Qatar as a hub of natural gas for the domestic Gulf market, is emblematic of drastically improved ties. In 1976, for example, Bahrain refused even to consider a bridge to Qatar financed completely by the Qataris – despite the obvious potential benefits to it. Newly solidified borders and a growing realization of common defence needs against a resurgent Iran have mitigated barriers to regional cooperation. Yet Bahrain eyes Qatar warily.

A recently leaked cable described King Hamad of Bahrain's "'annoyance" at Qatari behaviour, particularly the recent visit of Qatar's Chief of Staff of its armed forces to Iran, as well as Qatari rebuffs of Bahrani requests for natural gas'. Qatar's Chief of Staff, Major-General Hamad Al-Attiyah, had planned joint military exercises with Iran and even invited Iranian troops onto the Persian Gulf. King Hamad also noted that Qatar was able to send new gas to Mexico and the UK even as the Qataris claimed to be 'maxed out' of oil.[37]

Despite their geographic closeness and apparently similarities, good relations between the Gulf countries have never been automatic. In 1988 the United Nations Development Organization indicated that:

> trade among the six GCC economies is almost insignificant. Qatar imports les than 4 per cent of its import requirements from GCC states. Since the GCC countries are dependent to a large extent on the export of oil, the volume of trade between them is realtively limited.[38]

Active efforts by the leaders of the Gulf states have alleviated this past lack of regional economic cooperation to the extent that proposals to create the 'Gulfo', a currency equivalent to that of a financial regional superpower, are finally in the works. Qatar must, however, balance the economic opportunities of increased integration within the Gulf against its own highly independent interests.

Iran

On 3 October 2009 Reuters reported that Iranian sources, including the head of Iran's offshore operations, were claiming that Qatar National Bank was planning to finance Iran's oil development with a $400 million loan. One day later, the bank denied the existence of the loan.[39] Nevertheless, commercial relationships between Qatar and Iran are repeatedly reported as well as Qatari–Iranian cooperation over the North Field (Iran calls it the South Pars Field), the vast natural gas deposit whose ownership they share – it is divided by a maritime border. The ornate Iranian embassy is located on one of the most prominent parts of the Doha Corniche. One of the Emir's favourite restaurants was specially commissioned by him in a design based on Persian style. The multimillion-dollar building consists of a series of stunning chambers, where light reflects off walls inlaid with crystals, semi-precious stones and glass. In many ways, these dazzling Iranian chambers, where reality seems to fuse with mere image, perflectly symbolizes the complex relationship between Qatar and Iran.

Heir Apparent Prince Tamim has made several special trips to Iran and conservative President Ahmadinejad has accepted invitations to Qatar, despite Western protests. If it were possible to ignore the fact that Qatar is the headquarters of Central Command of the US military, one might mistake Qatar's supposed sympathy with the Iranian regime as genuine. However, the reality of Qatar and the Sheikh's views on Iran are, like so much of Qatari foreign relations, deliberately clouded in ambiguity and conditionality. While certainly wary of the possibility of Iran controlling the Persian Gulf should the US withdraw from the region, Qatar is also aware that such a withdrawal is highly unlikely. By developing relations with Iran independently of US interests, Qatar can secure and expand lucrative relations with its large Gulf neighbour. It could even be argued that Qatar is attempting to position itself as a secret negotiator between the USA and Iran, reaping the benefits of mediation yet again.

The appearance of neutrality and Qatar's reputation as an effective negotiator lie at the core of Qatar's sometimes spectacularly successful foreign policy. Despite the country's ability to broker disputes through remaining open and tolerating use of its economic and media resources by a wide range of parties and viewholders, Qatar seems to be overwhelmed by the dispute between its two most important international partners, the USA and Iran, however. One problem with Qatar's attempt to appeal to both Iran and the USA is that the techniques it has used to resolve, mitigate and ultimately gain prestige from other conflicts are subject to major risks. Qatar cannot appeal to both the USA and Iran in the way it has appealed to both Hamas and Israel, or to all the parties in the Lebanon conflict, or even to both Sheikh Qaradawi (a neo-traditional television cleric) and Saad Eddin Ibrahim (a liberal pro-democracy reformer who famously supported the overthrow of Saddam Hussein) and others with opposing ideologies. There are two reasons why Qatar's standard foreign policy formula will not work in this instance. First, unlike other conflicts in which it has been mediator, Qatar cannot be considered a neutral party in the simmering conflict between Iran and the USA. Not only does Qatar share the lucrative North Field with Iran, it also has an existential interest in maintaining the security of the Gulf and limits on the expansion of potential hegemonic powers in the region.

Historically, Qatar's location on the western side of the Arabian Peninsula puts it on the front lines of a long, historical struggle between Persians (Iranians today) and Arabs over control of the Gulf. The fact that Qataris – and most Gulf Arabs – are offended when the Gulf is called the 'Persian' Gulf, instead of the 'Arab' Gulf, reflects the continued tension inherent in the geography of the region. The sense of unease towards Iran is only heightened by internal political divisions between Sunni Arabs on the western shore. Iran has often staked a claim to the entire Gulf littoral, not only as a zone of influence but as an outright possession. Before the migration of Al-Khalifa to Bahrain and their assertion of authority over the island, Iran controlled and claimed it. In 1753, Nadir Shah, the great Safavid ruler of Persia, took the island of Bahrain. A combined force of Qataris and Al-Khalifa tribesmen sailing from Zubara, took it back in 1783, but Iran did not finally relinquish its claim over Bahrain until 1970.[40]

Iran is also a reminder of the political weakness of the Arab Gulf states. While Iran has long established political unity and dominance across much of the eastern Gulf, the Arab side of the Gulf has remained fractured. Even before the rise of Islam, areas on the eastern shore of the Gulf from Kuwait to Al-Hasa, the eastern province of Saudi Arabia that faces the Gulf, Qatar and the Emirates were claimed by Persians. The rise of Islam in Mecca, in western Arabia, relatively far from Persian influence, emboldened the Arabs of the Gulf, who converted alongside other Arab tribes and led the invasion of Sassanid Persia in the seventh century. The Arab Conquest of 632–44 led to the fall of this once-mighty Empire. Unlike Egypt or the Levant which eventually fell under the thrall of Arabic, however, Persians never fully embraced the Arabic language and culture even after most had converted to Islam.

The popular notion that the split between Persians and Arabs is founded on the original spilt between Shi'i and Sunni Muslims is false. It was some 800 years from the death of Ali, descendant of the Prophet Muhammad, to the rise of Ismail, the charismatic leader who founded the Shi'a Safavid Empire in Persia. Differences in geography, politics, ethnic identity, language and culture between the Iranian and the Arab sides of the Gulf are almost always more fundamental than religious differences. While religion remains a touchstone, Qataris prefer simply not to discuss differences between Shi'a and Sunni and overt conflicts between the two sects of Islam have remained almost non-existent in Qatar. Not all countries in the Gulf have such a placid attitude. In vivid contrast, Bahrain's ruling family is Sunni while the majority of the population is Shi'a, causing inevitable rifts as the Bahraini people demand more political control. In Saudi Arabia the Shi'a majority in the Al-Hasa region on the Gulf has long been the target of political suppression. While the Saudi Wahhabi doctrine was founded on the extermination of Shi'a and Sufi 'heresies' and Saudi raiders famously sacked Shi'a shrines at Karbala in the eighteenth century, Qataris were never as hostile to Shi'ism. With a comfortable Sunni majority that has maintained a co-dependent relationship with Al-Thani, the Qatari population seems content generally to ignore religious differences.

Despite a history of competition and conflicting claims over the Gulf, and despite their ostensibly Wahhabi Sunni offical doctrine, and Qatar's close relationship with the USA, Qatar has generally maintained friendly relations with Iran throughout its history. Persians have almost always been welcome to trade and establish themselves as merchants, and Iranian merchant families such as the Darwish and Al-Mana had important roles in Qatar's government and economy during the transition from British rule. While almost no non-Arabs, other than African slaves, were allowed to live in Qatar before the 1930s, the Persians maintained a significant presence on the Peninsula.

The regional power of Iran has not been completely hostile to Qatar's own interest in balancing the powers of the Gulf against each other. The present ruler of Qatar, Sheikh Hamad bin Khalifa, has maintained a strategic political relationship with the theocratic regime in Iran and blamed 'hidden hands' (implicitly meaning Western intelligence interference) for protests by opposition leaders after the Iranian presidental elections of 2009. Sheikh Hamad suggested that the USA deliberately fomented Iranaphobia among the Arab states.[41] Sheikh Tamim, the Heir Apparent, has been personally entrusted with maintaining ties to Iran.

Nevertheless, Qatar's and even Sheikh Hamad's personal friendship with members of the Iranian regime should be seen in the context of the country's explicit support of American and even Israeli interests. With Al-Udeid, the largest American base in the Gulf and the headquarters of US Central Command, on Qatari soil and within range of Iranian rockets, Qatar's overtures to Iran may, in fact, be an attempt to immunize itself against pre-emptive retribution from the Iranian regime. In a complicated twist, too, American interests may ironically be served by Qatar's diplomatic manoeuvering with Iran. Such gestures might induce Iran into thinking twice before attacking a 'friendly' Arab state, a state where plans are in place for 200 flights a month between Iran and Doha and for a policy to issue Iranians with 72-hour visas so that they can enter Qatar to trade and do business. Using soft diplomacy to avoid confrontation and support economic expansion, while deftly preserving Qatar's fundamental sovereign interests, Qatar's good relations with Iran have also served to deflect and hamper attempts by Saudi Arabia to dominate the Arab Gulf region.

Many Iranians, and high-ranking American military and foreign policy personnel for that matter, are also thankful to Sheikh Hamad for his personal role commanding a brigade of Qataris against Saddam Hussein, the great enemy of Iran, in the Persian Gulf War. The soldiers of the Hamad brigade were among the first coalition troops to engage Iraqi forces at Khafji.[42] The mutual respect between Qatar and Sheikh Hamad and both the United States and Iran, however, may reach a turning-point where the country will need to choose which side it is on.

The stablization of Iraq and the rise of Shi'a influence in the Gulf, not only in Iran but also in the Iraqi government, has forced Qatar, still a small, vulnerable but expensive country regardless of its fleeting international clout in mediation, to re-evaluate its most important international commitments. While the US influence in the region may come and go, Iran has a geographic and strategic interest in the entire Gulf. Iran not only shares major gas fields with Qatar, it also looks enviously at Qatar's superior gas liquifying and transportation facilities. Conflict between the USA and Iran may risk regional instability, but it may also be economically favourable for Qatar as oil and gas prices spike if Qatar is able to maintain its exports. While a full-scale armed conflict and the targeting of US bases on the Peninsula would cause a great deal of concern, the imposition of a powerful sanctions regime or the launching of strategic strikes on Iran's nuclear facilities and the resultant isolation of Iran have simply led Qatar to focus on alternatives for the distribution and sale of its oil and gas. The urgent focus on oil pipeline projects, such as the Dolphin project that by-passes the volatile Strait of Hormuz and a recent proposal for a pipeline to Turkey, would give Qatar the option of sending its oil and gas directly to customers in Europe. Also, taking a truly long-term view, the USA could be viewed as simply the latest in a long line of Western imperial powers – from Alexander the Great to Portugal and Britain – that will eventually withdraw from the region. As the USA begins its complete withdrawal from Iraq to focus on Central Asia and Afghanistan – the 'grand central station' of terrorism according to Anders Fogh Rasmussen, Secretary General of NATO[43] – Qatar has subtly developed close ties not only with the distant superpower the USA, but also with the regional powerhouse, Iran.

A recent major leak of secret diplomatic files through Wikileaks reveals how Qatar defended its relationship with Iran to American diplomats. After Assistant Secretary of Defense Alexander Vershbow pressed Qatar to distance itself from Iran, Crown Prince Tamim and Major-General Al-Attiyah 'repeated the Qatari position that they felt the need to engage all their neighbours and that Qatar could perhaps influence Iranian behaviour through its engagement'. Interestingly, the cable also revealed that the US government was hesitant to allow Qatar access to sensitive detection equipment such as the Large Aircraft Infrared Countermeasure (LAIRCM) system. This may have been because of Qatar's too-cosy relationship with Iran. At the same time, Al-Attiyah protested to the US that, while neighbours, Qatar and Iran were, 'not friends'.[44] In a meeting with Senator John Kerry, former US presidential candidate and chair of the Senate Foreign Relations Committee, the Emir of Qatar Sheikh Hamad said that 'based on 30 years of experience with the Iranians, they will give you 100 words. Trust only one of the 100.'[45]

Despite these apprehensions, the fact that Qatar shares the world's largest known gas field, the North Field/South Pars, with Iran means that it is unlikely that Qatar will ever fully break relations with it willingly. In 2005 Qatar's share of the gas field accounted for a massive 14 per cent of the world's proven reserves. Iran's share was 5 per cent.[46] A US State Department cable on preparations for the visit of Qatar's Prime Minister to Washington put it bluntly: 'Right now, we anticipate that Qatar would refuse to allow Qatari soil to be used to attack Iran, short of some sort of permanent USG [US Government] security guarantee to Qatar, to include its offshore natural gas field shared with Iran.'[47]

Al-Qaeda

One of the most significant international threats to Qatar's careful international balancing act comes from a non-state organization. Aware of the threat that Al-Qaeda poses, Qatar has publicly condemned the terrorist organization. From his public pronouncements, it appears that Sheikh Hamad is staunchly anti-Al-Qaeda and against the use of political violence as a tactic. According to University of Michigan Professor Juan Cole, Sheikh Hamad 'is said to have played a role in helping the United States capture Al-Qaeda operatives Ramzi bin al-Shibh and Khalid Sheikh Muhammad.'[48] Nevertheless, as mentioned previously, the US media has consistently reported contacts between Qatar government representatives and the leaders of Al-Qaeda. A US State Department Wikileaks cable also attests that 'Qatar, a generous host to the American military for years, was the "worst in the region" in counter-terrorism efforts'. Qatar's security service was 'hesitant to act against known terrorists out of concern for appearing to be aligned with the U.S. and provoking reprisals'.[49] That Osama bin Laden seemed to leak most of his tapes first to Al-Jazeera has led some to conclude that the Qatar-based satellite TV station functions as a publicity arm of the terrorist organization. These claims seem based primarily on speculation or on unconfirmed sources. Notwithstanding this, there may be strategic reasons for some in Qatar, if not the Emir himself, to justify limited, if secret, contact with Al-Qaeda.

First, Al-Qaeda is a thorn in the side of Saudi Arabia, and a direct threat to the Saudi monarchy. Contrary to the belief of most Americans and Europeans that Al-Qaeda is only focussed on attacking a 'Western' way of life, one of Al-Qaeda's primary objectives is to disrupt and eventually overthrow the Saudi monarchy. The near enemy for Al-Qaeda is not the USA but the corrupt and unIslamic rule of the Saudis, and, by extension, other corrupt Arab governments. Destroying a major oil terminal or disrupting trade in the Gulf would have a profoundly negative impact on the region and on the viability of the Gulf monarchs and their families, not only in Saudi Arabia but in Qatar as well. By disassociating itself from Saudi Arabia and maintaining its own channels of communication with Al-Qaeda, Qatar may be seeking to prevent destabilizing and economically destructive attacks in its own territory. Ayman al-Zawahiri, the intellectual spokesperson for Al-Qaeda, has accused the 'rulers of the Gulf' of fusing 'governance without the *sharia* with friendship for Christians and Jews'. According to al-Zawahiri, 'Any observer of the Arabian Peninsula, Gulf emirates, Egypt, and Jordan will see that they have been changed into bases and camps providing administrative and technical support to the Crusader's forces in the heart of the Islamic world.'[50] Qatar certainly fits al-Zawahiri's criteria of a monarchy that should be overthrown, though some in Qatar would doubtless want to be certain that al-Zawahiri's call for the overthrow of the Gulf monarchies is directed first at other 'decadent' monarchs.

Still, despite these threats, there is some indication that members of Al-Thani family, most importantly Sheikh Abdallah bin Khalid Al-Thani at the Ministry of the Interior, have in the past had sympathy toward and contact with Al-Qaeda – sometimes reaching back to the Cold War era when the *mujahidin* were fighting the Soviets in Afghanistan. Abdallah bin Khalid Al-Thani is currently under house arrest, but he retains the office of Minister of the Interior – an indication of the need to keep his family and power base satisfied.[51] Similar symphathies and contacts existed, it must be remembered, between the CIA and the *mujahidin* after the end of the Cold War. To suggest, however, that Qatar has a coherent, friendly policy towards Al-Qaeda or that its interests converge with Al-Qaeda's stated ambition to create a new caliphate that overthrows the monarchs and rulers of the Islamic world seems illogical. While Qatar may want to deflect the possibility of an attack, given the fact that it is the site of US Central Command, it would make no sense for Qatar or Al-Thani monarchy to support a group that ulimately plots the destruction of monarchy and of the nation-state in general in the Gulf and in the Islamic world.

In fact, multiple terrorist attacks by stateless actors aimed at Qatar, while somewhat unlikely and far-fetched, would be more of a direct threat to Qatar and its incredibly rich economic potential than any incursion by a recognizable state such as Iran. In the highly unlikely event of an invasion by Iran, for example, US airpower would simply annihilate Iranian ships. While the USA, Qatar's most obvious first strategic ally, has shown its ability to contain and even defeat nation-states, it has shown much less effectiveness in containing and defeating stateless actors in the region. For this reason, some in the Qatar government may simply be being prudent by maintaining secret contact with, if not actual support of, Al-Qaeda. Apart from a shooting incident on a US base in 2000, the only alleged Al-Qaeda attack in Qatar occurred in March 2005 at an English-speaking theatre during a performance of Shakespeare's *Twelfth Night*. An English teacher was killed and 12 were wounded.

Other than that tragic incident, aimed at foreigners rather than the Qatari government, Qatar has been largely immune from the sort of attacks carried out in Saudi Arabia. Indeed, the maintenance of Qatar's immunity from terrorist attack (even if that immunity has been obtained through secret means) may also be in the short-term interests of the USA.[52] The USA have greater strategic interest in the stability of Qatar than in the prosecution of possible Al-Qaeda sympathizers there. A large Al-Qaeda-style attack on Qatar would be an immediate blow to US strategic interests in the entire region since it could lead to a sudden lack of hospitality for US troops and bases in Qatar. Having already overextended its welcome in Saudi Arabia, and with other Gulf emirates wary of Al-Qaeda reprisals, the US military would find it challenging to locate a new base in the region should Al-Qaeda attacks become frequent.

Israel

In October 1993 Israeli officials leaked a report that they were in secret negotiations with Qatar to bring billions of dollars of natural gas through Israel and export it throughout the Mediterranean zone.[53] Qatar immediately denied the existence of the deal. Nevertheless, the commercial and economic ties between Qatar and Israel have a long and fascinating history. The history of Qatar and Israeli relations is a history of the limitations of a foreign policy of mediation and openness. While Qatar's tacit recognition of Israel may have pleased its Western protectors, especially the USA, it caused disgust in other Arab states determined to hold out the prospect of Arab recognition of Israel as a bargaining chip in regional negotiations on a peace deal.

The fact that Qatar shut the Israeli interest office in Doha in January 2009 after the Palestinians had endured months of blockades in Gaza shows that even Qatar's extremely flexible diplomacy has its limits. In March 2009 Sheikha Mozah even hired a US public relations firm, Fenton Communications, to increase awareness of the humanitarian crisis in Gaza. Fenton will support an 'international public opinion awareness campaign that advocates the accountability of those who participated in attacks on schools in Gaza'. [54] Sheikh Hamad also recently approved millions of dollars in food aid and supplies for Gaza.

Before 2009 and the Gaza blockade, however, the relations and open business contacts between Qatar and Israel were certainly well outside the norm for the Arabian Peninsula. The origins of Qatar's relationship with Israel were largely related to its increasing dependence on American power and protection – especially after the Persian Gulf War and the Iraqi invasion of Kuwait revealed the potential weakness of small Gulf States – and its ambition to shore up its position as a viable mediator between the USA, Saudi Arabia and Kuwait on one side and Iraq on the other.[55] Indeed, it was largely the desire to be considered a flexible and viable mediator, and thus an important player in a whole range of disputes in the region, that led Qatar to accept Israel's symbolic presence in Qatar. Indeed, as the specialist on Qatari–Israeli relations Uzi Rabi notes:

> While it may appear as though Qatar's relations with Israel constitute an undesirable source of contention between Qatar and its neighbours, Qatari foreign policy is formulated in a manner that not only anticipates an indignant Arab reaction, but also to a certain degree invites it. Maintaining relations with Israel has enabled Qatar to assert its independence in the Arab arena, and compete as a regional actor with not inconsiderable clout.[56]

Qatar's appeal to Israel to sponsor its 2005 non-permanent seat on the UN Security Council was certainly an example of Qatar's deft use of a flexible agenda in foreign policy. Israel and the USA agreed to sponsor Qatar but were quickly dismayed when Qatar became the only member of the Security Council to oppose setting a deadline for the cessation of Iran's nuclear enrichment in 2006. Having achieved its position on the Security Council through diplomacy, Qatar found ways of protecting its interests: using Iran as a counterweight to Saudi influence. Qatar also used its special relationship with Israel to increase its clout as a negotiator between the rival Palestinian factions Fatah and Hamas. In fact, it could be argued that Qatar has been at least as welcoming to Hamas, Israel's clear enemy, as to Fatah and other parties. After Jordan closed the offices of Hamas in 1999, Qatar offered to allow Khaled Mishal and some of his deputies to relocate to Qatar as long as they did not engage in overt political activities. It is reported that Khaled Mishal regularly shuttles between Doha and Damascus.[57] Although he described his 'relationship' with Sheikh Hamad and Sheikh Hamad bin Jassim as 'personal', Qatar's relationship with both Hamas and Israel should be seen largely within the context of its wider policy of forming contacts with highly divergent groups in order to increase its clout and position as a potential mediator.

Uzi Rami indicates that Qatar's relations with Israel were largely the result of the strategic independence it adopted in its foreign policy. Nevertheless, the relationship between Qatar and its US military protector cannot be underestimated. In fact, Qatar's abrupt repudiation of its relations with Israel in January 2009 may have had more to do with the changing political landscape in the USA – the inauguration of a US President less reflexively supportive of Israel – than the humanitarian crisis in Gaza. After all, Qatar had maintained its relationship with Israel throughout the humanitarian crisis of the Second Intifada but a very different US administration was then in power.

The United States of America

Although there had been some contact betweeen Qatar and America before the end of the British Protectorate, it was minimal and usually of a commercial nature. The close relationship between Al-Thani and the USA can be traced to the withdrawal of the British from the Gulf. In the early 1970s the Arab rulers of the Gulf secretly hoped that the USA would take the place of Great Britain as a military protector of their regimes. When the Emir of Kuwait visited the USA in 1968 he was told rather bluntly that there were 'no plans to take the unique place the UK once held' in the region. Similarly, although they were themselves in the midst of withdrawal, the British were sceptical of the capabilities of any American imperial replacement, the head of the Arabian Department D.J. McCarthy observing that the Americans were rather 'ham-fisted' when it came to Gulf and Arab affairs.[58] Regardless of the effectiveness of American or British protection, Qatar's relationship with the USA must be seen in the wider context of the new reality of US dominance in the Gulf region as a whole. It was in this context that the US established its embassy in Doha in 1973.

Whether through innate reluctance to become Britain's successor as an imperial guarantor of regional stability, or through fear that the British would be proven right and US meddling would only lead to more Vietnams, the USA attempted to remain on the sidelines. The Nixon Doctrine of 1969 favoured the use of proxies to support and maintain US interests. Allies of the USA would be expected to take care of their own defence, even though US arms and support would flow freely to American allies. Iran under Shah Pahlavi became a favourite buffer state for the USA. By blocking the encroachment of the USSR into the region and maintaining US interests in the free flow of Gulf oil, Pahlavi's Iran replaced Britain as the policeman of the Gulf. The USA maintained its support of the oppressive Pahlavi regime at almost any cost. According to the scholar Michael Klare in *Blood and Oil: The Dangers and Consequences of America's Growing Petroleum Dependency*, the Nixon Doctrine was only a prelude to more direct involvement in the region.[59] The 1979 Islamic Revolution in Iran dramatically changed the situation. No longer could the USA rely on Iran as a proxy. Saudi Arabia, although a close ally, did not have the resources or will to replace Iran and was rocked by its own internal rebellions, including the dramatic takeover of the Mecca mosque in 1979. The Carter Doctrine, proclaimed in 1980, changed US interests from indirect to direct involvement in the Persian Gulf. The Soviet invasion of Afghanistan in 1979 had only heightened the need for direct US involvement to guarantee Gulf security. President Carter could not have made US entrenchment in the region any clearer in his State of the Union Address:

> An attempt by any outside force [USSR] to gain control of the Persian Gulf region will be regarded as an assault on the vital interests of the United States of America, and such an assault will be repelled by any means necessary, including military force.[60]

At first, Qatar under Sheikh Khalifa not only acquiesced to the Carter Doctrine but actively supported it. Like many other Gulf States, Qatar refused to maintain substantial international relations with the USSR. Sheikh Khalifa remained a quiet and loyal dependant of US hegemony, largely following the anti-Soviet policy of his staunchly anti-communist neighbour the King of Saudi Arabia throughout much of the 1980s. During the Iran–Iraq War, the USA sent in ships and aircraft carriers to ensure oil shipments out of the Strait of Hormuz and prevented Iran from forcefully extending its claims on offshore reserves claimed by the Arab Gulf States. It was thus an unexpected and somewhat troubling surprise for US foreign policy when Qatar suddenly recognized the USSR on 1 August 1988, only a few short years before the fall of the Soviet Union. The USA was left unprepared for the small, plucky emirate to have the temerity to make such a direct challenge both to the supremacy of the Carter Doctrine and the inclination of America's main ally, Saudi Arabia.

The main reason for Qatar's rather late and untimely recognition of the Soviet Union, the year before the fall of the Berlin Wall, was regional; it wanted to acquire American-made Stinger missiles on the black market for defence of its border against Bahrain. The US had supplied similar missiles to Bahrain, but not to Qatar. Seeing its regional interests betrayed, Qatar, like many client states in the Cold War period, appealed to the USSR. Soon the USSR and Qatar began exchanging envoys.[61] In response, the US Congress banned arms sales to Qatar. The message from Qatar was clear: Qatar might be small and it might be a generally supportive partner in preserving US interests, but it would always put its own immediate regional, economic and political interests first. Qatar has continued this policy of both generally supporting the US while also pursuing its own local interests and creative and innovative foreign policy initiatives to the present day.

The end of the Cold War cost Qatar its regional bargaining position, and the invasion of Kuwait by Saddam Hussein temporarily refocussed Qatari policy. The Persian Gulf War saw Qataris fighting squarely on the side of the USA and its allies. Sheikh Khalifa agreed to destroy its 'illegally' procured Stinger missiles and allowed the USA to operate from Qatari soil. Qatar helped repel Saddam Hussein's attempt to expand into the Gulf and in 1992 Sheikh Khalifa signed a defence cooperation agreement with the USA.[62]

As the Qatar University scholar and respected Gulf specialist Steven Wright concludes in *The United States and Persian Gulf Security: The Foundations of the War on Terror*, the US relationship before 9/11 was based largely on the maintenance of the status quo.[63] The fall of the Soviet Union and the predominance of the USA seemed to guarantee continued and steady oil supplies from the Gulf States. The terrorist attacks on New York, however, caused the slow-moving ship of US diplomacy to change course dramatically.

Qatar's relations with the USA seemed to peak after Sheikh Hamad overthrew his father in 1995. In an historic visit to the USA in 1997, Sheikh Hamad spoke at Georgetown University about his plans for economic and political reform. Emphasizing his moderate position, he referred to Qatari interest in resolving the Israeli–Palestinian conflict and indicated that Qatar would allow Israel to attend an economic conference in Qatar despite the fact that the government had recently closed down the offices of the Israeli interest section.[64] Official relations between Qatar and the USA remained strong after 9/11. Sheikh Hamad personally pledged to combat terrorism. Despite Hamad's reassurances, however, many in the US security establishment seemed to doubt how much control Hamad truly had over his own family and ministers.

According to an official report by the Congressional Research Service, 'US officials have described Qatar's counterterrorism cooperation since 9/11 as significant; however, some observers have raised questions about possible support for Al-Qaeda by some Qatari citizens, including members of the Royal Family.'[65] The *9/11 Commission*

Report, commissioned to determine the causes of the attacks, detailed terrorist Khalid Sheikh Muhammad's activities in Qatar. Khalid Sheikh Muhammad is considered one of the most important operations officers in Al-Qaeda network. He was second only to al-Zawahiri and bin Laden himself. He was captured and held at Guantanamo, becoming a major source of information about Al-Qaeda:

> In 1992 ... After returning briefly to Pakistan, he moved his family to Qatar at the suggestion of the former minister of Islamic affairs of Qatar, Sheikh Abdallah bin Khalid bin Hamad al Thani. KSM [Khalid Sheikh Muhammad] took a position in Qatar as project engineer with the Qatari Ministry of Electricity and Water. Although he engaged in extensive international travel during his tenure at the ministry – much of it in furtherance of terrorist activity – KSM would hold his position there until early 1996, when he fled to Pakistan to avoid capture by U.S. authorities ...[66]

Officially and publicly the Qatar–USA relationship remained robust despite these somewhat troubling revelations. A recent Congressional Report summarized the rationale behind the muted US reponse to Qatar-based terriorism activities:

> U.S. concerns regarding alleged material support for terrorist groups by some Qataris, including members of the Royal Family, have been balanced over time by Qatar's counterterrorism efforts and its broader, long-term committement to host and support U.S. military forces engaged in ongoing operation in Iraq, Afghanistan and the global war on terrorism.[67]

If anything, the conclusions of the 9/11 Commission seemed to justify bolstering US support of Sheikh Hamad and his immediate family in order to avoid the unlikely but dire situation where a sheikh with Abdallah's sympathies might take charge. Sheikh Hamad's $100 million gift to Hurricane Katrina victims in New Orleans and his personal visit to the region was a public relations coup.[68] Qatar seems to be exceptional among US Gulf State allies in its genuine desire to reach out not only to the US government but to the US population. Liquified natural gas terminals set up in Texas have added a great deal of extra weight to bilateral trade between the USA and Qatar.

Finally, Qatar has become a convenient and effective force for diplomatic action and stability in the region. Qatari mediation efforts and the country's willingness not only to support peace but to finance it has been very beneficial not only to US interests but to the rest of the world. Nor has Qatar been the only accommodating partner in the USA–Qatar relationship. Recognizing Qatar's own sensitivities and learning from the hostile reaction to US troops in Saudi Arabia, the USA and Qatar emphasized that Al-Udeid base in Qatar would not be a 'sovereign' US entity but 'jointly administered'.

Qatar helped finance the construction of the base and provided some $400 million to update US facilities there in 2003.[69] In addition to Al-Udeid, Camp Al-Sayliyah in Qatar is the largest storage area for US military equipment in the region. Qatar has generally supported the USA in expanding operations on its bases despite the potential risks – a patriot missle was accidentially fired in October 2007 and the presence of so many young American troops in such a conservative country could lead to negative reactions from the Qatari people. American troops are largely prevented from living in or moving too freely in Doha. At the same time, the relationship between the USA and Qatar is not without its unresolveable complications: US officials have protested at Qatar's financial aid to Hamas and Gaza, calling it the financing of terror.

The USA also has substantial economic interests in the success of Qatar's natural gas production, a fact that has secured US investment in Qatar. Not only has Qatar signed agreements with several US energy companies, ExxonMobil and ConocoPhillips being the major players, it has also accepted major loans from the US Export-Import Bank. It was the Export-Import Bank that helped finance the development of natural gas facilities at Ras Laffan in 1996, despite the fact that the Qatari budget was highly constrained throughout the late 1990s. Most recently, in January 2010 Qatar and other Gulf countries agreed to allow the US military to station more missile defence installations on Qatari soil, and the USA has sped up its construction of such defences. The USA is also patrolling the gulf with Aegis missile ships at all times. Despite Qatar's more public diplomatic independence, Qatar is still clearly dependent on security arrangements provided by the USA.[70]

Asia and the Rest of the World

Qatar is at least as much South Asian as Arab. In terms of sheer numbers South Asian residents (Indians, Pakistanis, Sri Lankans, Nepalese and Bangladeshis) dominate the population and have entered into almost every aspect of the Qatari economy. China has also increased its interest in Gulf markets and Japan has historically been one of Qatar's chief trading partners, proving a steady supply of Toyotas and Land Cruisers – that symbol of the Qatari driver. South Korea has gained lucrative contracts to build liquid natural gas container ships.

QATAR'S USE OF MEDIA

Although Qatar excels at traditional nation-to-nation diplomacy, it has also invested heavily in soft-power diplomacy, utilizing international media at an early stage and hosting the recognized platform not only for Arabic news on Al-Jazeera, but for a new and bold internet age of Islamic jurisprudence.

IslamOnline

'I am a Muslim and my dad is an alcoholic – What should I do?' This was the question asked by a young Muslim woman on the Qatar-based and -funded IslamOnline website. One sign of the influence of IslamOnline.net is that fact that it was blocked in countries such as Tunisia, with its strict controls on information.[71] One of the most popular Islamic sites on the web, IslamOnline has been used to organize religious and political activism and opposition. Thus, because it is an active, community-based form of media, IslamOnline is more of a direct threat to and thorn in the side of authoritarian regimes outside Qatar. While online censorship is fairly effective, Al-Jazeera cannot be summarily blocked from illegal Tunisian, Libyan or Saudi satellite dishes. Yet, Qatar's control of IslamOnline, a truly remarkable operation with a dedicated coterie of approved Islamic scholars answering questions from users throughout the world, has certainly given it access to the mindsof the general Muslim public in a way that is as important as the Emir's more famous involvment in sponsoring Al-Jazeera.

Al-Jazeera

More than any other organization funded and controlled by Qatar, Al-Jazeera represents the difficulties and the risks of Qatar's attempt to simultaneously secure alliances with strategic partners while also claiming a prominent role within the Arabic-speaking and, with Al-Jazeera, English-speaking public at large. In 2003 the CIA believed that Al-Jazeera was encrypting messages and signals between Al-Qaeda operatives using TV signals and images. Although this seemed far-fetched, and probably highly ineffective weighed against all the less risky options available to Al-Qaeda online, there have been reports that during George W. Bush's administration some in the CIA were convinced that Al-Jazeera was the publicity arm of international terrorists. Likewise, Al-Jazeera became convinced of an American consipiracy against it.

Several suspicious bombings of Al-Jazeera headquarters in Iraq – one of which killed Al-Jazeera reporter Tarek Ayoub whose memorial is prominently displayed at Doha's Al-Jazeera headquarters – and in Afghanistan have only served to confirm Al-Jazeera's fears of US retaliation. Reporters without Borders was similarly outraged at these apparently accidental bombings.[72] A British official alleged that military personnel and certain members of the Bush administration were so concerned about Al-Jazeera, especially during the US siege of Fallujah in Iraq in 2004, that plans were hatched to bomb Al-Jazeera headquarters in Doha.[73] Later, the controversy over Al-Jazeera seems to have died down. Al-Jazeera has recently expanded its coverage and operations, opening an English-language channel and continuing to defend its status as the most watched Arabic-language news broadcaster.

In conclusion, Qatar's multilateral and bilateral relationships can be described as a mixture of both thoroughly modern opportunism and the traditional prestige of mediation. By making itself indispensible to a variety of diplomatic initiatives and by setting its own course between comparatively massive neighbours, Qatar is not only a maverick but also an effective broker. There seems to be little incentive for Qatar to modify its subtle diplomatic positioning in any significant way. As the next chapter will discuss, Qatar's political economy supports the international status quo.

7

Qatar's Political Economy – A Classic Rentier State?

Q atar appears to be a classic rentier state: dependent on one resource, 'rent' from oil and gas, Qatar is in a position of luxury that many a power-hungry ruler would envy – there is no need for it to rely on tax revenue from the population. Indeed, Qatar and Kuwait are at the very top of the worldwide list of countries most dependent on petroleum rent. While a rentier state can be defined as a state where 40 per cent of government revenue comes from rent, 87 per cent of Qatar's revenue comes from oil and gas.[1] Although Qatar has plans to introduce income tax – it will be one of the first Gulf countries to do so – the proportion of its revenue from rents [oil and gas revenue] is not expected to change significantly.[2] In Qatar almost everything in its social, economic and governmental structures, from 'per capita electricity consumption, to education levels, to literacy' has been profoundly shaped by oil revenue.[3] Also, unlike other oil-producing countries, Qatar has a very low price base – the point at which its oil or gas prices no longer ensure its financial stability. According to PFC Energy, a Washington DC consultancy, Venezuela requires an oil price of $95 a barrel to ensure macroeconomic security, Saudi Arabia $55. Qatar, however, could still remain financially stable even with oil below $10 a barrel, according to PFC. It is the only significant oil exporter that was *less* dependent on higher oil prices in 2008 than in 2000.[4]

While Qatar would probably be the last oil exporter to be seriously hurt by a catastrophic fall in the oil market, its heavy dependence on oil and gas has several implications. There is, for example, now a widespread assumption in studies of political economy that for a nation to depend for its wealth on its natural resources is at best a mixed blessing and at worst a curse for the national economy and a nearly impenetrable roadblock to democratization. Rentier states are often inflicted with the 'Dutch disease', the sudden inflation of prices and subsequent collapse of non-oil manufacturing and business named after the stagnation felt in the Dutch economy after its exploitation of petroleum reserves.[5] Oil crowds out other industry. Moreover, since there is 'no representation without taxation' those rentier states without an already established democratic culture are often ruled by authoritarian regimes. This divide between the state, the Emir, is often long term and only increases over time. As Jill Crystal observed:

> Oil based states are unusual in that their higher degree of autonomy from other social groupings is not the result of a momentary crisis, but part of a structurally determined, ongoing process. This independence is almost uniquely peculiar to oil. Almost any other export ... involves some accommodation between the rulers and the elite who control the workforce.[6]

Oil is uniquely de-democratizing. The political scientist Michael Ross determined after studying extensive worldwide data on rentier economies and political systems that 'the oil-impedes-democracy claim is both valid and statistically robust ... oil does hurt democracy.'[7] Nevertheless, some political scientists, such as Gulf expert Michael Herb, argue that the impact of reliance on a single resource, oil wealth, is not inevitable nor always predictable. As Herb remarked, 'different ways of dealing with this issue have an important impact on the results'.[8] Not simply the existence of natural resources, but how those resources are used has a major impact on the political and economic fate of states. For instance, a state could use oil revenue for economic development, for creating a middle class, paying for education, increasing diversification in the economy, or providing services. As political scientists have convincingly argued since the 1950s, development is correlated with democracy. Development enhances the potential for liberalization, though this is often offset by the still unaccountable nature of most state revenue. Even so, 'citizens have many reasons to want to hold their rulers accountable, even if they are not taxed'.[9] Qataris have come to expect the state's generous allowances, up to $7,000 a month, interest-free loans, free land and nearly guaranteed employment. Development and expansion of the state, especially a state controlled ever more closely by a powerful Emir, may lead to problematic social divisons and demands. According to Jill Crystal:

> As the state's scope grows, so with it grows the distance between the ruler and the popula-tion, as the popular perception of state services shifts from benevolence to entitlement. As the state's power expands, new actors appear who question the old arrangements.[10]

Few of these 'new actors' have so far appeared on the Qatari political scene and it is thus difficult to predict the particular ways Qatari society will deal with the distancing of the state and the Emir and the move away from their traditional, historic position as an accessible core of Qatari society.

Oil and gas revenue have had a major and obvious impact on Qatar's modern history. Nevertheless, even in the extreme case of Qatar where so much of its revenue, both current and forecast well into the future, derives from petroleum, the pre-oil economy, society and politics were not simply wiped away by a tidal wave of oil rents. Certainly, Qatar's economy was probably at its very weakest and poorest at the moment when oil revenue began to flow, thus compounding the effects of oil. Moreover, with such a small population, the effect of rentierism is more pronounced. Yet, even if Qatar were not so geographically blessed as to have a massive gas field of unfathomable proportions – a field of great magnitude even in a region of vast petroleum fields – many aspects of Qatar's social and political structure would probably not be incomprehensibly different from what they are today.

A study of the pre-oil, pearling industry reveals the deep historical roots of Qatar's present cultural and social structures. Indeed, what most studies in political science with their focus on measureable data miss is the lived experience, the totality of views and patterns of behaviour that determine culture. As Ruth Benedict, a founder of modern cultural anthropology, observed in *Patterns of Culture*, 'The significance of cultural behaviour is not exhausted when we have clearly understood that it is local and man-made and hugely variable. It tends to be integrated.'[11] Although a culture is not like an individual person, in that it cannot think or act of its own accord, it is determined by individuals who engage in a more or less consistent pattern of thought and action. By focusing on generalizations, data sets and comparisons between categories of 'Middle Eastern' and 'Islamic', political scientists may miss some of the particularities of sub-regional, localized cultures, particularities that can have a major impact on the shape and nature not only of social behaviours but of both externally visible and informally implied political structures.

While rentierism alone may not adequately explain Qatar's current authoritarianism, nor any other particularity of Qatar's government structure, neither should 'the ideological and cultural currents that are common to the Islamic world' be the primary explanation for low democracy scores tabulated according to measurements that may not capture traditional, informal means of representation. This is especially true in a very small country such as Qatar where actual, face to face contact between ruler and ruled was, until recently, not only feasible but common. The ideological and cultural currents of 'Islam' in the Middle East, if such generalized currents can even be said to exist at all, are characterized by recent anthropology as a complex dialectical tension between egalitarianism and authority. This is due not simply to oil but also to earlier economic history before oil.

In Qatar, the social cultural impact of pearling has been of real and longstanding importance, even if much of pearling culture has been recreated as the product of oil-financed 'heritage' preservation. While the economic measures may seem to indicate a radical change in almost every aspect of society, Qataris still feel an attachment to the past, even if some allege the economic viability of their past pearling culture has been blasted away by the petroleum economy. Yet, even by numerical measures, there is not necessarily 'consistent support for the thesis that rentierism has a harmful effect on democracy scores'. Kuwait, the country most like Qatar in many ways, has a 'democracy score' that is only .086 points below its current Freedom House democracy score if the data is crunched without the impact of oil.[12] Moreover, as the history of pearling in Qatar reveals, dependence on a single natural resource for much of its revenue was not new to Qatar.

FROM A PEARL TO AN OIL ECONOMY – CONSEQUENCES FOR GOVERNANCE

In 1863, five years before the treaty with Britain, Muhammad bin Thani told the traveller William Palgrave, 'We are all from the highest to the lowest slaves of one master, Pearl.'[13] Qatar had a higher proportion of its population then engaged in pearling than any other pearling centre in the world. Pearling, like oil a century later, was not a labour-intensive industry. Unlike oil, however, pearling involved almost the entire population in production. While oil involves mainly foreign agents and companies, pearling was a domestic activity that involved almost all settled Qataris. Even Bedouin were employed to guard pearling villages while the divers were away fishing from June to October.

Pearling in most parts of the Gulf involved an interesting system of profits and rents. It was financed by local merchants who loaned ships' captains and divers money to set themselves up and then kept them in debt. By paying cash in advance to divers, cash that needed to be repaid through pearling, the captain and the boat owner avoided Islamic prohibitions on usury. At the top of the loan pyramid, the sheikh financed his own financed pearl fleets and he could often be found travelling around the Gulf selling his people's pearls. Sheikhs could also levy taxes on those areas and villages they controlled.[14] In Qatar, however, the situation was slightly different. Although merchants were still important, they did not have nearly the same power as in other Gulf States. As Jill Crystal remarked:

> What set Qatar apart from Kuwait was the absence of an entrepôt economy ... Ecology and location dictated for it a complete dependence on pearling ... In particular the merchants were a weaker group .... Their control of the domestic workforce, which included a larger number of beduins [Bedouin] with independent ties to the desert beyond Qatar, was weaker. One measure of the merchants' weaker control was that Qatar's pearl divers were, for the region, uniquely free of debt bondage.[15]

The potentially isolating effect of the pearl economy was offset by the fact that pearls, a luxury item, had no really stable local market. In this respect pearls were like oil: highly dependent on foreign markets. Qatar's almost complete dependence on pearling had other important impacts too. Pearling was an industry with highly variable boom and bust prices and the resultant fluctuating and uncertain profits effected the attitude of many Qataris. While income from oil, even when prices are low, flows fairly steadily, the peaks and troughs of pearling could create a somewhat fatalistic and protectionist attitude among the pearl-fishers. Also, without alternative employment to pearling, non-religious education was not highly valued, which had something of an equalizing effect on the population. Unlike other Gulf societies, Qatar's pearling industry did not result in the same level of class stratification as in other emirates. Rarely were divers actually enslaved in Qatar and there was a much more fluid relationship between sheikh, merchant and diver than elsewhere. This fluid social arrangement steadily declined, however, as the Emir and his family almost exclusively gained more and more power and support from the British and, finally, from oil revenue.

Qatar's first major oil shipment did not occur until 1949, and the most dramatic changes caused by oil investment in Qatar did not occur until the 1960s: well within the living memory of older Qataris. Before the oil concession of 1935, a concession which guaranteed payments directly to the Emir, but not to the citizens of Qatar, the major and only significant source of revenue for the Emir and for the governance of Qatar came from levies on pearl-fishing ships and their captains. The transition from a pearling economy to an oil-based one dramatically shifted the Emir's principal source of revenue from Qatari divers, captains and pearl merchants to the revenue and rents of foreign oil companies.

Although pearl-fishing has essentially ceased except in cultural 'heritage' re-enactments, the impact of the pearl-fishing culture and economy can still be seen in the modern skyline of Doha. The names of various land development projects, most famously the reclaimed set of islands 'The Pearl', but also 'Al-Dana' (one of many names for pearls) also recall the country's once dominant pearling culture. Just as native peoples in in Arctic climates are said to have dozens of names for snow, there is similarly an entire, local lexicon dedicated to the pearl.

There are also constant reminders of the traditional pearl economy – pearling is an anchor of Qatari identity in the midst of hyper-modern development. Possibly the most photographed and most emblematic piece of public art is near the old port on Doha's manicured Corniche: a large concrete oyster, open wide enough to see a perfectly round pearl inside. The beloved shanties sung by the crews of pearling ships and their captains, used to maintain strict discipline and solidarity during long periods out at sea, are still remembered, passed down through the generations and memorized by Qatari schoolchildren. During the Asian Games Qatari women dressed in flowing black abayas performed the traditional dance to the sea. During the song the women dance in unison, dramatically hitting the sand with palm fronds and crying out against the sea for the return of husbands lost at sea. This cry of mourning is almost universally recognized by Qataris. A symbolic cry of profound cultural significance, it represents a yearning as much for a lost past as for lost husbands.[16]

Similar dances, songs and beliefs, although technically they contravene strict Wahhabi interpretations of Islam, involve pre-Islamic legends of whales swallowing the moon. The origins of the pearl have inspired a great deal of lore. According to recorded tradition, 'young shell-less oysters come to the surface when it is raining, or when the moon is full. The raindrop is the father of a good pearl and the oyster the mother while the moon produces the luster.'[17] If for Bedouin it was the desert, the camel and the well that defined cultural norms, for Qatari pearlers it was the sea, the ship and the oyster.

There are accounts preserved at Al-Khor Museum north of Doha of all-female pearling ships and female pearl ship captains competing with male rivals at sea. According to a publication by Al-Khor Museum:

> Ghilan and Mayy were the two characters of this legend which most probably originated in Al-Khor, Mayy was a woman in competition with a man, Ghilan. The woman proved to be more competent, in the beginning, even in that difficult task of navigation and looking for pearl oyster banks. Man has been favored by destiny ...[18]

If it is assumed that culture is a learned, collective behaviour, if cultural, linguistic and social norms can exist and solidify over centuries, there is, with the possible exception of land-based agriculture, little more profound and continuous, all-encompassing, collective behaviour than pearl-fishing in the Gulf. The cultural and historical roots of pearl-fishing are evidenced in an ancient cuneiform tablet found at Ur in Iraq and dated to 2000 BC, which refers to 'a parcel of fish eyes' or pearls from Dilmun, the ancient trading civilization that controlled Bahrain and Qatar. There is strong archaeological and written evidence that pearl-fishing continued, virtually non-stop, for four millenia until the discovery of oil. One of the most popular shops in the traditional, reconstructed Suq Waqif, prominently positioned at the main entrance, is run by a well-known old, pearl-fisher diver and body-builder. Filled with old photographs, fishing tackle and rare pearl specimens, his shop more than any other in the suq seems a bubble of lost time. Qataris still stream through the shop, examining the remnants of their recent past.

The decline and eventual complete disappearance of pearl-fishing and its replacement with oil development and refining has meant not only the decline of an economic activity but the loss of an entire way of ordering life and culture. There is a profound contrast between the social, political and cultural activities necessary to a pearl economy and those required for an oil economy. Qataris from the pearling generation are only too aware of the contrasts between the cultures of the pre-oil and oil economies. An uncle of one of my students commented, 'Pearling used to play an important role in strengthening social relations and ties. Diving and fishing were activities that required collective action. This created strong bonds between different parts of society.' The grandfather of this student, a senior member of a prominent Qatari tribe, remarked:

> Today, in contrast, we can see the laziness of the young men. They don't want to walk to the mosque because it is too far away for them. Modernity makes life easier in many ways but it also makes us separate from one another.

For instance, during the dramatic *al-Gaws al Kabir*, or first cold water, diving season, bands of ships left the port together, waving colourful flags, beating drums and chanting songs. Although almost exclusively male – excepting the women captains of Al-Khor legend – the crews and captains (*nakhodas*) of the pearling ship paralleled the ways of the Bedouin of the desert. They used profound, local knowledge of currents, sand colour, the presence of outcroppings, a knowledge inherited from generations, and roamed the sea in search of their rare prize. Most pearling fleets kept together and had an 'admiral' running the fleet, but the individual ships or *dhows* each relied on their own *nakhoda* to use his instinct and skill and keep the vessel over the virgin oyster beds. For fresh water the ship's men either went ashore or divers filled empty skins from submarine, freshwater springs. Pearl-diving required almost continual exposure to the water and long periods in the one of the world's saltiest seas.

There is a vast contrast beween the comforts available to the modern Qatari office worker and the sheer hardships experienced by the pearl-diver, of course. Wearing only a loincloth and perhaps some protection for the fingers, the divers, some of them black slaves brought over from east Africa, some of them free Arabs, would be attached to the boat with ropes tied to a stone or iron weight. The attendant on the ship had to pull the rope taut when the stone hit the bottom and pull up the diver when he felt him tugging the rope. There were several cases of divers perishing when the attendant above became distracted. Long exposure to the salt water caused trachoma. Saw fish, sharks and the Diadema sea urchin with its two-foot-long poisonous spines menaced divers. Many divers suffered from the bends and sheer exhaustion. They ate nothing during the day as the constant heat caused nausea, and for dinner consumed only handfuls of rice and dates. Whereas in the endless bounty of modern Qatar obesity and diabetes are serious health problems, during the pearling days the men suffered from malnutrition and exhaustion. Although Qatari divers were not quite as poor as some, there were instances when they went into extreme debt. In most of the Gulf death was no escape from the hard life of the diver, as the diver's debts to the ship's *nakhoda* would have to be paid off by his sons and family.

Importantly, however, and uniquely in the Gulf, most divers and ships' captains in Qatar were free men, free of indebted servitude.[19] Also, unlike other pearling centres Al-Thani ruler in Doha did not automatically receive a share of all, or even most, pearling revenue. Even as late as the early twentieth century, after Sheikh Jassim Al-Thani had achieved so much success in consolidating his power and Al-Thani family had solidly positioned itself as the premier family in Qatar, many tribal communites remained completely exempt from taxation. Al-Sudan in Bidaa according to Lorimer, were exempt from taxation and Al-Thani Sheikh in Doha received what Lorimer estimated to be a modest $8,400 per year. Several tribes in Wakra were exempt from taxation, and those who were liable made their payments to the Sheikh of Wakra, not Al-Thani of Doha. The Sheikh of Wakra received approximately $3,400 a year. A great deal of this revenue was spent on protecting the boats from raids and tending to the town while the ships were at sea. In all other ports no taxes were levied at all. There was little sense of monetary obligation to Al-Thani outside Doha.[20]

Gulf pearl-divers and captains were so protective of their traditional practices that the British were encouraged to impose a fine of $9,000 for diving with special gear or compression helmets and suits.[21] Whereas oil is discovered by modern, scientific equipment and by those with professional degrees conferred in Western institutions, severely limiting the role of Qataris and locals in production, those employed in pearl-fishing closely following ancient local knowledge and experience was the key to economic success. Although the education and literacy of recent generations far outpaces those of the past, this traditional respect for the knowledge and experience of elders remains a fundamental part of Qatari modern culture, though it is also a frequent source of friction between the generations.

Before the Japanese discovery of the cultured Mikimoto pearl and its increasingly wide distribution in the decades after 1908, pearl-fishing was a profitable business.[22] Although Qatar was not as large a producer of pearls as neighbouring Bahrain, a scholar from rival Dubai claims that Qatar's pearls were considered to be of the highest quality.[23] Pearling brought a great deal of currency into the region. The traveller James Wellsted claimed in 1835 that the pearling industry in the Gulf was worth £400,000, a true fortune for the time.[24] At a high point of pearling in the 1860s there were an estimated 817 pearling boats and some 13,000 divers in Qatar, 917 boats and 18,000 divers in Bahrain and 1,215 boats and 22,000 divers throughout what would become the United Arab Emirates. While Bahrain had a more diversified traditional economy and higher population, and the UAE also had revenue from agricultural production in its inland oases, Qatar, though it had a much smaller population and the fewest pearling boats, was dependent on pearling income for a much larger proportion of its total income.[25] At the top of its pearling economy, if not at its absolute centre, the Sheikh of Qatar received almost all of his revenue from taxes on boats around Bidaa and received a portion of their profits too.

The steep downturn in pearl prices after the depression of 1929 hit Qatar, if not the Sheikh himself, particularly hard. Unlike Bahrain which began oil production early in 1932, Qataris – if not the Sheikh himself who received an allowance from his 1935 oil concession, despite the fact that no substantial amount of oil would be shipped out until after the Second World War – were still highly dependent on pearl revenue. On top of the challenge of lower prices and profits, much of the Qatari pearling fleet had been destroyed in a dramatic flood in 1925, putting Qatari pearl captains and owners into severe debt. Qatar's overexposure to pearling and the fact that most food supplies, excepting dates, had to be imported only heightened the crisis. From 1925 to 1949 Qatar entered into probably its deepest economic depression, known as the 'years of hunger'. Entire families and tribes emigrated. The merchant classes were devastated. Al-Thani and the few persistent tribes left presided over a country nearly empty of its people. With fewer diverse powers and tribes to concede to, this great emptying of Qatar left the ruling family with even more power than it had possessed before. The British Political Agent described Qatar towards the end of the 'years of hunger'. He wrote of whole villages deserted and left in ruins, and even places of great historic importance such as Fuwayrat, where Al-Thani had orignally secured their power and their alliances, emptied.[26]

Even the traditional merchant classes represented by Al-Darwish and Al-Mani families were ruined. Salih Mani, the once proud patriarch of the merchant family, was reduced to roaming about the Gulf and renting out his motor launch.[27]

The emptying of the Qatari population immediately before the flood of oil revenue only served to heighten and strengthen the effects of Qatar's new oil-based economic and political system. With the merchants and the rest of the population completely impoverished, and Qataris either unable or too exhausted to maintain traditional claims, the incoming oil wealth in the hands of the Emir became an even more important source of power. Also, unlike pearl-fishing where the Sheikh had to rely on the cooperation of Qataris to provide him with revenue, the public is not the source of revenue for oil-based economies, though it can be a source of discontent and of demands.

Of course, the distinctions between a pearling economy and an oil economy are not absolute. There are, in some limited respects, parallels between the export of oils and pearls. Like the later export of crude oil to foreign refineries, Qatar exported raw pearls. The pearls were sometimes taken for sale abroad by Al-Thani Sheikh himself as he went on economic and diplomatic trips around the Gulf. They might be sent first to Bahrain and Lingah in Persia and then onwards to Bombay. From India came cotton and essential industrial items. In fact, Qatar was so tied to the Indian market that the Indian rupee was the offical currency of Qatar until 1966 when India devalued it. Most pearls that were shipped to India were processed, sold and turned into jewellery. As one observer noted in 1951, 'Peddlers may be found in most towns of the Persian Gulf with necklaces of Gulf pearls for sale; however, these have usually been imported from Bombay.'[28]

Although pearls were a raw material export like oil, pearling involved an intimate relationship between the Qatari ruler and the population, a relationship not needed in the oil industry. Almost as extradorinary as the long history of pearling in Qatar was how quickly it disappeared after the exploration of oil. After thousands of years of pearling and the deep-set traditions associated with it, the Qatari pearl industry simply vanished in a matter of years. In 1955 no pearling fleets left the shores of Qatar.

The advent of oil had two divergent impacts on Qatari politics and society. In one respect oil further enhanced the position of the Sheikh of Qatar. British oil companies signed personal contracts and concessions with the sheikhs, not with their populations. In other respects, however, oil production opened up new opportunities for Qataris to become wage-earners and to break away from their indebtedness to pearl merchants and, by extension, the Sheikh. Oil production, although dominated by foreign players and occuring outside the traditional centres of population, created a small, important, middle class. In Bahrain, where oil had been around much longer than Qatar, oil-workers became a locus of active opposition with ties to the Nasser movement in Egypt. In Qatar, however, the amount of explicit, 'middle-class' opposition was more muted.[29] This is true even when prices are in great flux.

OIL PRICES AND THE WIDER ECONOMY

From a breathless high of over $40 a barrel in June 2008, light sweet crude oil dropped precipitously to under $40 a barrel within six months. Even more important for Qatar's future, natural gas, another of Qatar's increasingly important exports, also fell, and by June 2009 had not regained its value nearly as much as oil. In June 2009 natural gas prices hovered just above lifetime lows.[30] With such extreme price fluctuation, Qatar could face serious difficulties in its long-term planning. Although the country's economy is administered conservatively, in the expectation of much lower oil prices, this did not protect it from going temporarily into deficit because of lower than expected petroleum prices in the 1980s. While oil prices have now stabilized, Qatar remains exposed to global economic trends.

For example, real estate in Qatar is intricately tied to price swings in the oil sector. Even though oil only employs 5 per cent of expatriates in the country and expats make up the vast bulk of the renters in the real estate market, oil prices drive the perception of real estate values. Doha's population doubled from 2001 to 2008 but plateaued briefly and then increased again – largely following oil and gas prices. According to a recent report by the Dubai-based consultancy Landmark Advisory, however, real estate prices in Doha are not necessarily dependent on population growth. This is mainly because the single, male construction workers, who make up 45 per cent of the workforce, are housed in industrial housing zones beyond the city.[31] According to Landmark, Qatar's real estate market, in the era of $140 oil seen as woefully undersupplied, may actually soon be oversupplied. According to a recent report by marketresearch.com

> The vacancy rate in Qatar's West Bay area stands at around 20% for 46 completed towers, despite government attempts to mitigate vacancy levels by leasing space. Real estate developers holding debt have also seen deterioration in their ability to repay loans on the back of declining rents in the country.[32]

'The Pearl', in many respects, is the iconic real estate project of Qatar, as important to its prestige as the Palm Jumeirah, a palm-shaped set of man-made islands, is to Dubai. The impact of The Pearl's success on Qatar's smaller economy is greater however. Qatar is not able to absorb losses as easily as Dubai and cannot go to a federal authority, such as Abu Dhabi, for a bail out. Nevertheless, even a major real estate boondoggle will not seriously threaten Qatar's long-term solvency as long as natural gas is in demand.

Lying outside the original lands of Qatar, properties on the artificial land of The Pearl, unlike other developments built on Qatar for which only a 99-year lease is available, can be bought outright. The possible acceleration in the decline of prices at The Pearl, however, may make the real estate development a burden on state finances rather than an envisioned engine of growth and investment. Sensing the potential for an embarrassing downward spiral, the Qatari government intervened and offered a package of about $5 billion to Qatari banks to enable them to buy up defaulted loans outright.[33] This may be a stop-gap measure similar to US buy-outs of toxic assets. Challenges remain, however. The lack of government transparency and the differences in and unreliability of statistical information on Doha's population and economy, and thus the difficulty of knowing rental values may prevent prospective expatriate buyers from entering the market.

Renting was also down significantly in 2008–9 and bank lending was curtailed. 'Despite government intervention, excessive lending and poor risk management have left Qatari banks over-exposed to real estate assets, which are now depreciating due to falling demand.'[34] This bursting of the real estate bubble in Qatar was largely due to over-speculation spurred by high inflation. The rapid rise of prices made interest rates effectively negative and encouraged buyers into the market, leading to further speculation. The awarding of the World Cup 2022 may have some positive impact on the real estate market but it may also lead to more oversupply as the state attempts to build enough space for the prospective fans and teams and others associated with the World Cup.

An excess of cash and an excess of political and personal manoeuvering have both hindered national projects to diversify the economy. Despite the often sincere adoration of the ruling family, the ambitions of Al-Thani elite often seem to come into irreconcilable conflict with entrenched social interest groups. These are people who, with little ability in English, despite being surrounded by the English language, often feel left out of the dreams and aspirations of the elite and are wary that little will be left of Qatar besides a museum re-creation or hazy memories of tribal ancestors.

Although it may come as something of a surprise given the vast wealth available to most Qataris, there is a problem with unemployment in Qatar, especially among the large number of young men who decide not to go to university, or if they do, major in Arabic and study of the Sharia. Young women graduates also face high unemployment; just 30 per cent of employees were female in 2004, according to Dr Lailah Dhiab of the General Secretariat of Development and Planning.[35]

Officially, the rate of unemployment of Qatari men is low, at 3.2 per cent. However, this statistic does not account for men who have chosen not to enter the labour market. There are resultant problems with these disaffected young men, who may gravitate towards other things that give their lives meaning, filling the space in their lives with alternative identities – even radical identities associated with Qatar's previously strict adherence to Wahhabi Islam may take root. Another cause for concern is the resentment of low-paid labourers from south Asia who make up the great majority of Qatar's workforce and who populate Industrial City, a depressing, sprawling warren hidden outside Doha. There are even instances where workers, deprived of rights and sometimes of pay, have repeatedly burned down their own buildings. In many ways the structural and real urban dilemmas in Doha, dilemmas as old as the first tribal settlements and yet as new as the highest skyscraper without an adequate car park, accurately reflect many of the overarching problems and opportunities in Qatar society as a whole.

AN END TO PETROLEUM DEPENDENCE?

Qatar may seem overly dependent on the expectation of high oil prices. Dr Khalid Bin Mohammad Al-Attiyah, Minister of State for International Cooperation, recently declared that 'there will always be demand for oil'.[36] Despite the overriding confidence in the oil market and the fact that no viable fuel alternatives have emerged, Qatar has still launched plans to free itself from dependence on this single resource. The Qatar Ministry of Finance declared 2020, the year crude oil reserves are expected to be depleted, if not natural gas, as the year when Qatar will have weaned its economy from its dependence on oil and gas revenue. In July 2009, Youssef Hussein Kamal, Qatar's Minister of Finance declared that that goal may need to be a delayed a couple of years because of falling petroleum prices.[37] Qatar's independence from petroleum revenue relies on investments, however. It needs revenue from oil and gas to wean itself from oil and gas. Higher petrol and gas prices allow the excess revenues required to purchase a host of diverse investments, from London real estate holdings to multinational stock portfolios.[38] These investments are meant to shield Qatar from full dependence on petroleum resources. The ruler of Qatar is particularly keen to maintain Qatar's extraordinary economic prosperity regardless of oil prices. This prosperity appears to justify the current structure of authority and government, a structure that vests all ultimate power with the Emir.

8

The Emir and the Exercise of Authority in Qatar

During the pearling years the Sheikh of Qatar was a 'merchant prince' whose interests were as much focussed outside of Qatar, on the markets of India and Persia, as on the internal workings of the village of Bidaa.[1] The income of the Sheikh from his pearling operations was only about as big as the tax revenue from the Qatari divers and boat captains. In many respects, the title of 'merchant chief' remains as true today and explains the tradition of the Sheikh pursuing the advancement of his own family's interests and his commercial and overseas operations, and his policy of encouraging the state to reach out to the wider world. In this way the whole state of Qatar has become almost a kind of corporation, with the Sheikh as CEO. At the same time, the level of control that the Sheikh has over the governance of Qatar is unparalleled by that of the CEO of any major corporate entity. It has certainly increased since the pearling years.

As Qatar expert Jill Crystal argued in her description of Sheikh Khalifa's Qatar, 'power remains uninstitutionalized. There is no meaningful distinction, either political or legal, between the person of the Emir and the institutions of the state. Sovereignty is unlimited.'[2] Despite his cultural and commerical reforms, little has changed in the actual structures of power during the reign of Sheikh Hamad. Historically, the lack of distinction between state and ruler has been more pronounced in Qatar than in other Gulf sheikhdoms. The proportion of total government expenditure spent on the royal family in Qatar in 1970 was 33 per cent, higher than the comparable figure for any neighbouring state. The total for Kuwait was 2.6 per cent and for Libya 0.8 per cent (in 1967–8).[3] With official net personal assets of over $2 billion (in 2009), and probably even greater undisclosed wealth, Sheikh Hamad bin Khalifa Al-Thani, aged 59 in 2011, is richer than the monarchs of much larger countries. Ranked seventh among the world's wealthiest royals by *Forbes Magazine* (in 2008), his personal wealth surpasses that of the Queen of the United Kingdom, the Sultan of Oman and the Prince of Monaco. Even the King of Morocco, who has similar power and authority in his society as the Sheikh, but who rules over a much larger country with a population of some 35 million people, has $500 million less in personal wealth than Sheikh Hamad.[4]

While it would have been difficult for the French monarch to walk away with almost a third of the income of the Ancien Régime, extraction of funds from Qatar's Treasury and the depositing of state income in their personal Swiss bank accounts was a common tradition for past Emirs, from Abdallah to Ali to Sheikh Khalifa. As late as 1989 the Emir personally signed all major cheques. Although Sheikh Hamad has promised to reform this unsavoury practice and to separate state finances from his personal accounts, he retains the power to reverse any such reform should he wish to do so. The increasing complexity of Qatar's economy and society has, to some extent, depersonalized the office and authority of the Emir. Many of the Emir's actions have reversed his father's abuses. Recently, Transparency International classified Qatar as a nation where rule is relatively transparent especially when compared to its neighbours: its score of 7 (in 2009) was not far from that of the USA at 7.5.[5] Nevertheless, while he has the expressed support of the population for most of his reform agenda, the Emir still holds has ultimate decision-making powers.

Personally involving himself in every sector of the country's development as his father did in the first years of his reign, Sheikh Hamad appears to be running his state through charisma and overseeing everything personally. In many respects this projection of Emiri power, the glossing over of internal disputes and the appearance that the Emir is the absolute captain of the state, is beneficial to Qatar externally. The Qatari Emir and his representatives abroad can give immediate backing or a guarantee of support without the time and delay or uncertainty of a drawn-out parliamentary process. The Emir can approve or disapprove of any project – the state coffers and the Qatar National Bank are in theory separate from the Emir, but in actuality he can direct Qatar's enormous gas and oil revenue if he wishes. Sheikh Khalifa, the deposed ruler of Qatar, allegedly allowed some 18.7 per cent of petroleum revenue in Qatar to go missing between 1990 and 1994.[6] As the sudden stripping and subsequent restoration of the Qatari citizenship of some 5,000 Al-Murrah tribesmen reveals, he can give citizenship just as rapidly as he can take it away.[7] Even though the new Constitution, supported by the Emir in the name of reform, and passed by popular referendum in 2003 with 96 per cent approval, calls for an Advisory Council where legislation can be passed, the Emir has the power of veto – a veto that can only be over-ruled by a two-thirds majority, which is unlikely given that one-third of the Advisory Council are appointed by the Emir. And in the almost impossible event that the Emir's veto is over-ruled, he can suspend legislation, 'for some time'.

National elections for the Advisory Council have, in any case, been suspended. Instead of calling regular nationwide elections, as the new Constitution of 2005 supposedly put into effect, the term of the current Advisory Council has simply been extended. In 2011 a vote was rescheduled, yet again, for the end of 2013. A Municipal Council, dealing with local issues, and with limited consultative powers, was set up, the first elected in 1999, following nationwide polls. Women voted in municipal elections and were considered as candidates.[8]

The legal system is similarly controlled by the Emir. He appoints all judges, many of them non-Qataris, making them vulnerable to deportation. Although an important constitutional step, the opening of the new Supreme Court, established by Law Number 12 in 2008, will probably not lead to any significant change in the power of the judiciary despite their remit to adjudicate on the 2005 Constitution. The Emir appoints all justices in the new Supreme Court. The mere existence of a constitutional court is extraordinary since most judges have steered clear of reviewing constitutional law, seeing it squarely within the power of the Emir. According to legal scholar Nathan Brown, 'not a single Qatari judge or lawyer could name one case in the history of the courts that had a constitutional dimension'.[9] As Jill Crystal noted, 'Qatar's courts have never served as a check on the ruler.'[10]

One of the few theoretical limitations on Qatari law still left open by the Constitution is that of Article 6, which requires the state 'to respect and implement all international agreements, charters and conventions it is party thereof'. Qatari labour sponsorship law, which requires all non-Qataris to be sponsored by a Qatari citizen, who has control over their status, visa, conditions, salary and potential expulsion, could in theory be challenged since Qatar is a member of the UN's International Labour Organization.[11] To 'respect and implement' however, are not the same as to enforce. Although some reforms may occur, there is a low probability that any policies significantly reducing the privileges of native Qatari citizens will be implemented. The liberalization, consultation and limited democratization allowed by the Constitution is limited to Qatari citizens. Citizenship law, according to Constitution Article 41, has the same force as the Constitution. This is in the interests of the Emir who has, through the Constitution, effectively formed an alliance with the citizen-elite of Qatar to maintain control and the social status quo while simultaneously increasing economic change and wealth.

Institutionally, economically and legally, the Emir seems to have effective, absolute power. According to Mehran Kamrava, the former acting Dean of Georgetown University, Qatar, the Emir will only increase and centralize his authority, using the rhetoric of liberalization only to shore up his power. Much reform has been about centralizing the power of the Emir, not limiting it.[12] However, there are several qualifications that need to be made to a simplistic view of Qatar as, in effect, the personal possession of the Emir with some formal concessions to democracy. Although it is tempting to cede to this projection of Emiri power as the 'reality' of power politics in Qatar, and his power over many elements of the state is almost absolute, the actual exercise of power in Qatar is much more complex, even as the Emir attempts to consolidate power around himself, his successor and immediate family. From the lofty heights of international summits and negotiations, Qatar's foreign policy seems remarkably nimble. Its Al-Jazeera media empire seems capable of a freewheeling judgement and style that galvanizes Arab public opinion. From a local perspective, however, the politics of Qatar has become increasingly sticky, increasingly complex and dependent on historical, local and tribal factors.

Internally, the power of the Emir is circumscribed in subtle ways, not by international threats but by internal political arrangements of a highly local, informal and tribal nature that is hard for Western political scientists trained in formal institutional politics and economics to understand or quantify. Although he discusses the importance of informal institutions, Douglas North, a major figure in current political science debate over the role of institutions in power and development, does not quantify or measure their actual impact. In many respects, informal institutions for political scientists appear analogous to the 'dark matter' of astrophysics: unknown in quantity, shape and real impact but known to be necessary and to exist.[13] Joseph Stigliz of the World Bank described informal institutions as functioning through 'social capital': tacit knowledge, a collection of networks, an aggregation of reputations and organizational capital.[14] In Qatar this 'social capital' is by no means completely monopolized by the Emir or even the ruling family. Sometimes the most effective forms of resistance appear silent to those outside the system, yet they are obvious to those within the particular system of rule. Seen from a purely institutional and economic framework, the Emir does indeed appear to monopolize power in Qatar.

Seen from within the traditional networks of obligation, authority, negotiation and independence – a tribal network of loyalty best described by the north African political philosopher Ibn Khaldun 600 years ago – the Emir is not so much an absolute monarch as an elected first among equals, a mediator between different power bases and interests, rather than a king. Ironically, it is the very institutionalization of informal authority and networks, a process supported by the West as 'democratization' that may ultimately lead to the fuller replacement of tribal identity by state nationalism of Emiri authority: social capital is not inexhaustible even if petrol capital appears to be. It is also possible, however, that the traditional networks of power, the flexible pools of *'asabiyya* 'tribal solidarity', that make Qatari society function are much more durable and capable of surviving the onslaught of modernization and institutionalization than at first appears. If the combination of traditional and innovative 'democratic' forms of civil society are strong and persistent enough in Qatar, the country could follow the model of Kuwait where the National Assembly has often questioned royalty-appointed ministers, despite the constant threat of dissolution by the Kuwaiti Sabah monarch. Instead of transforming itself into a fully democratic state, it is likely that Qatar will follow the pattern of 'liberalized autocracy' described by political scientists of the Middle East. In such a liberalized autocracy, many of the exterior and superficial trappings of democracy exist even as effective power remains with the autocrat. In some instances the trappings of democracy only serve to consolidate further the ruler's power.[15] Nevertheless, whatever the hypothetical extent of the Emir's scope and ability to exercise power, it would be inaccurate to suggest that it is limitless. Far from it. Important social actors and factors shape and direct his power.

THE SHAPE OF POWER IN QATAR

The shape and manifestation of political power and authority in Qatar is much more complicated than is recognized in formal law. The limits on the power of the Emir described below are not absolute, nor even consistent, but they do reveal the extent to which authoritarianism in Qatar is not simply imposed but is a part of a social consensus, a consensus that is itself manipulated by the Emir and the royal diwan at least as much as the social consensus itself limits the exercise and shape of power.

The Emir

The most effective and immediate limitations on the Emir's power come from the Emir himself. The Emir can decide to relegate his own authority, to allow press freedom or even municipal elections. However, the temporary relinquishing of power does not prevent the Emir from breaking his own self-imposed limitations.

Although Article 59 of the Qatar Constitution declares that the 'people are the source of authority ...', there is little or no specific legal support for this ideal. In effect, Article 67 appropriates to the Emir most specific powers:

1. Formulating the general policy of the State with the assistance of the Cabinet.
2. Endorsing and issuing laws. No law shall be issued unless endorsed by the Emir.
3. Convening meetings of the Council of Ministers, whenever public interest so requires. He shall chair all sessions he attends.
4. Appointing civil and military personnel and terminating their services according to the law.
5. Accepting the credentials of diplomatic and consular missions.
6. Pardoning convicts or reducing punishments in accordance with the law.
7. Bestowing civil and military honours in accordance with the law.
8. Establishing and organizing ministries and other government agencies and defining their authorities.
9. Establishing and organizing agencies to give him opinions and consultation to guide the policies of the State, to supervise these agencies and to define their authority.
10. Any other powers in accordance with this Constitution and the law.

There is no law in the Constitution that limits the Emir from checking his own power and authority or from limiting the reach of his office. As well as the plans to separate the public Treasury from his personal accounts, the Emir has approved some formal limitations to his authority. The most important of these self-imposed limitations was made in 1999 with the issuing of Emiri Decree 11 – a decree that called for a high-level commission to draft the Constitution.

The Qatari Constitution, effective June 2005, prevents the Emir from repeatedly declaring martial law without cause and approval from the Advisory Council (Article 69), from engaging in offensive warfare (Article 71) and from issuing decrees without the eventual approval of the Advisory Council. The likelihood of such extreme actions being taken by an Emir against the 'background of a rather uncontentious domestic political climate', with an Advisory Council where one-third of the membership is determined by the Emir and the other two-thirds are elected by a relatively small segment of the total population (Qataris that can prove a standard of nationality), seems nil. If anything, these limitations in *extremis* are more likely to protect the office of the Emir, in the unlikely event that the person of the Emir falls into a state of insanity or madness.

In addition to giving his approval to the new Constitution, the most public examples of the Emir ceding power or rights but then quickly backtracking relate to the thorny issue of a free press. Shortly after coming to power in 1995, the Emir declared a new era of press freedom. After this declaration, however, he shut down the Qatari Arabic daily, *Al-Sharq*, for being too openly critical of the Saudis. Similarly, the Emir's favoured wife Sheikha Mozah, whose activities are possible because of the authority of her husband, sponsored and founded the Doha Center for Media Freedom. Its director, the international freedom of the press advocate Robert Ménard, found himself unwelcome, however, after he publicly criticized the Qatari government and invited Flemming Rose, editor of the Danish newspaper which in 2005 published the controversial cartoons of Muhammad, to Doha. This caused uproar among Qataris.[16] Whatever the personal beliefs and the intentions of the Emir and his wife to bridge Western and Islamic culture, they are limited by those at both extremes of the politcal spectrum. A policy of mediation and reconciliation that has turned Qatar into a base of international cooperation has enormous benefits but also great risks, risks that may not be easily controlled.

Ultimately, however, the power of the Emir is limited not by international controversy but by his own mortality, as well as the stress and strain and possibly self-destructive temptations of rule. Sheikh Hamad, like his father, cannot prevent the possibility of internal coups or instability and a succession crisis should he die in office. Traditional Arab society has dealt with the vulnerability of individual sheikhs and rulers through cultural tradition. While most Western monarchies rely on clear and pre-established succession through primogeniture, favouring one branch of the royal family, Arab tribes in Qatar and the Gulf have made succession a wider family affair: primogeniture was not guaranteed and the royal family as a whole benefited substantially from power, not simply one brother and his offspring. This means Article 9 of the Qatari Constitution, which allows the ruling Emir to designate his son as successor, is an innovation from traditional practice. The social and tribal solidarity of the clan, Ibn Khaldun's *'asabiyya*, was an ultimate guarantee of power. Even if the ruler were assassinated, members of the family would be well positioned to preserve the status quo.

This family rule or 'clanocracy' preserved dynasties such as Al-Thani from overthrow. Those monarchies who did not rely on the family or did not distribute power amongst their kin but tried to concentrate all effective power in their own hands were much more vulnerable to revolution. King Idris of Libya (r. 1951–69), for example, actively avoided relying on the support of his own clan and family and did not attempt to establish support for dynastic succession – the result was Qaddafi's revolution. Sheikh Hamad's new moves towards a pseudo-primogeniture system, however, may threaten the cohesiveness and support of Al-Thani family. The future sustainability of Hamad's rule and that of his successors will depend substantially on how he shares power with the family.

Al-Thani Family

Conflicts within Al-Thani date to before the first major oil payments. However, it was not until July 1949 when a major oil concession payment was made personally to Sheikh Abdallah bin Jassim that internal family disputes had a serious impact. Believing the concession to be his personally, Sheikh Abdallah refused to share the money with other members of the family. Since 1938 the descendants of Ahmad bin Muhammad bin Thani, the designated successor to Jassim who had died before him in 1905 (not to be confused with the Emir Ahmad bin Abdallah who was overthrown by Khalifa in 1972) had been petitioning the British, complaining of their poverty and of being left out of their rightful share to the oil (see Table 1 of Al-Thani Rulers). Since the 1935 concession Abdallah and his successor Hamad, who died in 1948 before he had the chance to succeed, had secretly put much of the oil concession payment into private funds. This concentration of wealth in the Emir's immediate family caused serious rifts with the rest of Al-Thani. The ruler was forced to raise payments to other Al-Thani sheikhs; by 1958, they reportedly received some 45 per cent of state revenue.[17]

The Emir continues to answer to his family. Although technically he has the ability to appoint ministers and review government decisions, some ministries function as miniature fiefdoms. 'If dynastic regimes are susceptible to strife and ill-will among the members of the ruling families, Al-Thani, the ruling family of Qatar, should have fallen from power a long time ago.'[18] Also, as Zahlan remarked, 'Al-Thani, unlike

Al-Sabah (of Kuwait), do not appear to have a corporate identity ... Factionalism inevitably occurs, particularly when so many rulers enjoyed unusually long reigns.'[19] Because of this potential factionalism and the need to placate their demands, the Emir is often compelled to put prominent members of his own family into important ministerial posts. The heads of Qatar's main government posts are almost entirely Al-Thani (see Table 1, p. 135).

One of the main reasons for Al-Thani family's bargaining power is its role in determining the succession. Sheikh Hamad's changes to the Constitution, especially his placing of the power of determining succession squarely within the hands of the ruling Emir, could curb this and hence the tradition of factionalism within the family. At the same time, the changes may open up the possibility of challenges not only to the Emir but also to the entire system of rule itself. It was only with the confidence that he had established effective control over the factionalism of his family and other power players in Qatar that the Emir made the move to change the Constitution, sidelining traditional allies and traditional power compromises. It may not be 'all in the family' for the Emir and his successor in Qatar, but rather 'going it alone'. No matter how powerful and convincing the current Emir has been in establishing the new arrangement, however, the Gulf is a treacherous place to 'go it alone'.

Until Sheikh Hamad's recent changes, the Sheikh needed to secure the support of his family before declaring a successor. This made for succession crises and uncertainties, with opportunities for Al-Thani family members to demand concessions. Family demands have now, to some extent, decreased in importance, as the family is not powerful or united enough to cause any serious fissures or instability in the continuity of the current, largely absolutist and monarchical system of rule. Instead of relying on the approval of a 'family council' to designate the successor, the revised Qatari Constitution gives the Emir almost exclusive power to designate one of his sons as successor. Although Article 9 of the Constitution stipulates that he 'consult' the family council, he need not have their complete approval. Able to secure his succession and nominate his successor from his immediate family long before his death, the Emir can bypass the traditional jockeying between prominent uncles and relatives vying for power. Indeed, in this important respect Sheikh Hamad has even more power than his father Khalifa whose first choice as successor, according to some reports, was not Sheikh Hamad, but his favoured son Abdalaziz.

Qatari and Arab society in general does not have an established tradition of primogeniture. Historically, the tribe as a whole designated tribal sheikhs or hakims, and successors did not even need to be from the same immediate family. As the historian J.C. Hurewitz observed, the tradition of primogeniture did not even extend to powerful kings or rulers:

The absence of fixed rules of succession was an important generator of military politics in Islam. The principle of primogeniture, almost universally applied in Europe, was not recognized in Islam, least of all among the Muslim dynasties of the seventeenth and eighteenth centuries. All male members of an extended royal family were acceptable candidates for the throne ... Islamic polities, hovering between hereditary and 'elective' monarchies, became inured to violent and disorderly succession whenever the reigning monarch's wishes were not honored after his death.[20]

Primogeniture and guarantees of 'orderly' succession are effectively European innovations. The tribe as a whole must approve of the new Sheikh through the *baya* or oath of allegiance. Yet the *baya* was never guaranteed and several times tribes rejected the favoured son of their sheikh. This oath of allegiance is still used ceremonially but has no effective weight since no Al-Thani sheikh would so openly defy the power of the Emir and expect to remain in the country or in their ministerial post. Although couched in 'tradition', the current Emir's establishment of hereditary primogeniture and complete power over succession imposes Western notions of personal rule and monarchy upon Qatari society. If they are sidelined to too great an extent and no longer respected or called upon to participate in the succession, however Al-Thani family may be less willing to jump on the 'bandwagon' and support en masse the Emir's chosen successors. Clean succession from father to chosen, often eldest, son may reduce uncertainty, but it may also inspire members of the family more ardently to support rivals. The health of the Emir, who had kidney replacement surgery in the USA in 1997, is not necessarily guaranteed and the issue of succession is a constant worry and concern.

The choice of Tamim, Sheikh Hamad's fourth son, and the passing over of his first three sons shows the difficulty of the succession issue and its potential for sparking conflict, not only within the family but with Qatar's most important allies and supporters. By constantly changing successors, Sheikh Hamad can avoid a situation where one of his sons gains enough support to overthrow as he had overthrown his father before him. Jassim bin Hamad, replaced Mish'al bin Hamad as successor in 1996, but according to unsubstantiated reports, Jassim supposedly had no interest in ruling. It is also possible that Jassim's absolute loyalty to Sheikh Hamad was somehow in doubt. Born in 1978 as the eldest son of Sheikha Mozah, he graduated from Sandhurst and supports his brother Tamim as head of the Higher Committee on Coordination and Pursuance. It has been reported that the Emir's second son Fahd was overlooked entirely because of his religious conservatism and alleged association with the *mujahidin* while they were fighting the Soviets.[21] Indeed, clean primogeniture is not necessarily the path of succession. The eldest son Mish'al was passed over because he seemed to lack the leadership abilities of his younger brothers. Sheikh Tamim was made the successor in August 2003. He was also educated at Sandhurst (an honour that has become almost requirement for rule) and was president of the Doha Asian Games and has cultivated close ties with the United States. Athough he has been given substantial responsibilities, including the Iran diplomatic portfolio, his power is still very much circumscribed. There are still more brothers in Al-Thani family from the three wives of the Emir, Noora, Mariam and Mozah, who could easily take his place.

Despite new limits and clearer procedures imposed by the current Emir, the power and prestige of the ruling family remains. Al-Thanis continue to monopolize the most important government posts and ministries. Another more obvious indication of the power of the Emir's family is the way in which members of this family have elevated themselves above the rest of the Qatari population. Although in the past any important tribesman could call himself 'sheikh', it has become customary that only members of Al-Thani identify themselves as 'sheikh' or 'chief' or, in the case of women, 'sheikha'. Al-Thani family thus monopolize these titles and effectively denies sheikhly traditions to other tribes in Qatar.

Al-Thani Family in Positions of Influence

Hamad, following the policy of his predecessors, has successfully concentrated wealth and power among his closest relations. Nevertheless, marriage is one significant way that lineage groups outside the close-knit Al-Thani clan of Hamad can access real influence and power in the central government. The mother of the current Emir, for instance, is from Al-Attiyah clan. The Attiyah have enjoyed special privileges in the current government, gaining lucrative posts and positions including the coveted Energy Ministry run by Abdallah bin Hamad Al-Attiyah until January 2011. Although he was replaced as the powerful Energy Minister by Mohammed Saleh al Sada, Abdallah is currently chairman of Qatar Petroleum and Deputy Prime Minister. He was also appointed 'Head of the Emir's Court' after leaving the Energy Ministry. He is credited with the development of Liquified Natural Gas exports, a strategic move considering that Qatar only exports some 825,000 barrels of crude while its natural gas exports are now much larger.[23] Had Abdalaziz, another son of Khalifa and a serious contender to reign, whose mother was one of Al-Suwaidi clan, succeeded, the Suwaidi may have gained more prominence in government.

As the following list of major government posts demonstrates, all of the top positions and ministries of major significance in Qatar are dominated by Al-Thani and, to a much lesser extent, Al-Attiyah. Some secondary posts are held by close allies of Al-Thani including Al-Kuwari, Al-Suwaidi, Al-Ghanim and Al-Dosari. Clearly, there is a recognition of the need to distribute some power and influence either to technocrats, Yousef Hussein Kamal at the Ministry of Finance being a prime example, or to members of prominent Qatari tribes. These two lists are by no means meant to be comprehensive.

TABLE 1. Al-Thani and Al-Attiyah in Prominent Government and Economic Positions

Positions	Names
Emir	Sheikh Hamad bin Khalifa Al-Thani
Heir Apparent	Sheikh Tamim bin Hamad Al-Thani
Prime Minister and Foreign Minister	Hamad bin Jassim bin Jabor Al-Thani
Deputy Prime Minister	Abdallah bin Hamad Al-Attiyah
Cabinet Affairs Minister	Sheikh Nasser bin Muhammad bin Thani
Interior Minister	Sheikh Abdallah bin Khalid Al-Thani
Commerce Minister	Sheikh Fahd bin Jassim bin Muhammad bin Thani (d. May 2009)
Communications and Transport	Sheikh Nasser bin Muhammad bin Thani
Agriculture and Municipal Affairs	Sheikh Abdulrahman bin Abdulaziz Al-Thani
State Minister for Internal Affairs	Sheikh Abdallah bin Nasser bin Khalifa Al-Thani
State Minister for International Cooperation	Dr Khalid bin Muhammad Al-Attiyah
State Minister (at Large)	Sheikh Hamad bin Abdallah bin Muhammad bin Thani
State Minister (at Large)	Sheikh Hamad bin Suhaym Al-Thani
Central Bank Governor	Abdallah Saud Al-Thani
Qatar Chamber of Commerce and Industry Chairman	Khalifa bin Jassim bin Muhammad bin Thani
Head of Reach Out to Asia international charity	Sheikha Mayassa bint Hamad Al-Thani

The various sheikhs and branches of the ruling family do manage to serve as a check on the Emir's power, however. In the initial years after the first export of oil in 1949, armed Al-Thani sheikhs were able physically to threaten the Emir into giving them cash payments. Al-Thani sheikhs also drove many of the Emir's foreign-born ministers, such as Abdallah Darwish, out of office, depriving him of a buffer between himself and the demands of his family members. Although such direct threats are no longer feasible, Al-Thani continue to exert a powerful pull on the Sheikh and their demands are rarely refused. In the past few years, however, Sheikh Hamad has effectively limited the power and influence of Al-Thani factions outside his immediate family and has mainly provided opportunities and new organizations to serve only his most loyal or closest relatives.[22]

Tribes and Informal Powers

A survey taken shortly after the Qatari municipal elections in 1999, elections open only to Qatari voters who could prove residency on the Peninsula before the oil boom, revealed that almost all respondents voted primarily according to their tribal affiliations.[24] As effectively self-governing, social entities with loyalties independent of the state, tribes in Qatar, and the inherent limitations of centralization in a society based on tribal ties and identity, are the one major impediment to complete centralization of power. It is for this reason, more than any other, that tribes have been effectively invited into the 'democratic' process through the setting up of elections and institutions that allegedly represent the people, and thus the tribes – most Qataris vote according to tribe and most seats are divided according to tribal affiliation.[25]

TABLE 2. Non-Al-Thani in Significant Positions

Positions	Names
Most public and prominent wife of the Emir	Sheikha Mozah bint Nasser Al-Misnad (ranked No. 79 in *Forbes Magazine*'s list of the world's most powerful women)
Justice Minister	Hassan bin Abdallah Al-Ghanim
Finance and Economy	Yousef Hussein Kamal
Energy Minister	Mohammed Saleh al Saba
Labour	Dr Sultan bin Hassan al Dhabit Al-Dosari
Religious Affairs	Ahmad bin Abdallah Al-Marri
Public Health	Abdallah bin Khalid Al-Qahtani
Education	Saad bin Ibrahim Al-Mahmoud
Culture, Arts and Heritage	Ahmad bin Abdulaziz Al-Kuwari
Social Affairs	Nasser bin Abdallah Al-Hemaidi
Environment	Abdallah Al-Midhadhi
State Minister for Foreign Affairs	Ahmad bin Abdallah Al-Mahmoud
State Minister for Energy and Industrial Affairs	Muhammad Saleh Al-Sada
RasGas Managing Director	Hamad Rashid Al-Mohannadi
QatarGas Chair and CEO	Faisal Al-Suwaidi
President of Qatar University	Dr Sheikha Abdallah Al-Misnad (Aunt of Sheikha Mozah)

The current, appointed Advisory Council, its term extended until the Emir finally approves a nationwide election, consists primarily of representatives from tribes and lineages outside the royal family.[26] Although most of the 35 members of the Council are from lineages closely allied to Al-Thani, they are not themselves Al-Thani. Instead, there is a healthy representation from other historically prominent Qatari families, families mentioned in previous chapters as holders of historic claims and powers in Qatar. Rather than stuffing the council with his closest relatives, a policy that might be expected in a system of 'family rule', the Emir, like his father, has used the Council to ensure the vital support and consensus of Qatari tribes. Instead of providing these representatives of non-Al-Thani tribes with power, however, the Council serves to diffuse dissent. Even less than the parliament promised in the 2003 Constitution, the current Advisory Council has very limited authority: it cannot formulate the budget but only approve it, its laws can be easily overturned by the Emir. Also, it typically meets for only a few hours a week. Nevertheless, it has provided the Emir with a source of legitimacy and support from other tribes, even as he attempts to balance the demands of his own family. 'Shaykh Hamad's early promises of liberalization arose out of elite factionalism, and more specifically, intra-family competition within Al-Thani.'[27]

Although some have claimed that non-Al-Thani Qatari tribes have effectively been marginalized from the explicit political process, they remain an important part of the less explicit, informal relations within Qatar. Al-Thani and the Emir have attempted to erase traditional segmentary bounds on power. Nevertheless, there is not a complete 'absence of meaningful competition from other, non Al-Thani families', as argued by the political scientist Mehran Kamrava.[28] I have mentioned several instances where the claims of Al-Thani were challenged and where other tribes have, in fact, made claims to independence from Al-Thani rule.

The history of Qatar's tribes, such as Al-Sudan and Al bin Ainain, includes historic claims at least as compelling as those of Al-Thani. Although Al-Thani have attempted to appropriate this history, the pull of tribal affliliation remains strong. As Jill Crystal observed, 'In the Gulf the expressions of political power lie below the surface. Rules, while real, are publicly uncodified and social groupings sometimes lack clear institutional analogs.'[29] It remains to be seen if the Qatari state and the Emir will or will not be successful in completely co-opting lineage groups, especially considering the lack of industrial anomie and and the surprising lack of an expected disjunction and disruption of linage tribes in Qatar as discussed at the beginning of this book. New states according to Durkheim try 'to ulitize existing organization and assimilate it ... The segments, or at least groups of segments united by special affinities, become organs.'[30]

Time will tell whether the Emir and the state will be able to turn Qatar's tribes into organs of state and Emiri power. Indeed, Qatar's lineage groups, institutionalized by a state electoral system that seemingly supports the status quo, appears to be almost as resilient as the monarchy itself, perhaps for many of the same reasons that Al-Thani have remained in power. The development of 'democracy' in Qatar, a development that has largely appropriated and controlled traditional means of representation and expressions of power in Qatari tribes, may be as much an instrument of assimilation as an instrument of liberalization.

Although a complete comprehensive description of Qatar's many lineage groups and loyalties must be left to future sociologists and anthropologists, a brief sample of some of the less well-known lineage and social groups of Qatar reveals the continued relevance and complexity of Qatari tribal identities. That several groups have been left out of this analysis is in no way an indication of their lack of importance.

AL-ATTIYAH

Although they were once almost equal to Al-Thani, they are now the second-most prominent family in Qatar. Al-Attiyah have married strategically into Al-Thani clan and continue to fill important, lucrative posts. Nasr Al-Attiyah, who originally gained influence through marriage, became the most influential adviser of Sheikh Abdallah bin Jassim Al-Thani. Muhammad Al-Attiyah was the first chief of police. The current Minister of Energy is similarly related to Sheikh Hamad through marriage. In 1963 Hamad Al- Attiyah was the leader of a popular uprising against Al-Thani.

AL-THANI

Although disputed, many claim Al-Thani are themselves members of the larger Al-Ma'adhid confederacy, the Ma'adhid, in turn, were descended from al-Tamim. The founder of the Ma'adhid, Ma'adhid bin Musharraf, was once the powerful governor of the Jabrin Oasis in the middle of Saudi Arabia. The name means 'alliance of the brave'. This has lead some other Ma'adhid tacitly to question the special status of Al-Thani. There are some 3,000 of the most well-connected of Al-Thani family, but most no longer have as strong a claim to power as a few deades ago when Al-Thani sheikhs could, often through force, effectively dictate the Emir's choice of technocrats and ministers. Several are descendants of Sheikh Ahmad who was sidelined after the coup of Khalifa. Similarly, the direct descendants of Sheikh Jassim are favoured, with the major exception of Hamad bin Jassim (a different Jassim).

The sheer size of Al-Thani clan, especially compared with the overall population of Qataris, is important. There were some 20,000 Al-Thani, or half the population, in the 1980s and their swelling number has lead to some divisions in the ranks as various branches of Al-Thani attempt to secure influence. Several sheikhs were known to drive out and make arbitrary land claims in the 1950s. Centralized control of land distribution has recently been consolidated by the Emir.

AL BIN ALI

Al bin Ali come from Ha'il and Jabrin in central Saudi Arabia. Al-Thani generally deny their relationship with this tribe, even though Al bin Ali claim Ma'adhid heritage. Al bin Ali were often prominent leaders in Qatar before the rise of Muhammad bin Thani in the 1860s. Al Badi, relative of the ruler of Qatar before Al-Thani, Al-Ghanim and Al-Hitmi are from Al bin Ali.

AL-SUDAN

A *hadari*, or settled coastal tribe, some of Al-Sudan have lived in the Doha area since before the nineteenth century. In that early period their chief, Sulaimann bin Nasir, was, for some years before the 1850s, the most prominent man in Doha. Although there were only around 400 in the clan between 1908 and 1939, according to Lorimer, the group of houses in Fareej al Sudan (the neighbourhood where Al-Sudan lived) in the centre of modern Doha attests to their historical presence in the Qatari capital.[31] Before the last of the tribe moved to Doha in the 1970s, the original homeland of Al-Sudan was the now nearly abandoned village of Fuwayrat in the north of Qatar. Like Al-Thani, Al-Sudan inhabited Qatar long before the arrival of the Utubi tribe in 1783. As a result of their deep historical association with Qatar and the distance of Fuwayrat from Doha, the sheikh and *majlis* (tribal council) of Al-Sudan have generally enjoyed a great deal of autonomy. In fact, those from Al-Sudan tribe living in Doha before 1970 were exempt from taxes on the pearl trade.[32]

BANI KHALID AND AL-AINAIN

Rulers of Al-Hasa and Qatar before the rise of the Saudi, the Bani Khalid have lost almost all of their influence in the Peninsula, despite their deep historic presence in eastern Arabia. Al-Ainain is perhaps the most prominent of the Bani Khalid clans in Qatar, and controlled Doha before their forced exile in the 1820s. Having settled in Wakra, their 1908 population was 2,000. The tribe did not, however, forget their former position of influence and often resented interference in Wakra by Al-Thani. They considered themselves exempt from the taxes levied on other, less prominent tribes. It was reported in 1907 by the British Political Agent in Bahrain that:

> A member of the Al bu Ainain tribe by name Jabr was recently called upon to pay his portion of the tax levied annually from the pearling boats by Abd al Rahman [Al-Thani governor of Wakra] Jabr refused to pay ...[33]

AL-SULUTA

Ancient merchants of Qatar, Al Nasr of Al-Suluta tribe was one of the most powerful merchants in Doha. They retain some influence and some symbolic importance in the Advisory Council.

AL-MAHANDA

The most important clans of the Mahanda include Al-Ibrahim and Al-Misnad of Al-Khawr to the north of Doha. Sheikha Mozah bint Nasser Al-Misnad is currently President of Qatar University. Abdallah Al-Misnad was involved in some of the riots and uprisings of 1963.

HUWALAH

The Huwalah Sunnis migrated regularly between the Persian and Arabian shores of the Gulf, once settling near Hormuz, and they are a historical link to both. They are now concentrated in Doha and Wakra. The Huwalah have regularly occupied important positions as advisers and leaders of the merchant community. They include the Darwish, the 'Abd al Ghani, Nasr Allah, Haydar and Ibn Muhammad. Two other prominent merchant families, Al-Mullah and Jayda, have been less successfully intergrated into government roles.

AL-KUWARI

Displeased with Jassim bin Muhammad bin Thani's alliance with the Ottomans, the Kuwari left Doha in 1879 and settled in Fuwayrat. They have recently cooperated closely with Al-Thani, however, and occupy some important government posts. They are currently among the most influential families of Qatar. Al-Thani trace their bloodline to Al-Kuwari and a common ancestor – Tamim.

AL-DAWASIR

Incorporating Al-Dawasir, inhabitants of the Hawar islands, into the government has allowed Qatar to justify its claims over that territory.

'NOMADIC' TRIBES

AL-MURRAH (MARRI)

Mentioned several times in this book, Al-Murrah have long been the border guards for Saudi Arabia and the frontiers that came under Saudi influence. Although some Murrah clans still occupy some important positions in the Qatari military, their position in Qatar is largely one on the sidelines because of a history of interaction with the Saudis. As mentioned earlier, one clan of Murrah were stripped of their Qatari citizenship and sent to Saudi Arabia.

BANI HAJR

From Al-Hasa, the Bani Hajr were originally allied to the Wahhabis, paid *zakat*, or Islamic taxes, to the Saudi Wahhabis and even received regular payments from the rulers of Doha.[34] Usually a land-based Bedouin tribe, they were also famous for their piracy at sea in the 1870s. The Bani Hajr supported Sheikh Jassim bin Mohammad Al-Thani's successful defiance of the Ottomans at the Battle of Wajbah, cementing their alliance with Al-Thani. Although maintaining many of their independent Bedouin values, the Bani Hajr remain a prominent part of the Emir's personal guard and the elite police forces.[35]

140

AL-NAIM

Al-Naim have fulfilled the same role for the Bahrain Sheikh that the Bani Hajr fulfilled for Al-Thani – Bedouin body guards. With historic claims to the north of Qatar and Zubara, the Naim maintain the conceit of independent status. While a branch of Naim recognized the authority of Al-Thani in Qatar, they remain somewhat precariously on the sidelines of government in Qatar.

AL-MANASIR

Orginally from Trucial Oman, Al-Manasir have found a solid place in Qatari society.

AL-AJMAN

Like the Bani Hajr, the Ajman are from the province of Al-Hasa. They have extensive connections with the UAE as well.

AL-DARWISH

The wealthiest of the merchant families in Qatar during British colonial rule, the Darwish still wield some influence, especially in commercial matters.

AL-MANI

Another merchant clan, Al-Mani were often out-manoeuvered by Al-Darwish, who seized many development contracts. They returned to influence, however, after Abdallah Al-Darwish was expelled from Qatar for his closeness to the British. They continue to have large commerical interests in Qatar.

AL-MANNAI

The patriarch of this clan arrived in the 1940s from Bahrain. They mainly own or owned foreign company interests in Qatar, such as General Motors.

AFRICANS (FORMER SLAVES AND FREE AFRICANS)

A digression into the history of slavery in Qatar illuminates the importance of outsiders in the balance of power between the ruler, his family, and the prominent tribes of Qatar. Little discussed in Qatar today, slavery existed in Qatar well into the twentieth century. Although the open trade in slavery then ceased and many slaves and their descendants had been welcomed into Arab tribes, adopting the tribal name of their masters, it was not until the 1950s that all slaves were manumitted.

Slaves from the East African coast were part of Qatari society probably for almost as long as the trade existed, mostly under the auspices of Omani merchants and their contacts on the island of Zanzibar (once a part of Oman). One of the earliest descriptions of slavery in the Gulf is in Lieutenant Macleod's 1823 commentary on the General Treaty of Peace of 1820. The General Treaty with the Persian Gulf sheikhs, including the Sheikh of Bahrain who officially represented Qatar, seems expressly to forbid trade in slaves by the 'friendly Arabs'. In this respect, it 'officially' adheres to the Slave Trade Act of 1807.

According to Article 9 of the Treaty, 'The carrying off of slaves, men, women, or children, from the coasts of Africa or elsewhere, and the transporting them in vessels is plunder and piracy, and the friendly Arabs shall do nothing of this nature.' Yet, as Macleod admits, the British never actively enforced either this ban or subsequent bans on slavery itself, except in the most egregious of instances. As Macleod said revealingly in his commentary, 'The Article in regard to the slave trade does certainly not bear the construction that has been hitherto put on it. It evidently only alludes to descents made on the coast of Africa for the purpose of making slaves.'[36] Acknowledging the strength of the anti-slavery movement in Britain, led by the irascible William Wilberforce (1759–1833), the British imperial powers saw the necessity of officially banning the slave trade across the empire. At the same time they limited the actual enforcement of this ban in the Gulf for political reasons. Further complicating the situation, the Arab sheikhdoms were protectorates, so their internal affairs were not under the direct control of the British, who had little interest in interfering in them. The situation became somewhat more delicate after the passage of an outright slavery ban throughout the British empire with the Slavery Abolition Act of 1833.

African slaves, initially without any particular clan loyalty, became powerful agents of the Sheikh. In fact, slaves were often used as proxy rulers, representatives and informers. After one inter-family conflict, for example, 'Sheikh Jassim is much disappointed about his sons and has kept a faithful negro in Doha to inform him of the movements there.'[37] Following a traditions stretching back to the time of the Abbasid Caliphs and the Mamluks of Egypt, the Sheikhs of Qatar also used slaves to provide armed support – if on a much smaller scale than anything seen in Baghdad or Fustat. Sheikh Jassim often bragged about this slave army when travelling abroad to sell his pearls: 'While in Bahrain he stated that he had with him in Katar about 400 slaves who are being trained to handle arms for the purpose of fighting in case of need ...'[38] In many cases slaves came to embody and defend the honour of their masters, often fighting with other slaves as they adopted the identity of their sheikh's own tribe. This would occur even when no Arab master was around. For example, in 1914 the following incident was reported:

> ... a Persian boat full of goats came to Doha. Sheikh Abdallah's negroes went on board to instruct the *nakhoda* [captain] to land the goats in the market and not to sell them from the boat direct. Negros of Ahmad's sons also had gone on board to buy goats there and then. Sheikh Abdallah's negroes told them not to buy from there but from the market. Ahmad's sons' negros did not hear them and both parties fought. Ahmad's negros were wounded by Sheikh Abdallah's negroes. Upon this Ahmad's sons became very angry and on the third day caught one of the Sheikh Abdallah's negroes and thrashed him very seriously ...

Sheikh Abdallah was reprimanded for this act by several of his brothers and other sheikhs. But Sheikh Abdallah would not apologize for the incident. Instead, he became 'more and more excited and declared that under the circumstances he would leave Qatar and the rulership ... then the people of Qatar approached Abdallah to desist from his resolution.'[39]

Before the mass influx of expatriates, slaves served an important role in maintaining the Qatari social hierarchy. Providing a buffer between the ruler and his family, slaves could be a loyal source of support. This might explain Abdallah's reluctance to apologize for his slaves and likewise his reluctance to give up slavery entirely, despite formal British protestations. Even after slaves in Qatar were manumitted in the 1950s, as oil exploitation and the use of expatriate labour began in earnest,[40] freed slaves, still used the names of their former masters. This continued to be an important, if not explicitly recognized, part of Qatari society. Qataris have yet to open up this rather difficult and contentious chapter of their history.

The issue of slavery is particularly sensitive as various groups have now begun to describe the situation of expatriate workers from poor countries who remain dependent on the sponsorship of Qatari nationals as akin to it. Even Sheikh Hamad bin Jassim Al-Thani, the Foreign Minister and Prime Minister, has compared the situation of some expatriates to 'slavery'.[41] In many respects, indeed, the expatriate workforce in Qatar does serve a similar role as the African slaves of the past. These workers provide a buffer both between the Emir and Qatari society and between groups within Qatari society, delaying the necessity of involving Qataris directly within the government or in the technocratic decisions and compromises necessary for a modern political economy.

THE MILITARY: COUP MECHANICS

Despite the importance of Qatar's lineage groups and tribal affiliations for understanding Qatar's cultural and social history, centralized political power, if not all political decisions relevant to the tribe, remains fairly securely with Al-Thani. The Emir has only really needed to make symbolic concessions to tribal groups at the national level. Nevertheless, some of the instruments used by Al-Thani Emir to guarantee his security, especially the military, may themselves be a threat to his rule.

Whereas in the nineteenth century neighbouring tribal Emirs and sheikhs might have been the most potent threat to a ruler, today it is is the military that is often the source of coups. Historical examples abound of the risk associated with maintaining a standing army in authoritarian states or monarchies. Anwar Sadat, President of Egypt, was assassinated not by the external enemies and rivals of Egypt but by officers in his own disgruntled army during a military parade. Gamal Abdel Nasser, his famed predecessor, was an officer in the army which overthrew the monarchy. Likewise, Qaddafi, a colonel, ousted King Idris of Libya. More than any other social or state sector, the army appears to be most capable of changing the status quo. Al-Thani of Qatar, along with rulers of other Gulf States such as Saudi Arabia, however, have not faced any serious challenge to their power from military officers outside their own families. It could be that the social conditions are simply not ripe for a military coup, especially from the middle ranks. Unlike Egypt or Libya with their much larger domestic constituencies, there would be almost no internal support for a military government in Qatar. Most coups are stopped long before they are executed.

Another reason for the de-fanging of the threat of internal military coups is the careful manipulation of military officers and positions. Al-Thani are firmly in control and distributed throughout the high ranks of the military. Most of the army is dependent on their state salaries. Any rebels are easily ousted. Moreover, much of the military is largely symbolic or ceremonial. Qatar hardly has a need for its own army, except perhaps to provide a bodyguard for the Emir. The USA provides much of the protection needed for the Qatar state itself. This does not mean, however, that Al-Thani have not had to take precautions. Historically, the Bedouin have made up the personal and most loyal bodyguard of the Emir and they fought to protect his interests as far back as the Battle of Wajbah. The Emir's summary denial of Qatari citizenship to Al-Murrah Bedouin should, however, be seen as a warning to other Bedouin groups who question the status quo or are considering abusing their position as the traditional guards of last resort. The last thing Al-Thani want is a Praetorian guard dictating its own interests.

If anything, however, it is not Al-Thani monarchy that is at risk of overthrow but the Emir himself. The Emir has most to fear from his own family, especially those family members who may be covertly or even overtly associated with the Saudis. Recent reports and rumours circulated by the Arab press, mainly Al Bawaba news, and the Stratfor news agency, suggested that on 30 July 2009 a military coup planned against Sheikh Hamad was thwarted.[42] According to these reports, Major-General Hamad bin Al-Attiyah was involved in the coup attempt. The coup was not fully executed and many reports of it were exaggerated, but there have been several other failed attempts to use the military as a platform for changing the ruler. Like the coup attempts in 2002 and 1996, the 2009 coup was likely supported by Saudi Arabia as a warning gesture to Qatar. Saudi Arabia has often been perturbed by Qatar's increased international stature and the Emir's refusal to keep in step with Saudi foreign policy. Nevertheless, the reports must be treated with some scepticism. They may have been simply an elaborate public relations ruse by Saudi Arabia to paint the Emir's position in Qatar, falsely, as unstable. As Michael Dunn, editor of the *Middle East Report* claimed, the rumours may in fact be little more than 'coffeehouse gossip'.[43] Even as Al-Thani family and the military is highly controlled, so is the promised 'democratization' process.

DEMOCRACY?

Qatar's most recent and largely symbolic moves toward democratization are far from new. Although it is often portrayed as new and revolutionary by those who see the promotion of democracy as a solution to extremism in the Middle East, Qataris, in fact, experienced previous experiments with democracy decades before the events of 2001 and US efforts to 'democratize' its Arab allies. Qatar was not always a sleepy place, unaffected by the larger revolutionary trends of the wider Middle East. An episode during the crucial period between 1960 and 1969 when British power in the Gulf was both at its height and beginning to wane provides an important anecdote about the previous, largely failed, attempts at democracy in Qatar.

In February 1963 noisy crowds demonstrated in Doha, responding to the violent end of Abdul Karim Jassim, the nationalist Prime Minister of Iraq who was overthrown by the Ba'ath party and with the probable assistance of the CIA in that year. Footage of his execution was broadcast. Mostly Yemeni and Iraqi workers, the demonstrators carried pictures of the Egyptian President and nationalist Gamal Abdel Nasser. They had been encouraged to rise up by the Egyptian nationalist radio station Saut al Arab, 'Voice of the Arabs' Al-Jazeera of the 1960s. In the following weeks, demonstrators came out again, this time to celebrate the creation of a pan-Arab union between Syria, Egypt and Iraq on 18 April and to demand an end to European colonialism and British-supported monarchies such as that of King Hussein of Jordan. Egypt began to increase pressure on Qatar, supporting attacks on the ruler on Egyptian radio when the Emir refused to go along with Egyptian policy towards Yemen. At a demonstration on 20 April, the protests were so fierce that police killed three people. There was a general strike by oil workers. Aramco oil reported 'usual threats' to demolish the Ras Tanura oil refinery.[44] Protesters called for the 'appointment of Qataris to head government departments, the total Arabization of security forces, and equality before the law'.[45]

In the face of all this, the Emir had to call on loyal Bedouin tribes, much as Sheikh Abdallah and Sheikh Jassim had done decades before during battles with rival tribes, to reassert control. The Bedouin patrolled the streets in their trucks. Thus, it was tribes external to Al-Thani family, not the fractious Al-Thani family itself – which was as much a problem as a help to the Emir – that helped guarantee the security of the Emir. The British, represented by the Political Resident, Sir William Luce, supported the the restoration of 'law and order', but they also demanded that Sheikh Ahmad reform the government and the distribution of revenue. Much like the Municipal Council elections held in 2003, an election was called for 4 August 1963 and a law passed forming a 'Doha Council'. Largely done to placate the British, just as the recent Municipal elections were intended to please Western observers, most Qataris were 'unaware that an election was taking place. Meanwhile, one of the winners announced that he had been elected about a week before the election was held.' The Council was unable to convene because the ruler had not appointed the three members he was required to select.[46] Rather than being a democratic outlet, the Municipal Council turned into a flop.

With passions quelled and the Emir's power established by security forces, the threat of violent overthrow and pan-Arab nationalist fervour subsided. In 1964 a new law was passed establishing an 'Advisory Council' composed only of members of Al-Thani family. Yet again, the Council failed to meet – the Political Agent in Doha remarked that the law was not worth 'the paper it is written on'.[47] There was still concern, however, that some Qataris held a 'deep seated resentment against Al-Thani family'. Although a low simmer instead of a frequent boil, this resentment still exists to some degree among Qataris today, especially since the extravagant expenditure lavished on the immediate members of Al-Thani royal family evidently continues.

It should be noted there that although these protests were couched in the rhetoric of pan-Arabism and Nasserism two of the leaders of these strikes, Hamad Al-Attiya and Abdallah Al-Misnad, were distant relations of Al-Thani. They complained not at the lack of direct, liberal democracy but at the way the government had 'usurped' their 'historical' roles. Sheikh Hamad protested that his family had not been given the requisite, high positions in government and Abdallah Al-Misnad complained that the state had effectively taken over his power and position as chief of the Muhanda tribe.[48] Clearly, Al-Thani had been attempting to usurp 'traditional' claims to power for some time.

There are many parallels but also important differences between Qatar's experiments with democracy in the 1960s and more recent democratic reforms. In both cases, Al-Thani Emir has been either forced or quietly cajoled into establishing some form of democracy. In the case of the British in the 1960s, there was a real threat of internal rebellion. In the case of the United States, there was a need to demonstrate to the US public after 9/11 that alliances with Arabian states and absolute monarchs, so important to US grand strategy for energy security but so seemingly contradictory to stated US ideals, did not lead to extermism but to 'democracy'. Another parallel with the 1960s is that recent democratic steps taken by the Emir are, according to one scholar, less than profound: 'In spite of the remarkable democratic steps taken by [the] Qatari government, it is hard to claim that they are conducive to an authentic democracy...'.[49] Before explaining why Qatar's recent democratic reforms have been described as largely ineffective or 'inauthentic', however, I will briefly summarize the era of state-controlled reform from 1998 to 2007 that preceded a much more recent slow-down.

In 1998 the Emir held elections for membership to a Central Municipal Council. All Qataris, both men and women, could participate and run as candidates for the 29-member assembly, a largely advisory institution that would be attached to, and ulitmately subordinate, the Ministry of Municipal Affairs and Agriculture. Some 280 male and

8 female candidates put their names forward, a remarkable amount of participation and a high percentage of Qataris voted. Other ministries and government bodies were also encouraged to hold elections, including the Board of the Qatar Chamber of Commerce, which replaced appointments made by the Emir to the 17-member body. Students were encouraged to vote in elections and create representative bodies, student councils, at universities and schools. A series of conferences from 2002 to 2005 sought to educate Qataris about womens' rights and political participation.

The Doha Forum on Democracy and Free Trade has provided a platform for the Emir to demonstrate his claimed reform credentials to the world. In April 2003 a referendum gave Qataris the chance to approve a new 150-article Constitution. In all, 96 per cent of voters approved of the Constitution which, along with giving the Sheikh more power over the succession, established the legal framework for a 45-member parliament with four-year terms. Although all ministers would still be appointed by the state, parliament could question them and query their budget proposals. The Constitution banned political parties but provided women with the right to vote and to hold elected office.

The parliament has not yet been effectively set up. In fact, the only section of the new Constitution that appears to have taken real effect is the award of more power over the succession to the Emir. Even if the parliament were to be convened, 'The Constitution continued to guarantee the primacy of the ruling family ...'.[50] Most importantly, however, there may simply not be the same demand for democracy from Qataris as there was during the heady days of pan-Arabism and Nasserism. The Qatari youth distracted by investments in sports and clubs, the creation of a quasi-civil society that is still dependent on state revenue, the fundamental problem of being a rentier state and a US government less intent on demanding formalized democratization have led to a hollowing out of the promise of any real democratization in Qatar. Yet, while reforms in Qatar have largely stalled, there is always the posibility that external threats, such as a Saudi succession crisis or revolt by Shi'as in Al-Hasa or major changes and developments in pan-Islamic and pan-Arab ideology, could, as in the 1960s, encourage renewed demands for a distribution of power in Qatar. Unlike the 1960s however, when Egyptian radio fomented revolt within Qatar, it is Qatar and Al-Jazeera that is now in control of a large portion of the the collective media voice of the Arabic-speaking world. Civil society, long seen as a promising foundation of effective democracy, is similarly controlled through the auspices of the state.

A pamphlet entitled *Civil Society Organizations in Qatar*, published by the State of Qatar, speaks of an 'institutional framework that supports the efforts of civil society institutions'. Yet most civil society organizations in Qatar are not independent of the state but, as the pamphet admits, must work to 'get more organizational and administrative independence' from the state. Those civil organizations not controlled by the state or by elite loyalists, such as Sheikh Eid bin Mohamed Al-Thani's Charity Institution, are rather less than spectacular in their ability to demand change. Proudly listed among 24 active civil society institutions in the 2004 pamphlet, for instance, are the Qatar Photographic Society, the Environment Friends Centre, the Qatar Amateur Radio Society and the Qatar Philatelic Club. Although a relatively small country, and there are probably more societies that have emerged since 2004, this is still a rather paltry listing of open, civil organizations.[51] As Mehran Kamrava has elucidated, civil society has largely been monopolized by state-sponsored, and state controlled, quasi-civil groups such as Reach out to Asia and the Qatar Foundation, controlled and led by the Emir's closest family members and loyalists.

Like the ostensible promotion of civil society organizations, democracy in Qatar today is much more organized and actively controlled by the state than it was in the 1960s. *The First Democratic House in Qatar*, a book in Arabic for the domestic Qatari audience by Ibrahim 'Abd al Rahman al Hidous, representative of the Central Municipal Council, reveals something of the current shape of limited democratic change in Qatar. Although some of the electoral districts for the election of council representatives are geographic, such as Airport or Al-Markhiyya, most are based on tribal settlements and compounds such as Bin 'Amran and Saluta Jadida, allowing for representation according to traditional lineage designations, designations now officially defined, mapped and contained. A map of municipal voting districts has become, in essence, a map of the new officially determined sectors of identity in Qatar.[52] As the Qatari scholar Ali al-Shawi has shown, most Qataris vote almost entirely according to self-professed 'tribal' affiliation.[53] While the Municipal Council remains relatively powerless, these elections thus can be an effective way of diffusing and dividing the claims of non-royal Qataris. In the same way that tribal Emirs were transformed into *Rais al-Baladiyya* (mayor of the neighbourhood) but given no real power, so too will tribes themselves be transformed into geographical constituencies for a body with no real power.[54]

It is possible, however, that having tasted institutional representation, Qataris will demand more. Nevertheless, as the scholar Marina Ottaway has argued, a distinction needs to be made between cosmetic reform and substantive democracy, a democracy that involves not only elections.[55] A real paradigm shift in the structures of power will be necessary before substantive democracy takes hold. The so-called 'transition paradigm', the notion of immediate democratic change occuring through simple reform of formal structures, needs to be reconsidered. A long-sustained shift in the power paradigm of Qatar seems unlikely today.[56] Abdallah Al-Misnad's 1963 protest against the government's attempts to take away traditional power from tribes may still have some resonance in Qatar today, but there is little that tribes can do except within the very proscribed limits defined by the government. Most existential threats and demands on a rentier state such as Qatar are external in nature, however, without markets for their exports, rentier governments would lapse into ineffectivness.

INTERNATIONAL MARKETS

It has long been argued that Al-Thani were largely exempt from challenges to their authority, challenges brought by the powerful merchants of other Gulf monarchies. According to the argument outlined by Jill Crystal in her book *Oil and Politics in the Gulf*, Qatar, unlike Kuwait, lacked a significant merchant class, especially after the devastation of the 'years of hunger' during the Second World War. Nevertheless, Qatar's recent, major forays into the international finance and real estate markets should give pause to the claim that Al-Thani and the Emir have effectively cornered the whole of Qatar's political economy. In order to attract the most prestigious brands and financial institutions, Qatar and Al-Thani have been forced to loosen some of the country's protectionist regulations. The Qatar Financial Centre, for example, does not have the same restrictions on the percentage of a corporation that must be owned by Qataris. Also, The Pearl development properties can be held by foreigners. The massive movement of bonds and currencies across international markets are also largely outside the control of the Emir. As the default of Dubai World in November 2009 showed, these markets can have a major impact on the region. The popping of the Dubai bubble led to a run on the Gulf markets.

While Qatar is no Dubai – Qatar has a vast amount of potential natural gas revenue while Dubai has little oil left – it is not entirely certain that the international supply and demand of natural gas, Qatar's main and most important export for decades to come, will remain at ideal levels for Qatar. Gas, like oil, is subject to wild fluctuations in price. Even as gas prices went through the roof during the economic expansion of the middle 2000s, natural gas was the 'worst performing commodity investment of 2009'.[57] According to one analyst, 'We have more gas than we know what to do with in the US, we have more waterborne gas floating around the world's oceans that doesn't have a home.'[58] Moreover, newly discovered natural gas reserves in the USA will compete with Qatar's liquid natural gas exports to drive down prices. While not destroying all Qatar's potential profit, such natural gas oversupply may decrease future returns.

Like Saudi Arabia's oil, Qatar's natural gas is some of the cheapest in the world to extract, allowing for profits on gas even when the price was as low as $2.40 per million BTU. Gas has been known to peak at $13.00. While this has shielded it somewhat from the effect of lower prices, a drop in natural gas futures will certainly hamper Qatar's ability to fabsorb the current clip of expansion and investment. Although Qatar has joined the Gas Exporting Countries Forum, a gas cartel similar to OPEC, it is unclear how effective this organization will be in stabilizing prices in the future. With no clear, dominant player like Saudi Arabia, Qatar will need to negotiate and form coalitions with major gas-exporting partners such as Russia and Iran. These increased ties to the East may cause some rifts with the USA, Qatar's major ally, the financier of much of its natural gas infrastructure expansion after the Emir's coup in 1995 and its main security guarantor. Abdallah Al-Attiyah, the Energy Minister of Qatar until 2011, has already announced that Qatar has the right to divert exports away from terminals in the USA to emerging markets in countries such as China. Clearly, the vagaries of the international gas market and the expansion of Qatar's international economic ties will lead to tough decisions for Qatar and may limit its ability to maintain its professed neutral stance on international issues.

Single resource dependence has inherent risks, risks that may disintegrate the Gulf's expansion and development as quickly as it was created. Qatar is certainly not immune to a paradigm shift in the extraction of energy or in the development of non-petrol technologies, a shift that becomes increasingly likely as resource-dependent nations invest in research in 'alternative' energy and technology. While the replacement of gas and oil seemingly lies in the distant future, the likelihood of such a development only increases over time. While the possibility of complete market collapse appears to be highly unlikely, it is nearly impossible to hedge. Yet, if it did happen, it would, obviously, lead to severe internal social, political and economic breakdown.

RELIGION

Qatar's Constitution guarantees religious freedom and the Emir has even sponsored the building of the first churches on the Peninsula for hundreds of years. However, the main religious concern for Al-Thani is not with the faith of its visiting workers but with the power of Islam as a religio-political ideology that could challenge the state. It has become the accepted wisdom of political scientists that religion and religious institutions have been effectively marginalized by emiri power in Qatar. When compared with Saudi Arabia, Qatar's religious establishment does seem especially weak. This comparison, however, does not take into consideration the fact that Saudi Arabia holds a particular position in the Arab and Islamic world, not only as guardian of the holy sites of Medina and Mecca but as the place where Wahhabism was born. Unlike Ibn Saud who made a pact with Muhammad ibn 'Abd al Wahhab in 1745, Al-Thani did not empower the creation of a new religious movement as part of their founding ideology.

When compared with any state or society other than Saudi Arabia, Qatar and Qataris are remarkably religious. Religious considerations and limitations to the power of the Emir should not be taken as simply symbolic, even if religious decision-makers and imams in Qatar largely come from outside it and are thus vulnerable to manipulation by him. Some 73 per cent of Qatar's religious employees are non-Qatari, allowing the Emir to deport most uncooperative clerics at will. However, Qatar's more senior religious clerics are Qatari citizens.[59] This has not stopped clerics from speaking out about Qatar's liberalizing reforms. In 1998 a religious scholar was detained for three years.[60] Also, some clerics, such as Sheikh Yusuf al Qaradawi, an Egyptian who was given Qatari citizenship along with much of his family, have used Qatar and the satellite station Al-Jazeera as a base for spreading a conservative interpretation of Islam that may not be exactly in line with the opinions of Qatar's elite or the interests of the royal family's main guarantor of security in this volatile region, the USA.

Although Sheikh Qaradawi has denounced the use of terrorist violence in Qatar, and although he relies primarily on emiri patronage for protection and financial support, his message is not completely dictated by the emiri establishment. It remains unclear if his loyalites are really to the wealthy, Qatari elite or to Egypt's Muslim Brotherhood. Qaradawi, perhaps the most well-known and respected popular TV cleric in the Middle East, the Oprah of televised Islamic jurisprudence, is an international social and political symbol. He is certainly no stooge of Al-Thani family.

As the case of Qaradawi reveals, who is using whom is not always clear in Qatari religious politics. While Al-Thani may be interested in benefiting from the prestige of hosting Qaradawi, and Qaradawi may be interested in benefiting from Qatar's hospitality, the centuries-long history of religion being used by scholars as a subtle, but effective means of critiquing state power should not be overlooked. Even if Qaradawi has never criticized Qatar directly, his neo-traditionalist discourse, consumed so readily by Muslims around the world, including Qataris, implicitly seeks to limit the scope and nature of Qatar's own, largely Westernized development and to question the rationale behind it.

Moreover, Qatari society is sometimes more conservative than Al-Thanis. Less experienced in international circles and apt to attend the gender-segregated Qatar University, Qatari tribes still follow and enforce Islamic rules, even without the guidance of official religious representatives of the state. There have been numerous reports of informal *muttawa*, or enforcers of public virtue, who have appeared on the campus of the Qatar Foundation in Doha to oppose the socially liberalizing effects of Westernized education. The replacement of Arabic, the language of the Qur'an, with English has similarly caused a general, popular rection against the speed of the Emir's educational reforms.[61] Although portrayed as purely of benefit to the nation and the future of Qatar, education has also been used as a subtle means of exercising and negotiating power. Although often associated with democractization and liberalization, state-sponsored education can also have centralizing consequences. Indeed, education may be the ultimate avenue for facilitating the transition of Qatar from a segmentary to a unitary society in ways that benefit the entrenched powers of Al-Thani.

EDUCATION EFFORTS

Of the entire population of Qatar, there are but a handful of Qataris seriously interested in some aspect of professional classical music performance. This fact, however, did not stop Sheikha Mozah and the Qatar Foundation from courting the Julliard School in

New York, possibly the most prestigious institution for classical music in the world, to encourage it to establish a campus in Doha. While the attempt to create a world-class musical institution in Qatar is still in its planning phase, other world-class institutions such as the Georgetown School of Foreign Service, Virginia Commonwealth University School of the Arts, Carnegie Mellon and Weill Cornell Medical College, have had branch campuses in Qatar for up to a decade. Qatar has deliberately chosen to make education and the industry of ideas one of its most important investments, an investment that Al-Thani family hopes will position Qatar as a leader in educational excellence in the Gulf. Money seems to be no object in this mission overseen by the Qatar Foundation, or in any project associated with education for that matter. The country spent some 19.7 billion Qatari riyals, or around US$4 billion, on education in 2008. Between 2005 and 2006 spending on education was only about a quarter of the 2008 amount.[62]

A similar project with similarly almost limitless funds is the Museum of the Islamic Arts, a massive and imposing building on the Corniche, designed by the famous architect I.M. Pei who was enticed out of retirement to design it. The museum aims to be the largest and most significant collection of Islamic arts, crafts and visual heritage anywhere. Like the future and even bigger National Library, and like Education City itself, the museum is dedicated to public education and is intended to highlight Doha, and Qatar, as a recognized centre of culture and knowledge.

What all these recent initiatives have in common is that they have been initiated by the Emir or his family. Like every modern state, modern education is controlled by the state, allowing the state, and the Emir and Al-Thani family, either directly or indirectly, to consolidate ideological and national loyalty around an imagined 'status quo' of emiri authority. Education as a top-down, state-controlled affair, however, is only a recent phenomenon in Qatar.

History of Education in Qatar

The modern history of education in Qatar is the history of the gradual, if not entirely successful, replacement of traditional forms of identity with those defined by the state. Seen as a great benefit to the 'nation', modern education implicitly breaks the flow of generational transfer, putting the state in the position of the Sheikh and the elder, a process that replaces local histories with those of the nation. Before the exploitation of oil in the 1950s, education in Qatar was controlled within lineage groups. The educational curriculum for most boys, if they were privilieged, meant the basics of reading and writing and the recitation and memorization of the Qur'an during the pearling off-season. At most, boys would be taught at an informal, local school, or *kuttab*, or within the mosque in the neighborhood where their tribe settled. Girls learned to read and write at home.

Only the very wealthiest were able to send their children overseas to private schools, usually in Britain.

Most pre-petroleum education in Qatar occurred within the family and the lineage group. Pearl-farmers would teach their sons how to find the perfect oysters and sail the *dhow*. Mothers and grandmothers would teach girls the essential skills of survival. They would also serve as *mutaween*, traditional teachers and enforcers of moral order. In fact the memory of traditional teaching is not so distant. Both male and female *mutaween*, unrecognized and uncontrolled by the state, still exist in Qatar, even if the state has appropriated most formal educational functions.

Oil exploitation in the 1950s, however, rapidly transformed Qatari society and educational expectations. The first formal, state-funded school in Qatar opened in 1952. It was not until Sheikh Khalifa began his reign in the early 1970s, however, that educational reform began to accelerate.

Sheikh Khalifa bin Hamad Al-Thani built the foundations of Qatar's educational system almost from scratch. Nevertheless, for decades under his centralized rule the educational curriculum maintained much of its traditional, religious focus. Even so, enterprising reformers began to consider the possibility of changing and modernizing the curriculum. Two leading women were especially important in planting the early seeds of curriculum development in Qatar: Sheikha Ahmad Al-Mahmoud and Sheikha Abdallah Al-Misnad. Currently President of Qatar University, and author of important studies and evaluations of Qatar's education system, Sheikha Al-Misnad was instrumental in creating the basic foundations of a systematic and modern curriculum structure in Qatar. Sheikha Ahmad Al-Mahmoud, Minister of Education, created the foundation of assessment and evaluation procedures, encouraging Qatar towards the adoption of modern pedagogical techniques in the early 1990s. She also spearheaded the appointment of women at the highest levels of Qatar's educational system.

Although the new systems provided the framework for the systematic evaluation of student learning and teaching supervision and assessment, they were often not fully implemented because of bureaucratic hurtles. Education and society entered a new era of rapid modernization with the assumption of power by Sheikh Hamad Al-Thani, the son of Sheikh Khalifa, in 1995. Almost immediately, Sheikh Hamad and his wife, Sheikha Mozah, who has taken a personal interest in educational reform in Qatar, set up the Qatar Foundation to reform the country's science, arts and language teaching programmes. The Qatar Foundation started with higher education, including reform of Qatar University and the establishment of satellite campuses of American universities such as Cornell and Georgetown at Education City.

This chapter has focussed primarily on the formal expression of power in Qatar. Power seems to be unmistakably concentrated in the Emir. In conclusion, however, one major caveat to this apparent truism must be considered. There is an important, unspoken, informal pact between the Emir and Qatari citizens, a pact that is more essential to the maintenance of power in Qatar than any formal, dry, and rather arbitrarily proclaimed constitutional parameter. In this pact, the same sort of pact that has cemented the Qatari people to their leaders for centuries, the Qatari people are compensated with the wealth of the state in exchange for handing over the traditional distribution of power through tribal skeikhs and independent families. The Emir cannot simply relinquish his ultimate obligation to the Qatari people of this still-relevant, informal pact. True, it might be argued that the Emir has sufficiently isolated himself and the state from his people through the importation of labour and the guarantees of foreign powers. Yet he has also gone to incredible lengths to rewrite the history of Qatar, focusing on Al-Thani lineage as the key to Qatar's very existence.

Conclusions – Change or Continuity?

Qatar is famous for its shifting sand dunes. Entire mountains of sand can appear on once-flat ground. The direction of the prevailing wind, the *sebkha*, that produces these shifts, however, has not changed. On satellite images Qatar's desolate land appears etched or scarred by great diagonal lines that run north-west to south-east with the winds. Similarly, the extraordinary economic growth and modernization of Qatar has seemingly created a mountain of wealth. The prevailing influences and the social conditions that have shaped Qatar and its politics for centuries, however, remain, in many ways, the same. According to some political scientists, Qatar, like many of its Gulf neighbours, is just as vulnerable to disruptive, political, change as are the famously shifting mountains of sand of Udeid. Others, however, believe that Al-Thanis' lasting power has been underestimated and that it will remain and persist under the current political system for decades to come. It is these two possibilities – stubborn persistence and dramatic change – that continue to beguile political scientists and thinkers about the Gulf emirates in general.

With the Arab Gulf States poised on the geographic, diplomatic and political gulf that divides Iran and the USA, their governance and relative vulnerability have become strategically vital subjects of enquiry for the USA. Political scientists and scholars of international affairs have long predicted the downfall of the oil-rich Gulf States and governments. In the introduction to *Oil Monarchies: Domestic and Security Challenges in the Arab Gulf States*, the political scientist Gregory Gause described the general tendency to assume that the Gulf monarchies will soon disappear.[1] The scholar and commentator Kenneth Pollack recently claimed that the Gulf was drowning in the riches of the present oil boom and that misspending of oil money may lead to disaster for small Gulf emirates such as Qatar, the United Arab Emirates and Kuwait. In his recent book *Dubai: the Vulnerability of Success*, Christopher Davidson emphasized the vulnerability of Dubai's recent, spectacular economic boom.[2] During the 2008–9 financial crisis and the collapse of oil prices, Western newspapers such as *The New York Times* engaged in a bit of lightly veiled *schadenfreude* when describing the oncoming doom for the Gulf. They dramatically reported car-parks full of abandoned vehicles and an apocalyptic decline in property values.³ In *The Rise, Corruption and Coming Fall of the House of Saud*, Said Aburish predicted the disastrous crumbling of the Saudi monarchy and the regional instability that that decline would entail.⁴ The question is easily posed, if Saudi Arabia, the economic, political and religious powerhouse of the region could fall like a house of cards, how more easily would its small neighbour Qatar? Although a consensus has begun to form that the Gulf States are more stable than once thought, Gulf expert Gary Sick, in 'The Coming Crisis in the Persian Gulf', still questions the long-term sustainability of the Gulf monarchies.⁵

While accurate in their portrayal of the potential of long-term weaknesses and vulnerabilities, these largely pessimistic studies give little credence to the deep historical and social roots of Gulf monarchies. While many studies of the Gulf are heavy on financial analysis and descriptions of sheikhs' personalities, they are less balanced in their use of history and historical methods or in giving due consideration to cultural aspects. As A. Montigny-Kozlowska, perhaps the only scholar to study seriously the sociology of Qatar, commented on recent works on Qatar, 'Their spotty character, their weaknesses of uncertainty and their focus above all else on "economy" – in the most qualitative manner possible – makes synthesis and sociological interpretation especially challenging.'⁶ While the economy of Qatar has fluctuated wildly and while labour, development, investment and technology has transformed the superficial appearance of Qatar, the fundamental social and political system, a system based on consensus between Qatari nationals, has remained stable and based on informal contracts established between the ruling tribe, Al-Thani, and other Qatari tribes at least a century ago. Since the nineteenth century Gulf monarchies have faced and survived many of the same economic and even geopolitical challenges that commentators such as Kenneth Pollack cite as mortal dangers for Gulf countries such as Qatar today.

Qatar's past does not reveal a weak political and social system doomed to failure in a modern, complex environment, but rather a surprisingly robust, durable and socially cohesive tribal society in which Al-Thani, the ruling tribe, were first among equals. Tribal consensus, not simply top-down totalitarianism, characterized and continues to characterize some aspects of decision-making in Qatar. Several scholars have wondered at the 'persistence' of powerful monarchies in the Middle East. While other regions of the world have progressively abandoned traditional monarchical systems, the Gulf has remained a region dominated by royal families. As Lisa Anderson, political scientist at Columbia University observed, 'The only major ruling monarchs in the world today reside in the Arab world.'⁷ In *All in the Family: Absolutism, Revolution and Democracy in the Middle Eastern Democracies*, Michael Herb, explained how the royal families of the Gulf region 'formed themselves into ruling institutions in control of the newly powerful bureaucratic states of the oil era'.⁸ While his thesis applies to Qatar and Al-Thani have used the bureaucracy of the oil state to their advantage, the careful management of oil revenue is not the entire story of their success.

Unlike other rentier states based on personal rule, such as Qaddafi's Libya, reliant almost entirely on oil wells for its strength and legitimacy, in Qatar Al-Thani can draw upon an even deeper well, a well of historical myth and solidarity linking the success and independence of Qataris to the historical leadership of Al-Thani. As Robert Vitalis made clear in his book *America's Kingdom: Mythmaking on the Saudi Oil Frontier*, this manipulation of national myths to serve the interests of the ruling family is not unique to Qatar.[9] Like the Saudis, Al-Thani have maintained their power not through force or domination but through their historical legitimacy as leaders and defenders of the idea of Qatar and Qatari independence decades before the discovery of oil. Despite their appropriation of the oil bureaucracy, Al-Thani legitimacy and power remains dependent on historical, tribal relationships from the pre-oil era and on the loyalty and solidarity, the *'asabiyya*, of Al-Thani family and other Qatari tribes. In Qatar a citizen can only vote if his or her family has been living on the Peninsula since before 1930, or before the discovery and development of oil. This rule exists despite the fact that the vast majority of Qatari residents, including Bahraini or Shi'a families living in Qatar for decades, do not qualify. Even as 'democratization' progresses, it is a democratization based on a select group of citizen elites, most coming from tribes that at least publicly agree to a narrative of Al-Thani primacy in the pre-First World War era. Even within Al-Thani family, there is a system of consensus and discussion. Challengers within Al-Thani family to the stated policies of the Emir are still appointed to senior ministerial posts as a way of silencing them by giving them formal titles. The Emir constantly attempts to bypass traditional obligations and tribal systems in the name of benevolent totalitarianism and progress. Indeed, there is often a disconnect between the social morals of traditional Qataris and the progressive internationalism of the Emir and his immediate family.

To some extent, but perhaps not quite to the extent that it may appear, Qataris have gone along with the Emir's modernization projects, seemingly content as long as they retain their place as part of an elevated, citizen elite with all the guarantees that that entails. While monarchies in other larger Middle Eastern states such as Morocco and Saudi Arabia must elevate their own families above the citizenry, in Qatar the number of 'original' citizens is so small, under 20 per cent of the entire population, that Qataris have become a 'citizen aristocracy', elevated above the masses of migrant labourers, European and American residents, and even other Arabs who are a major part of modern Qatar but who remain largely at the mercy of their employers and the Ministry of Interior.

The cohesiveness of Qataris and their loyalty to Al-Thani, key reasons for the survival of the current system, are explained by Qatar's long-term history and the way in which Qatari citizens view their independent historical rights. Economists have emphasized oil wealth and the classic rentier pattern as the fundamental reasons for Qatar's success and the stability of the royal family. More specialized scholars such as Jill Crystal at Auburn University have emphasized the limited co-dependence between foreign, usually Iranian, merchants and Al-Thani rulers in Qatar. The coming of oil and the collapse of the pearl industry severed much of this dependence, limited as it was. While the booming economy and relations with the merchant class are important factors, factors detailed by Jill Crystal, the legitimacy and power of Al-Thani is based at least as much on an historical myth of co-dependence between Al-Thani and the Arab, Qatari citizen elite, as it is on oil, bureaucratic and institutional development or the distribution of wealth. As discussed at the beginning of this book, Qataris seem less impacted by the anomie of modernization than by the inheritance of tradition. This does not mean that 'tradition' as the qualifier of Qatari social life remains static. Far from it. The core Al-Thani elite, the Qataris themselves, are constantly engaged in attempts at defining and redefining 'heritage' and 'tradition' for its own ends, to transform mythologized historical traditions into nationalist symbol in a way that justifies Al-Thani power.

The Future of Tradition

Bureaucratic and technocratic achievements are not easily mythologized. It is stories of bravery and honour and 'independence' that are most cherished and provide a narrative around which an imagined community or a nation forms. For example, more Americans will remember the story of Paul Revere's ride during the Revolutionary War than the specific contents of the Constitution, even if the latter has a much more immediate bearing on their personal rights and welfare. Although its historical myths are almost completely unknown outside the country, Qatar is certainly not lacking in these myths, myths that have been used to legitimize the current political system. There were the many battles for Zubara in 1878 and 1937 and finally, most recently, in the international courts, when Al-Thani, with the crucial support and loyalty of other Qatari tribes, asserted their independence from Bahrain. There was the bravery of Emir Jassim Al-Thani who in the late nineteenth century, again with the support of Qatari tribes, successfully rallied the Qataris against the Ottomans. In all of these stories it is the leadership of Al-Thani, supported by loyal tribes, that establishes and assures the independence of Qatar.

In addition to the promotion of shared historical myths affirming the legitimacy of Al-Thani, there have been other more active ways in which Al-Thani have asserted the importance of a common Qatari identity. One prominent example is the camel-racing at the Shahaniya race track, which was built in the middle of Qatar out of sight of modern skyscrapers. While foreign staff may dominate banks and universities, and malls may be filled with expatriates, the Shahaniya race track preserves a strictly 'Arab' tradition. The scholar Sulayman Khalaf at Harvard University has explained how 'the annual celebrations and activities surrounding the glorification of the camel as a cultural icon are given new meaning, rhetoric, and direction for a community reconstructing itself as a modern nation-state within shifting global contexts'.[10] Qatar's tribes have transformed 'traditional' ways of living into cultural artefacts pursued by the elite for both legitimacy and the preservation of identity.

A new property development called Qatar Cultural Village, whilst it will be built in its entirety by migrant labour and designed primarily by outsiders, will make a similar attempt to manifest a mythical historical authenticity. Located in the new West Bay area of Doha, and occupying a total area of 245 acres, the Cultural Village 'was conceptualized to reflect the heritage of Qatar through traditional architecture that accommodates a large number of activities arranged in such a way as to reflect a historical and cultural theme throughout'.[11] With the Cultural Village and a host of similar heritage projects, the myth of tradition is preserved in a thoroughly modern, climate-controlled space. The most visible way in which Qataris assert their identity is through dress. By wearing the *thob,* the long white garment used by men, in a specific way, Qatari men assert their historical identity as Qataris in bodily terms. This means of assertion remains striking as Qataris enter into an otherwise thoroughly modern or Westernized physical space. While the body remains clothed in tradition, the environment in which the body moves has been radically changed.

Carefully controlled and sanitized assertions of Qatari heritage serve to support the 'heritage' and alleged 'tradition' of monarchy even if that monarchy never really existed in its current form. This use of tradition and heritage by monarchy is not restricted to the Gulf. Even in the UK, the modern monarchy is adept at justifying its existence through the preservation and continuation of 'heritage'. In an intriguing example of the international bonds of heritage and the association between heritage and monarchy as a justification for preserving the monarchy, the UK's Prince Charles's recently appealed to his fellow royal prince Hamad bin Khalifa Al-Thani of Qatar to intervene in the matter of a new and, in Prince Charles's opinion, unsightly property development in London financed by Qatari money. The concept of monarchy as a bulwark of identity-preserving heritage was effectively globalized. There was high irony here – a practically powerless British royal appealed to the ruler of a former British protectorate for aid in the defence of his own definition of Englishness. While Prince Charles's intervention was met with howls of protest in the British press, decisions taken by the Emir of Qatar and his family fundamentally to reshape the character and development of Qatar have occured largely without public debate.[12] While such criticism also exists in Qatar, it is almost always expressed informally or through indirect channels.

Not only physical architecture is controlled and shaped by Al-Thani family and the Qatari government. Qatar's written history has followed the same carefully constructed contours as its architectural heritage projects. While the heat of the desert can be controlled by massive government projects creating artificial interior climates, the heat of history can be similarly regulated into the carefully packaged, cooled and subdued category of national heritage. Both the ruling family and the leaders of individual Qatari tribes manage their history and historical myths carefully – something that has made the writing of this book particularly challenging. A recent call from the National Library for Qataris to deposit their family and tribal archives yielded a disappointing response, although the existence of these archives and oral histories are generally known and they appear occasionally, often in relation to land claims.

The nearly complete lack of critical and independent historical research and publication of Qatar's recent history can be partly explained by Qatar's deft management of its historical image, both for the sake of its international standing and to ensure the internal cohesion of Qatari society. While there are a comparatively large number of studies on Qatar based on British, and even Ottoman documents related to the region, the lack of a critical bibliography on Qatar since independence can be accounted for not only by a lack of sources on sensitive subjects but by the efforts of Al-Thani, and of Qataris themselves, to control information, or perhaps to avoid having to enforce the rigid rules of honour. A dishonour committed in the past is more quickly repaired if it is not set down in writing. If history remains inert, it remains possible to avoid past grievances and maintain unity in the face of external threats. Glossing over history means turning tribal affiliation into a sanitized form of 'heritage' and conveniently maintains the power of the Emir and the state.

With its academic institutions, including American institutions in Education City, monitored and dependent on government funds, and with its press corps composed mainly of powerless expatriates, Qatar's ruling family and government have managed to remain beneath the radar of critical historical scrutiny.

Despite the ironies and inconsistencies of this historical, heritage myth-making, the history of Qatar has had real implications. History has shaped Qatari ambitions and national character as much as Qataris and Al-Thani have shaped historical myths to preserve the status quo. From the middle of the nineteenth century, Al-Thani rulers of Qatar and their Qatari allies from a select group of Arab tribes residing on the Peninsula kept both the Ottoman and British Empires at bay. They prevented Persian, Saudi or Omani incursions and maintained a lucrative trade in a single natural resource with a fluctuating price (pearls – not oil) in the nineteenth and early twentieth centuries. The challenges of maintaining a fragile balance between the new American imperialism and Iranian regional influence and dealing with oil fluctuations are not so terribly different from the challenges of the past. The one major risk to Al-Thani rule, however, is that power becomes too concentrated in a small part of Al-Thani family.

If there is one major constant in Qatari history it is that the Emir and his immediate family cannot risk standing too far apart from the rest of the Qatari population. Attempts to do so would add an element of internal risk to a geopolitical neighbourhood that is inherently dicey. Indeed, the option of appealing to the migrant population as a means of countering the informal power of Qatari citizens would be, in the end, self-defeating. Although an expression of Emiri power, attempts to isolate, repress or disenfranchise dissident tribes, as in the case of Al-Murrah, are also somewhat futile. Such actions would severely erode the legitimacy of the Emir in the eyes of the international community. Indeed, it was probably international scrutiny that forced Sheikh Hamad to reinstate the 5,000 Al-Murrah as Qatari citizens. It is because of this strategic calculation of the sway of internal politics, more than any sense of paternal obligation, that the Emir has concentrated so much on the promotion of Qatarization of the workforce and education of Qataris. Even as Al-Thani continue to concentrate power, it is only by maintaining an active role of Qataris, both Al-Thani and non-Al-Thani, in Qatari society over the long term that the emirate will survive.

Although the risks to Al-Thani are not nearly as visible as the risks facing the King of Bahrain, where protests have often erupted on the streets, there are many potential fissures in the fabric of Qatari society that may open if Al-Thani move too far and too fast in promoting their own over the rest of Qatari society. While Qatar's Al-Jazeera cable television service covered the fall of President Ben Ali in Tunisia in the confidence that its own sponsor, Al-Thani, would surely never face the same fate, there are potential hazards ahead for Al-Thani if they make strategic blunders. As much as Mehran Kamrava's observation about the increasing differences between Al-Thani elite and the rest of Qatar may be true, the international community, including the USA, might ultimately see an internally isolated Qatari Emir and his family as a situation potentially too vulnerable to withstand in such a strategic ally. It is likely, and it is hoped by many, that the Emir and his immediate family will not test the limits of their power or the extent to which they can stand far apart from the already small segment of the population that is Qatari. After all, as the accounts of ancient sailors tell us, the calm, warm waters of the Gulf are deceptive. They can sink even the wealthiest, the most confident, and the best prepared.

Timeline

55,000 BC	Stone Age peoples in Qatar leave behind basic stone tools.
Eighth–Sixth millenium BC	Arabia and Qatar enter a much wetter period. Hunter-gatherers store wild grain on the Peninsula.
2450–1700 BC	The Dilmun trading culture, famous for its burial mounds in Bahrain, leaves behind distinctive Barbar pottery at sites around Qatar.
1700 BC	The murex marine snail is harvested at Khor Shaqiq in Qatar. Extracts from the snail are used to produce royal, Tyrian purple.
Second–third centuries AD	Persian settlers leave behind glazed ware at Umm al Main Qatar.
627–9 AD	The Arab Christian governor of Al-Hasa and the ruler of Bahrain convert to Islam. The Arab tribes of Qatar and Bahrain send ships to fight in Muslim fleets during the expansion of Islam.
***c.* fifteenth century AD**	A group of Al-Thani tribesmen of the Maʿadhid branch of the Tamim line of Arabs migrates from a small village in central Saudi Arabia to Qatar.
1521 AD	Bahrain becomes a possession of the Portuguese.
1602	Shah Abbas, with the help of the British, captures Bahrain from the Portuguese.
1660	Oman occupies Bahrain and allows the Huwalah Arabs who migrated there to settle on the island.
1753	Nadir Shah of Persia captures Bahrain, determined to assert control over the entire Gulf.
1760	A group of Utubi Arabs from Kuwait migrate to Zubara on Qatar's northern coast. The Khalifa and the Jalahimah branches of the Utubi Arabs turn Zubara into a substantial trade and pearling city.
1780s–1826	Rahmah bin Jabir of the Jalahimah branch of Kuwaiti Utubi Arabs harasses Bahraini shipping from his base at Kawr Hassan in Qatar.
1783	A group of Utubi and Qatari Arabs storms Bahrain and captures the island from Persia. The most powerful Al-Khalifa

Arabs settle in Bahrain. Ahmad bin Khalifa becomes ruler of Bahrain establishing the Khalifa dynasty.

1792–1813 Abd Aziz bin Saud and his son spread Wahhabi Islam to the eastern shores of the Gulf and Qatar. Rahmah forms temporary alliances of convenience with the Wahhabis.

1820 The British Government of Bombay concludes a General Treaty of Peace signed by the tribes of the east Arabian coast. Qatar is not awarded a separate flag and is considered a part of Bahrain by the British until the 1860s.

1821 Doha is bombarded by the *Vestal* of the British East India Company. Buhur bin Jurban of the Al bu-Ainain tribe professes to be ignorant of the reasons for British action against it.

1828 Qatar, left without a single powerful leader, is bullied by Al-Khalifa of Bahrain. One of Qatar's most distinguished chiefs, Muhammad bin Khamis of Al-Ainain tribe, is imprisoned. Bahrain evicts Al-Ainain from Doha and sends them to Fuwayrat and Ruways, villages in the north of Qatar. Saliyman bin Nasir, chief of the Sudan tribe, fills the power vaccum in Doha.

1840 Egyptians, then in control of Al-Hasa, plan but fail to send a force to collect *zakat*, or religious taxes, from the Naim tribe under Jabir bin Nasir.

1841 Doha is bombarded again by British ships as the pirate Jassim bin Jabir Raqraqi takes refuge in Qatar.

1843 Isa bin Tarif (d. 1847) of the Al bin Ali tribe opposes the co-ruler of Bahrain and leads revolts from Qatar.

1850 Faisal bin Turki, Wahhabi of Saudi Arabia, enters Qatar, gains the support of Qatar's residents and prepares to invade Bahrain. He is stopped by the British Persian Gulf Squadron.

1867 An attack on Qatar by Bahrain and Abu Dhabi for its sympathy towards the Wahhabis allows Muhammad bin Thani, the notable Doha chief, to rebel successfully against the Bahraini governor.

12 September 1868 British Colonel Lewis Pelly compels the ruler of Bahrain to pay damages to Qatar. He meets and recognizes Sheikh Muhammad bin Thani as the representative of the people of Qatar. The 1868 treaty between Qatar and Britain is put into force.

1871 The Ottomans arrive in Doha after occupying Al-Hasa. Jassim bin Muhammad bin Thani, son of Muhammad bin Thani, accepts the Ottoman flag in Qatar.

1876	Jassim appointed Qaim Maqam or regional governor of Qatar. Jassim asserts his authority over all of Qatar. He manipulates both the Ottomans on land and the British at sea.
1878	Jassim and a force of 2,000 sack Zubara and punish Al-Naim tribe for its 'piracy' and allegiance with Bahrain.
1893	Qataris prevail over the Ottomans at the battle of Wajbah.
1913	Sheikh Jassim dies. Sheikh Abdallah comes to power. Abdallah's relatives dispute his government.
1916	Treaty is signed between Sheikh Abdallah and the British affirming his power. Abdallah agrees to enforce laws against piracy, the arms trade and the slave trade. A separate telegram allows him to ignore the Article on slavery.
1921	Abdallah asks for protection against the Saudis. Abdallah's brothers receive Saudi support. Abdallah appeals to the British.
1926	Abdallah grants exploration rights to D'Arcy Exploration of the Anglo-Persian Oil Company. The USA sends its own negotiators and oil companies to compete with the British. Abdallah uses this competition as leverage.
1935	An oil concession to the Anglo-Persian Oil company is signed by Abdallah, who personally receives 150,000 Indian rupees a year. The British recognize Abdallah's heir, Hamad.
1937	A war between Bahrain and Qatar over Zubara leads to the split of the Naim tribe between those loyal to Al-Thani and those loyal to Bahrain. Many Naim are exiled, only to return to their lands after the Second World War. Qatar captures Zubara.
1939	Oil is discovered but the Second World War prevents further exploration.
1942	All oil development is halted. Qatar enters the 'years of hunger'. The Sheikh is forced to mortgage his own home.
1942–8	Most Qatari families and merchants are forced to flee Qatar out of economic hardship. Al-Thani family, shielded by continued oil concession revenue, remains and consolidates its internal power.
1949	Oil exports start again. Abdallah designates Ali as his successor (Abdallah's chosen heir Hamad having died in 1948) and Khalifa as second in line. Several Al-Thani sheikhs go on strike and buy weapons threatening the sheikh unless they receive higher allowances from the oil contracts. Abdallah abdicates.
1950s	Petroleum Development Qatar Limited (PDQL) expands operations in Dukhan. Several strikes are mounted by Qatari

	labourers. Not much oil is discovered offshore until the 1960s. Shell, an American company, is given the offshore concessions.
1956	The Pan-Arab nationalist movement touches Qatar. Al-Attiyah brothers demand more involvement in government from the British. The Qatari sheikhs attack the role of Abdallah Darwish, Sheikh Ali's principal advisor and a close confidant of the British.
1957	Possible mines are discovered in the house of Sheikh Ali. Blame is cast on unruly younger sheikhs jockeying for more power and payments.
1960	After a decline in oil revenue, Ali concedes power to his son Ahmad.
1961	Citizenship law grants full citizenship only to Qataris residing in Peninsula before 1930.
1964	A new law stipulates that all industry and businesses must be at least 51 per cent Qatari-owned.
1970s	Sheikh Khalifa invests heavily in infrastructure. Qatar University is founded. The oil industry is nationalized.
1971	Qatar becomes an independent state.
1972	Khalifa overthrows Ahmad in a coup after receiving support from Al-Thani sheikhs and other prominent Qataris.
1980s	A drop in oil prices in 1986 leads to austerity measures and a decline in allowances to sheikhs.
1982	A group of Bahrainis write 'Bahrain' on the Zubara fort during a field trip. Bahraini and Qatari relations deteriorate over the disputed Hawar islands.
1986	Fasht al-Dibal Island (a coral reef) is claimed by Qatar and Bahrain. Iran supports Qatari claims.
1991	A contingent of the Qatari Army tanks rolls against Saddam Hussein's invasion at the Battle of Khafji, Saudi Arabia.
1995	Sheikh Hamad bin Khalifa Al-Thani seizes control of Qatar while his father is in Switzerland. Sheikh Hamad establishes the Qatar Foundation for Education, Science and Community Development to promote education and the creation of Education City as well as other social and international initiatives.
1996	An Emiri decree establishes Al-Jazeera television channel.
1996	A counter coup attempt fails. Sheikh Hamad bin Jassim bin Hamad al Thani and other conspirators are put on trial.

2003	Qatar becomes a base for the US attack on Iraq during the second Gulf War.
2004	A new Constitution is launched.
2005	A suicide bomber strikes the Doha Players Theatre. Most believe the attack on the Arabian Peninsula was carried out by Al-Qaeda.
2006	Citizenship Law Number 38 of 2005 expands citizenship to include limited citizenship to those proving they had resided in Qatar for 25 years.
2010	Qatar is selected to host the 2022 FIFA World Cup.
2011	Qatar actively supports Arab Spring even as it limits internal political participation. Qatar sends air force to support anti-Qaddafi rebels.

Notes

CHAPTER 1

1 Qtd. in Jill Crystal, *Oil and Politics in the Gulf: Rulers and Merchants in Kuwait and Qatar* (Cambridge, 1990), p. 117.

2 A. Montigny-Kozlowska, 'Histoire et changements sociaux au Qatar', *La Péninsule arabique d'aujourd'hui*, Vol. 2 (1982), p. 483.

3 Qtd. in Miriam Joyce, *Ruling Sheikhs and Her Majesty's Government, 1960–1969* (Portland, OR, 2003), p. 45.

4 Qtd. on homepage of Dohadebates, http://www.thedohadebates.com/, accessed 20 January 2011.

5 Citation CIA World Factbook 'Qatar'. Available https://www.cia.gov/library/publications/the-world-factbook/rankorder/2003rank.html?countryName=Qatar&countryCode=qa&regionCode=mde&rank=1#qa and Theodora.com 'Qatar' http://www.theodora.com/wfbcurrent/qatar/qatar_economy.html, accessed 15 November 2011.

6 On the routes of the Naim see *Bedouins of Qatar* by Klaus Ferdinand and Ida Nicolaisen of the Carlsberg Foundation's Nomad Research Project (New York, 1993).

7 J. C. Wilkenson, 'Nomadic territory as a factor in defining Arabia's boundaries', in M. Mundy and B. Musallam (eds), *The Transformation of Nomadic Society in the Arab East* (Cambridge, 2000), p. 44.

8 Montigny-Kozlowska: 'Histoire et changements sociaux au Qatar', p. 493.

9 In his chapter on Qatar, National Public Radio reporter Eric Weiner described his immediate impressions of the country as a place without any real culture or history. *The Geography of Bliss: One Grump's Search for the Happiest Places in the World* (London and New York, 2008).

10 Although Qatar is a particular case, a nuanced view of the ways tradition and modernity are viewed *within* the Middle East more broadly can be found in Stephen Humphreys, *Between Memory and Desire: The Middle East in a Troubled Age* (Berkeley, updated edition, 2005).

11 Émile Durkheim, *On Morality and Society: Selected Writings*, ed. R. Bellah (Chicago, 1973), p. 70.

12 G. E. Von Grunebaum, *Modern Islam* (New York, 1964), p. 338.

13 Durkheim: *On Morality*, p. 70.

14 R. Tapper, 'Anthropologists, historians and tribespeople on tribe and state formation in the Middle East', in P. Khoury and J. Kostiner (eds), *Tribes and State Formation in the Middle East* (Berkeley and Los Angeles, 1990), pp. 54–5.

15 *Muqaddimah*, Vol. 1, p. 267.

16 On the history of Qatari labour in the early periods of oil field development see Ragaei Mullakh, *Qatar: Development of an Oil Economy* (London, 1979).

17 'Qatar population put at 1,580,050', *The Penisula*, 2 December 2009.

18 See the President's webpage. 'Biography' http://www.qu.edu.qa/offices/president/biography.php

19 'Obesity reaches epidemic proportions in the Gulf Region', *AME Info*, http://www.ameinfo.com/123855.html, accessed 18 June 2007.

20 According to Human Rights Watch, authorities are failing to curb sexual abuse of maids, particularly from Sri Lanka. See 'Sri Lanka abuse Rampant in the Gulf', *BBC News*, posted 14 November 2007, http://news.bbc.co.uk/2/hi/south_asia/7093842.stm

21 'Expatriates – A liability?', *Khaleej Times*, 14 December 2009.

22 In 2008 at the opening of the 37th session of the Advisory Council, a body composed of mainly non-royal Qatari tribal representatives, the Emir remarked, 'A number of bottleneck areas have risen in the economy, caused by the big increase in expatriate labour'. Online. Available http://www.diwan.gov.qa/english/the_Emir/the_Emir_speeche_83.htm (14 June 2009).

23 Ibid.

24 Local merchants used these strikes to galvanize Qataris against foreign company interests as well. Crystal, *Oil and Politics*, p. 162.

25 Rosemarie Said Zahlan, *The Creation of Qatar* (London, 1979), p. 99.

26 Emile A. Nakhleh, 'Labor markets and citizenship in Bahrayn and Qatar', *Middle East Journal*, Vol. 31, No. 2 (Spring 1977), pp. 143–56, 144.

27 See homepage of the Qatar National Food Security website. Online. Available http://www.qnfsp.gov.qa/ (23 October 2010).

28 The glacier surfaced in 2009 with one of the most vehemently discussed topics in the active Qatari blogosphere in 2009. Comments criticizing Qataris and their celebration of their national day (the author described reckless driving and somebody apparently in an Osama bin Laden mask) by a Western art history professor who had been teaching in Qatar for several years sparked outrage against expatriates. According to a leader of a Facebook group of Qataris set up to challenge the professor's comments, 'They have called us names such as pigs, uncivilized, racist barbarians ... They say that we cannot survive without them and that we cannot

handle or manage our country ...' *All Headline News*. Online. Available http://www. allheadlinenews.com/articles/7017362017 (26 December 2009).

29   'Qatar: Public outrage rises with demand for Saudi Maids', *Los Angeles Times* blog. Online. Available http://latimesblogs.latimes.com/babylonbeyond/2009/08/qatar-public-outrage-as-demand-for-saudi-maids-rises-amid-fears-of-black-magic.html (12 August 2009).

30   These publications have a long pedigree and are often financed outright by public relations firms. See *This is Qatar*, a quarterly that was distributed by Gulf Public Relations starting in 1978. Also *Spotlight Qatar* (London, 1979). Bernard Gérard's *Qatar* (London, 2000) was published by the Ministry of Information and remains a popular and regularly updated coffee-table book. Although written in an appealing manner with many fine colour photographs, it is perhaps the most notorious example of this glossy form of historical myth-making.

31   London, 1979.

32   *Oil and Politics in the Gulf: Rulers and Merchants in Kuwait and Qatar* (Cambridge, 1990).

33   'Abu Dhabi and Qatar build museums to recast national identity', *New York Times*. Online. Available http://www.nytimes.com/2010/11/27/arts/design/27museums. html (27 November 2010).

34   Michel Foucault, 'What is enlightenment?', in P. Rabinow (ed.), *The Michel Foucault Reader* (New York, 1984), pp. 39–40.

35   Leonard Binder, *Islamic Liberalism* (Chicago, 1988), p. 293.

36   Qtd. in ibid., p. 294.

37   As Rosemarie S. Zahlan aptly commented, 'The Al Thani are relative newcomers as a ruling family. But then, so too is the establishment of Qatar as an independent state', *The Making of the Modern Gulf States* (London, revised edition, 1998), p. 99.

38   Ibid.

39   J. E. Peterson, 'The Arabian Peninsula in modern times: A historiographical survey', *The American Historical Review*, 96/5 (December 1991), p. 1437.

40   Joseph Kéchichian, *Power and Succession in Arab Monarchies* (London, 2008), pp. 194–8.

41   The *CIA World Factbook* claims that Qataris had the highest per capita GDP in 2008. https://www.cia.gov/library/publications/the-world-factbook/geos/qa.html; Qatar's per capita income has been among the highest in the world for several decades. In 1978 the *Financial Times* reported Qatar's per capita GDP at $11,400, the third highest in the world: 'Qatar', 22 February 1978.

42   Montigny-Kozlowska: 'Histoire et changements sociaux au Qatar', pp. 475–517.

43 Electoral districts fall almost perfectly in line with tribal boundaries. For these maps see Ibrahim al Hidous, *Awal Bait lil-Dimaqratiyya fi Qatar* (Doha, 2001), an officially published book that provides an insider's view of the 'democratization' process.

44 According to one confidential source who was present in the Majlis, the boisterous and informal style of George W. Bush during his visit to the Qatari diwan and the Majlis al-Shura in 2004, the first visit to the country by a sitting US President, created something of a minor diplomatic disaster.

45 'German Federation asks FIFA for inquiry', BBC website http://news.bbc.co.uk/ sport2/hi/football/13613314.stm, accessed 31 August 2011.

46 'Move to Gulf by key unit could set staff for Iraq War', *New York Times*, 12 September 2002. Online. Available http://www.nytimes.com/2002/09/12/us/ vigilance-memory-military-move-gulf-key-unit-could-set-staff-for-iraq-war. html?scp=7&sq=udeid&st=cse (4 August 2009).

47 In January 2009 Qatar closed the Israeli interest section after bombings and incursions in Gaza. Qatar's alignment with Syria and Hamas as an 'alternative camp' drove policy on the ground. Besides Israel, There have been a few such breaks in Qatar's record of befriending almost all possible positions and parties. Qatar has attempted to position itself as a stalwart against terrorism in the Arabian Peninsula even as some nations have suggested that Qatar has paid off terrorist organizations. Ethiopia recently called the bluff politically and broke off ties with Qatar, accusing it of supporting and financing Islamist groups in Somalia and Eritrea. *The Peninsula*, 24 April 2008. Sheikh Hamad explicitly called for the evacuation of Ethiopian troops from Somalia in his speech to the Advisory council on 6 November 2007:

As for the situation in Somalia, we stress the unity of this fraternal country and its independence, as well as bringing about security and stability, one condition of which is the evacuation of foreign troops and sincere endeavour for national reconciliation that includes all categories and sectors of the Somali people.

http://www.diwan.gov.qa/english/the_Emir/the_Emir_speeche_77.htm (14 June 2009). See also Gary Sick, 'The coming crisis in the Persian Gulf', in *The Persian Gulf at the Millenium* (Basingstoke, 1997), pp. 12–21.

48 Some of this support seems to have a financial motivation as Qatar seeks to gain access to contracts. See 'Special report – Qatar's big Libya adventure', *Reuters Africa*. Online. Available http://af.reuters.com/article/energyOilNews/idAFLDE7570PX20110609 (9 June 2011).

49 Ahmed Saif, 'Deconstructing before building: Perspectives on democracy in Qatar', in A. Ehteshami and S. Wright (eds) *Reform in the Middle East Oil Monarchies* (Reading, 2008), p. 125; Durkheim: *On Morality and Society*, p. 70.

50 The influence of Persian merchants such as the Darwish and the Fardan on the ruling families of the Gulf is the central argument of Jill Crystal's book *Oil and Politics in the Gulf: Rulers and Merchants in Kuwait and Qatar* (Cambridge, 1995).

51 http://www.qsa.gov.qa/Eng/News/2008/Articles/13.htm (29 June 2009).

52 This is dramatically demonstrated by the Qatar Statistics Authority population pyramid: http://www.qsa.gov.qa/Eng/populationpyramid/PopulationPyramid.htm (29 June 2009).

53 Sick, 'The coming crisis'.

54 'Oil plays excessive role in Qatar economy', Gulfnews.com. Online. Available http://gulfnews.com/business/opinion/oil-plays-excessive-role-in-qatar-economy-1.848076 (7 August 2011). For *Quarterly Statistical Bulletins* in 2008 see http://www.qcb.gov.qa/English/Publications/Statistics/Pages/Statisticalbulletins.aspx

55 The reasons and motivations for former intelligence officers to make such revelations are often problematic and difficult to ascertain. Robert Baer, *Sleeping with the Devil: How Washington Sold Our Soul for Saudi Crude* (New York, 2003). Melissa Boyle Mahle, *Denial and Deception: An Insider's View of the CIA from Iran-Contra to 9/11* (New York, 2004); Patrick Tyler, 'Intelligence Break Led US to Tie Envoy Killing to Iraqi Qaeda Cell', *New York Times*, 6 February 2003. According to Tyler's unconfirmed information, the CIA discovered that a member of the royal family in Qatar, Abdul Karim Al-Thani, provided shelter to Abu Mussab al-Zarqawi, the former leader of Al-Qaeda in Iraq.

56 Ali al Allawi remarked,

In the past, the Shariah [Islamic law] connected Muslims' outer world with their inner realities. The eclipse of the Shariah by secular civil, commercial, and criminal law severed that connection. Some people see a desacralized world as a fertile ground for nurturing the private faith of the individual ... But Islam cannot easily co-exist with a political order that takes no heed of its inner dimensions. The integrity of Islam requires a delicate balance between the individual's spirituality and the demands of the community as a whole.

Chronicle of Higher Education Review. Online. Available http://chronicle.com/free/v55/i40/40allawi.htm?utm_source=cr&utm_medium=en (29 June 2009). See also Ali al Allawi's book, *The Crisis of Islamic Civilization* (New Haven, 2009). The theme of Stephen Humphrey's book, *Between Memory and Desire: The Middle East in A Troubled Age* (Berkeley, 2001), is similarly the long struggle between modernity and tradition in Islamic society. Unfortunately, most news reports only reveal the dramatic breaches between cave-dwelling terrorists and mile-high towers, ignoring the more widespread crisis in Islamic civilization as a whole.

57 'Secret US Embassy Cables'. Online. Available http://cablegate.wikileaks.org/cable/2009/12/09DOHA728.html. (28 November 2010).

58 Ibid.

59 Dale Eickelman, *The Past in Search of a Public: Folklore and Heritage in the Emirates and the Arab Gulf* (Zayed Center for Heritage and History, Dubai, 2000).

60 *Sacred Space and Holy War*, p. 189.

61 'Facebook Page calls for removal of Qatar's Emir', Reuters website. Online. Available http://in.reuters.com/article/2011/02/24/idINIndia-55131320110224 (21 September 2011).

62 See the Facebook page – http://www.facebook.com/the.Qatar.revolution.2011 (21 September 2011).

63 See 'Abortive coup in Qatar', Ennahar Online. Online. Available http://www.enna-haronline.com/en/international/5904.html (21 September 2011).

64 See her Facebook page, http://www.facebook.com/pages/HH-Sheikha-Mozah-Bint-Nasser-Al-Missned/10208116846 (21 September 2011).

65 Ali al-Shawi, 'Political Influences of Tribes in the State of Qatar: Impact of Tribal Loyalty on Political Participation', PhD dissertation (Mississippi State University, 2002).

CHAPTER 2

1. Qtd. Rosemarie Said Zahlan, in *The Creation of Qatar* (New York, 1979), p. 64. The Kingdom of Saudi Arabia did not come into existence until the unification of the kingdoms of the Nejd and the Hijaz in 1932.

2 Lieutenant Kemball notes that 'Qatar ... is so called from the greater fall of rain therein than in the other portions of Bani Khalid territory', *Records of Qatar*, p. 91.

3 United Nations Industrial Development Organization, *Qatar: Towards Industrial Diversification of an Oil-Based Economy*, 1988, p. 33.

4 'Bahrain, UAE launch summer hours work ban'. Online. Available http://www.ara-bianbusiness.com/560616-bahrain-uae-launch-summer-hours-work-ban (2 August 2009).

5 Fran Gillespie, a Qatari resident, has popularized the study of Qatar's flora, fauna and geography. See the first chapter of *Qatar*, a book financed by the Qatari Foreign Ministry (London, 2000).

6 'Saudis demand say in Emirates pipeline', *International Herald Tribune*, 12 July 2006. See *New York Times* archive. Online. Available http://www.nytimes.com/2006/07/12/business/worldbusiness/12iht-pipe.2180611.html (31 August 2011).

7 Fortunately the culture and practices of the the Bedouin of Qatar were recorded shortly before the disappearance of their way of life. See the rich and informative *Bedouins of Qatar*, by Klaus Ferdinand and Ida Nicolaisen of the Carlsberg Foundation's Nomad Research Project (Thames and Hudson, 1993).

8 Rosemarie Zahlan remarked in the late 1970s that 'Placed in the context of the Arab shaykhdoms of the Gulf ... Qatar is only strikingly different in one respect: it has never had any permanent inland settlements.' *The Creation of Qatar* (New York, 1979), p. 13.

9   Lorimer's Gazetteer was classified as secret when it was published by the British government in 1915. *Gazetteer of the Persian Gulf, Oman and Central Araiba,* 6 vols, (London: 1986), Archive Editions. It is interesting to note, as well, that the Naim did not yet convert to Wahhabi Islam until the late twentieth century. Qtd. in Ferdinand and Nicolaisen: *Bedouins of Qatar,* p. 41.

10   Qatar's inland was 'remarkably rich in wells, which was an essential precondition for the existence of the pastoral bedouins': Ferdinand and Nicolaisen: *Bedouins of Qatar,* p. 39. Many of these wells were masonry-lined.

11   Ferdinand and Nicolaisen: *Bedouins of Qatar,* p. 35.

12   Ibid.

13   Qtd in Ferdinand and Nicolaisen, *Bedouins of Qatar,* p. 49.

CHAPTER 3

1   Carnegie Mellon University heritage project, 'Zubara Town', *Heritage of Qatar,* http://www.heritageofqatar.org/

2   Charles Lindholm, *The Islamic Middle East: Tradition and Change,* revised edition (London, 2002), p. 6.

3   James Onley, 'Britain and the Gulf Sheikhdoms, 1820–1971: The politics of protection', *Center for International and Region Studies Occasional Papers* (2009), p. 1.

4   Tixier Jacques and Marie-Louise Inizan (eds), *Mission archéologique française au Qatar,* 2 Vols (Paris, 1980).

5   'Archaeological discovery in Western Qatar sheds new light on early man', *Gulf Times,* 7 September 2008.

6   Beatrice de Cardi, *Qatar Archaeological Report* (Oxford, 1979); Fran Gillespie, 'Steeped in antiquity', *Gulf Times,* Friday, 16 May 2008.

7   Isaac of Qatar should not be confused with the earlier, sixth-century Isaac the Syrian. H. Alfayev, Metropolitan of Kiev et al., *The Spiritual World of Isaac the Syrian* (Collegeville, Minnesota, 2001).

8   'Lost town unearthed by Lampeter archaeologist', *BBC Wales.* Online. Available http://www.bbc.co.uk/news/11032699 (20 August 2010).

9   'Affairs of the Persian Gulf', *Records of Qatar,* Vol. 1 (Oxford, 1991), p. 597.

10   Francis Warden (ed.), 'Uttoobee tribe of Arabs', *Records of Qatar,* pp. 397–8.

11   Francis Warden et al., 'Utub migration to the Qatar Peninsula and Bahrain: Historical sketch of the "Utub, 1716–1853" ', *Records of Qatar,* Vol. 1, p. 403.

12   *Porte* refers to the *Sublime Porte* of the Ottoman Sultan. Ibid, pp. 3–67, 59.

13   Ibid, p. 598.

14   See *Arabian Treaties 1600–1960*, Vol. 2, ed. P. Tuson and E. Quick, Cambridge: Cambridge archive Editions, 1992.

15   Routledge, 1986.

16   Lieutenant Kemball, 'Tribes inhabiting the Arabian shores', *Records of Qatar*, p. 88.

17   *Emergence of Qatar*, p. 10.

18   Kemball, *Records of Qatar*, p. 89.

19   J. G. Lorimer *Gazetteer of the Persian Gulf*, Vol. 1, Part 1B (Dublin, reprinted 1984) p. 832. 'The ability of the Sheikh of Doha to prevent piratical outrages was not entirely clear …'

20   Kemball, *Records of Qatar*, p. 99.

21   This is according to an analysis of Lorimer's figures: Lorimer, *Gazetteer of the Persian Gulf*, See also Zahlan, *The Creation of Qatar* (New York, 1979), p. 22.

22   Lorimer, *Gazetteer of the Persian Gulf*, Vol. 1B, p. 793.

23   Ibid, p. 802.

24   The Bani Khalid emirate ruled over much of the Persian Gulf and Al-Hasa fell to the Wahhabis in the 1790s. On the prominence of Al-Huwailah see Wilkinson, John, *Arabia's Frontiers: The Story of Britain's Boundary Drawing in the Desert* (London and New York, 1991), p. 42. Al-Musallam became a tributary of the Khalid, Bani. Zahlan, *The Creation of Qatar*, p. 18, describes Al- Musallam in Al-Huwailah, Al-Sudan in Fuwayrat and Al bin Ali in Doha/Bidaa before 1783.

25   According to Colonel Francis Beville Prideaux who visited the Sheikh at Al-Wusail in 1905 to gather information for Lorimer's *Gazetteer*: 'Sheikh Jassim bin Thani gives the pedigree of his grandfather as follows: Thani bin Muhammad bin Thani bin Ali bin Muhammad bin Salim bin Muhammad bin Jassim bin Sa'id bin Ali bin Thamir bin Muhammad bin Ali bin Ma'dhad bin Musharraf. He says that Ma'dhad [*sic*] governed the Jabrin Oasis, whence the family, at a later date, removed on account of the unhealthiness of the climate; after a sojourn at Kuwait they finally settled in Qatar.' The Ma'adhid did not come from Kuwait until around 1750. *Emergence of Qatar*, p. 17.

26   This was the obvervation of the Bombay Marine Coastal survey, *Emergence of Qatar*, p. 5.

27   Captain Brucks, 'Navigation of the Gulf of Persia', *Records of Qatar*, Vol. 1, p. 109.

28   Lorimer, *Gazetteer of the Persian Gulf*, p. 794.

29   Constable, 'Persian Gulf pilot', *Records of Qatar*, Vol. 2, p. 25.

30   Lorimer, *Gazetteer of the Persian Gulf*, Vol. I, p. 800.

31   This was subsequently ruled an invalid argument, see *Sacred Space and Holy War*, p. 189.

32   Rosemarie S. Zahlan, *The Making of The Gulf States*, p. 100.

33   Reproduced in a letter from Lieutenant-Colonel Lewis Pelly to C. Gonne, Secretary of the Government of Bombay, *Records of Qatar*, Vol. 2, pp. 124–5.

34   United Nations, *International Court of Justice, Reports of Judgments, Advisory Opinions and Orders* (2001), p. 307.

35   *Records of Qatar*, Vol. 2, p. 132.

36   The rather contrived meeting on board the *Vigilant* is described by Colonel Pelly in his letter to the Secretary of the Government of Bombay, *Records of Qatar*, Vol. 2, pp. 124–5.

37   *Records of Qatar*, Vol. 2, p. 131.

38   Ibid, p. 132.

39   Lisa Anderson, 'Absolutism and the resilience of Monarchy in the Middle East', *Political Science Quarterly*, Vol. 106, No. 1 (Spring 1991), p. 7.

40   Frederick Anscombe, *The Ottoman Gulf: The Creation of Kuwait, Saudi Arabia and Qatar* (New York, 1997), p. 2.

41   Qtd. in Rahman, *Emergence of Qatar*, p. 98.

42   Ibid.

43   Ibid, p. 106.

44   Ibid, p. 112.

45   http://www.ndqatar.com/english/index.php?page=about-nd (19 December 2009).

CHAPTER 4

1   New York, 1999.

2   *Ruling Families of Arabia, Qatar*, p. 272.

3   Ibid, p. 209.

4   From Major Knox, 'Political resident of Persian Gulf to foreign secretary of government of India', *Ruling Families of Arabia, Qatar*, p. 224.

5   Qtd. in Arnold T. Wilson, *The Persian Gulf: An Historical Sketch from the Earliest Times to the Beginning of the Twentieth Century* (London, 1954), p. 192.

6   Clive Leatherdale, *Britain and Saudi Arabia, 1925–1939: The Imperial Oasis* (London, 1983).

7   Shakespear, for instance, played a personal role in the rise of the House of Saud, perishing at a battle of Al Jarrab against the Rashid, the great rivals of the Saud. See Zahra Freeth and H. V. F. Winstone, *Explorers of Arabia: From the Renaissance to the End of the Victorian era* (London, 1978).

8   See Perceval Graves, *The Life of Sir Percy Cox* (London, 1941).

9   *Ruling Families of Arabia, Qatar*, p. 267.

10   Ibid, p. 268.

11 Abdallah refused the offer but it is striking how far the British were willing to go in securing the personal authority of Abdallah, *Ruling Families of Arabia, Qatar*, p. 272.

12 *Ruling Families of Arabia, Qatar*, p. 271.

13 Ibid, p. 266.

14 From a letter from J. H. H. Bill, 'Deputy political resident, Persian Gulf', *Ruling Families of Arabia, Qatar*, p. 279. Allegedly 'A good deal of arms smuggling' still went on in Doha after the agreement, p. 286.

15 *Ruling Families of Arabia, Qatar*, p. 265.

16 Ibid, p. 271.

17 Ibid, p. 272.

18 See, for instance, the incident described in a report in *Ruling Families of Arabia, Qatar*, p. 255.

19 Deputy Secretary to the Government of India to Political Resident in the Persian Gulf, 8 August 1921, qtd. in *Ruling Families of Arabia, Qatar*, p. 296.

20 Qtd. in Michael Herb, *All in the Family: Absolutism, Revolution and Democracy in the Middle Eastern Democracies* (New York, 1999), p. 30.

21 Rosemarie S. Zahlan, *The Making of the Modern Gulf States*, p. 101. The issue of the number of salutes given to a particular Emir in the Gulf led to that particular game of quantifying honour so peculiar to British society and culture. Fewer gun salutes meant that the Empire was somehow displeased with a particular sheikh or held him in lower regard.

22 Zahlan, *The Making of the Modern Gulf States*, p. 27.

23 *Ruling Families of Arabia, Qatar*, p. 302.

24 Ibid, p. 303.

25 From a conversation with Abdallah recorded by Captian Prior, Political Agent, Bahrain, 1930, qtd. in *Ruling Families of Arabia, Qatar*, p. 318.

26 From the Persian Gulf Political Resident Lieutenant-Colonel Haworth's account, *Ruling Families of Arabia, Qatar*, p. 344.

27 Ibid, p. 345.

28 Political Resident, Bahrain, to Resident Bushire, qtd. in *Ruling Families of Arabia, Qatar*, p. 349.

29 R. W. Ferrier, *The History of the British Petroleum Company* (Cambridge, 1982), Vol. 1.

30 Rosemarie Said Zahlan, *Creation of Qatar* (London, 1979), p. 71.

31 Ibid.

32 Ibid, pp. 74–5.

33 Nasser Othman, *With their Bare Hands: The Story of the Oil Industry in Qatar* (London, 1984), pp. 137–46. Petroleum Development Qatar Ltd. was later named Qatar Petroleum Company and then simply Qatar Petroleum.

34 Zahlan, *The Making of the Modern Gulf States*, p. 103.

35 Ibid. 103.

CHAPTER 5

1 See Joseph Kéchichian, *Power and Succession in Arab Monarchies*, p. 199.

2 Sheikh Khalifa bin Hamad Al-Thani, *Speeches and Statements* (Qatar, 1978), Preface.

3 Economist Intelligence Unit, *The Arabian Peninsula: Sheikhdoms and Republics*, first quarter 1978, p. 16.

4 Jill Crystal, *Oil and Politics in the Gulf* (Cambridge, 1990), p. 155.

5 Ibid, p. 158.

6 Kéchichian, *Power and Succession in Arab Monarchies*, p. 201.

7 United Nations Development Organization, *Qatar: Towards Industrial Diversification of an Oil-Based Economy*, Industrial Development Review Series (1988), p. 13.

8 United Nations Development Organization: *Qatar*, p. 16.

9 Ibid, p. 19.

10 Ibid, p. 32.

11 Economist Intelligence Unit, 'Country Profile: Bahrain and Qatar, 1995–96', *Middle East Economic Digest*, 10 May 1996, p. 3.

12 Kéchichian, *Power and Succession in Arab Monarchies*, p. 199.

CHAPTER 6

1 According to an official announcement to the Advisory Council by Sheikh Hamad, http://www.diwan.gov.qa/english/the_Emir/the_Emir_speeche_83.htm (14 June 2009).

2 This is according to the US Energy Information Administration statistics, http://www.eia.gov/cabs/qatar/Full.html (September, 2011).

3 Ibid.

4 United Nations, *Qatar*, p. 31.

5 'Such biological resources could ultimately be used to develop oil spill remediation', Renee Richer, 'Conservation in Qatar: Impacts of increasing industrialization', *Georgetown Center for International and Regional Studies*, Occasional Paper (Doha, Qatar, 2008), p. 2.

6 http://www.qatarembassy.net/Emir.asp

7 Although conflicting accounts and rumours abound, one of the best accounts synthesizing news reports of the 1995 coup can be found in Michael Herb, *All in the Family: Absolutism, Revolution and Democracy in the Middle Eastern Democracies* (New York, 1999), pp. 116–19.

8 Kéchichian, *Power and Succession in Arab Monarchies*, p. 213.

9 Ibid, p. 219.

10 A. Guillaume, *The Life of Muhammad* (Oxford, 1955), pp. 84–7.

11 'Qatar, playing all sides, is a nonstop mediator', *New York Times*. Online. Available www.nytimes.com/2008/07/09/world/middleeast/09qatar.html (9 July 2008).

12 'Qatar, playing all sides, is a non-stop negotiator', *New York Times*. Online. Available http://www.nytimes.com/2008/07/09/world/middleeast/09qatar.html?pagewanted=print (9 July 2008).

13 This is the argument of political analyst Dr Fahd bin Abdul Rahman Al-Thani, 'Qatar's foreign policy: Small country, big ambitions'. Online. Available http://www.islamonline.net/servlet/Satellite?c=Article_C&pagename=Zone-English-Muslim_Affairs%2FMAELayout&cid=1213871606942 (8 July 2008).

14 'Qatar discloses mediation in Iraq, Libya and Sudan', Arabicnews.com. Online. Available www.arabicnews.com/ansub/Daily/Day/040101/2004010111.html (1 January 2004).

15 'Qatar extends its influence still further', *Daily Telegraph*. Online. Available http://www.telegraph.co.uk/news/worldnews/middleeast/qatar/7701689/Qatar-extends-its-influence-still-further.html (11 May 2010).

16 For a description of the coup attempt see Joseph Kéchichian, *Power and Succession in Arab Monarchies*, London and Boulder, 2008, p. 200.

17 'Sudan to review chad peace deals in Qatar', Reuters.com. Online. Available http://www.reuters.com/article/homepageCrisis/idUSLU641448._CH_.2400 (30 April 2009).

18 'Qatar discloses mediation in Iraq, Libya and Sudan', Arabicnews.com. Online. Available www.arabicnews.com/ansub/Daily/Day/040101/2004010111.html (1 January 2004).

19 'Qatar emerges as a mediatior between Fatah and Hamas', *New York Times*. Online. Available http://www.nytimes.com/2006/10/10/world/middleeast/10mideast.html (10 October 2006).

20 'Qatar steps into the breach', *International Security Network* (Zurich). Online. Available http://www.isn.ethz.ch/isn/Current-Affairs/Security-Watch/Detail/?ots591=4888CAA0-B3DB-1461-98B9-E20E7B9C13D4&lng=en&id=98148 (24 March 2009).

21 Wikileaks, 'Secret US embassy cables'. Online. Available http://cablegate.wikileaks.org/cable/2009/02/09CAIRO231.html (28 November 2010).

22 'Qatar steps into the breach', *International Security Network* (Zurich). Online. Available http://www.isn.ethz.ch/isn/Current-Affairs/Security-Watch/Detail/?ots591=4888CAA0-

B3DB-1461-98B9-E20E7B9C13D4&lng=en&id=98148 (24 March 2009). The Georgia State University scholar Isa Blumi's account of Al-Houthi rebellion provides new information about the complexities of the conflict and Qatar's involvement in resolving the dispute: *Chaos in Yemen: Societal Collapse and the New Authoritarianism* (New York and London).

23 'Western Sahara: Annan welcomes release of 100 Moroccan prisoners-of-war', *UN News Centre*. Online. Available http://www.un.org/apps/news/story.asp?NewsID=9869&Cr=western&Cr1=sahar (24 February 2004).

24 Political Agent of Kuwait to Political Resident in Bushire, 1934, *Ruling Families of Arabia* (Qatar), p. 399.

25 'Sixty-nine per cent of Qataris felt that the description [cold war] fitted their current relations with Saudi Arabia – with only 40% of Saudis sharing the view, 30% disagreeing and 30% who said they didn't know', See 'This House believes that after Gaza Arab unity is dead and buried', *Doha Debates*. Online. Available http://www.dohadebates.com/debates/debate.asp?d=47&mode=opinions (20 September 2011).

26 'Politics and defense', *Gulf States Newsletter*. Online. Available http://www.gsn-online.com/SSIs/GSNs_WORLD/Saudi_Arabia/documents/Saudi-447.PDF (1992).

27 Ibid.

28 'Thousands in Saudi Arabia After Losing Qatari Citizenship', Gulfnews.com. Online. Available http://gulfnews.com/news/gulf/qatar/thousands-in-saudi-arabia-after-losing-qatari-citizenship-1.283103 (September 2011).

29 *Bedouin of Qatar*, p. 50. Also, see Cole, Donald, *The Al Murrah Bedouin of the Empty Quarter* (Chicago, 1975), p. 2.

30 Jill Crystal, 'Political reform and the prospects for transition in the Gulf', *FRIDE Working Paper*, No. 11, p. 1.

31 Ahmed Saif, 'Deconstructing before building: Perspectives on democracy in Qatar', in Anoushiravan Ehteshami and Steven Wright (eds), *Reform in the Middle East Oil Monarchies* (London, 2008), p. 104.

32 Juan Cole, *Engaging the Muslim World* (New York, 2009), p. 110.

33 Qtd. in Jill Crystal, *Oil and Politics in the Gulf* (Cambridge, 1990), p. 113.

34 'Al-Jazeera no longer a hammer to the Saudis', *International Herald Tribune*, 12 January 2008.

35 'Persian Gulf states Bahrain and Qatar to be linked via Causeway', *Associated Press*, 11 June 2006.

36 'Qatar-Bahrain causeway to be ready by 2015', http://www.thepeninsulaqatar.com/qatar/150343-qatar-bahrain-causeway-to-be-ready-by-2015.html (20 September 2011).

37 Wikileaks. Online. Available http://cablegate.wikileaks.org/cable/2009/07/09MANAMA442. (28 November 2010).

38   United Nations: *Qatar*, p. 24.

39   'Qatar national bank denies investing in Iran oilfield', http://www.reuters.com/
       article/GCA-Oil/idUSTRE59318Y20091004 (4 October 2009).

40   Rosemarie Said Zahlan, *The Creation of Qatar* (London, 1979), pp. 28–9.

41   'Envoy calls for "leap forward" in Qatar-Iran ties', *Gulf Times*. Online. Available
       http://www.gulftimes.com/site/topics/article.asp?cu_no=2&item_no=305738
       &version=1&template_id=57&parent_id=56 (28 July 2009).

42   Anthony Cordesman, *Bahrain, Oman, Qatar and the UAE: Challenges of Security*
       (Boulder, Colorado, 1997), p. 213.

43   CNN.com, 'New NATO Chief warns of Afghan Terror Grand Central'. Online.
       Available   http://articles.cnn.com/2009-08-03/world/nato.rasmussen_1_new-
       nato-strategic-concept-international-security-assistance-force?_s=PM:WORLD
       (September 2011).

44   Wikileaks. Online. Available http://cablegate.wikileaks.org/cable/2009/08/09
       DOHA502.html (28 November 2010).

45   Wikileaks. Online. Available http://cablegate.wikileaks.org/cable/2010/02/10
       DOHA70.html (28 November 2010).

46   *Qatar Petoleum Annual Report* (2005), p. 25.

47   Wikileaks. Online. Available http://cablegate.wikileaks.org/cable/2009/12/09
       DOHA733.html (28 November 2010).

48   Cole, *Engaging the Muslim World*, p. 106.

49   Qtd. in 'Cables obtained by Wikileaks shine light into secret diplomatic chan-
       nels', *New York Times*. Online. Available http://www.nytimes.com/2010/11/29/
       world/29cables.html?_r=1&hp (28 November 2010).

50   Raymond Ibrahim (ed.), *Al-Qaeda Reader* (New York, 2002), pp. 101–2.

51   Mehran Kamrava, 'Royal factionalism and political liberalization in Qatar', *The
       Middle East Journal*, 63/3 (Summer 2009), p. 414.

52   On alleged Qatari contacts with Al-Qaeda, see the controversial 1 May 2005 report
       in *The Times*, 'Qatar buys off Al-Qaeda attacks with oil millions'. According to the
       article, senior Qatari officials claimed they had agreed to send Al-Qaeda millions
       in protection money. One official allegedly said, 'We are a soft target and prefer to
       pay to secure our national and economical interests. We are not the only ones doing
       so.' There are several reasons to question the veracity of this article. First, there is
       the fact that the name of the source is not revealed. There is also the fact that the
       article was published at a time when the British press were focussed on terrorist
       threats, and indeed, two months later, on 7/7, the UK was subject to a terrible and
       unforgiveable attack on its citizens; in a country previously largely considered 'safe'
       for foreigners, this provoked press outrage. Whether *The Times*' claims are true or
       not, the lack of transparency in the Qatari government will only invite further

speculation about the 'true nature' of Qatar's contacts with international terrorist networks.

53   *New York Times*, 29 October 1993, p. A10.

54   'Israelis may stay home to avoid arrest in Europe', *Washington Post*. Online. Available   http://washingtontimes.com/news/2009/oct/13/israelis-may-stay-home-to-avoid-arrest/?feat=home_top5_shared (13 October 2009).

55   Uzi Rabi, 'Qatar's relations with Israel: Challenging Arab and Gulf norms', *The Middle East Journal* 63/3 (Summer 2009), pp. 443–60.

56   Uzi Rabi, 'Qatar's relations with Israel', *Telavivnotes: An Update on Middle Eastern Developments by the Moshe Dayan Center*, 7 October 2008, pp. 3–4.

57   Matthew Levitt, *Hamas: Politics, Charity and Terrorism in the Service of Jihad* (New Haven, 2009), p. 198.

58   Simon Smith, *Britain's Revival and Fall in the Gulf* (London and New York, 2004), pp. 138–9. Following the Wikileaks saga, the British Foreign Office, of course, has a reputation for being rather less than diplomatic in much of its offical correspondence!

59   New York, 2004.

60   Jimmy Carter, 'State of the Union Address' (23 January 1980). Online. Available from USA-Presidents.org website. http://www.usa-presidents.info/union/carter-3.html (11 August 2011).

61   'Qatar opens ties to Moscow at times of strains with U.S.', *New York Times*, 2 August 1988.

62   Christopher Blanchard, *CRS Report for Congress: Qatar: Background and U.S. Relations* (Washington, DC, 2008), p. 8.

63   London, 2007.

64   The Israeli interest section would reopen and close (sometimes only partially) again. The presence of the Israeli 'ambassador' (there was no embassy, so technically ambassadorial status was not granted) during the endless circuit of official conferences and conventions in Doha would often lead to a somewhat comical shifting of chairs as foreign diplomats and Qataris moved to avoid the appearance of favouring Israel by sitting next to the Israeli envoy. Adding further irony, the Israeli interest section in Doha practically neighbours the villa of Khaled Mishal, leader of Hamas.

65   Christopher Blanchard *CRS Report for Congress: Qatar: Background and U.S. Relations* (Washington DC, 2008).

66   *9/11 Commission Report*, p. 147.

67   Christopher Blanchard, *CRS Report for Congress*, p. 9.

68   http://www.qatarkatrinafund.org/

69   'US will move air operations to Qatar base', *New York Times*, 28 April 2003.

70   'US speeding up missle defenses in the Persian Gulf', *New York Times*. Online. Available http://www.nytimes.com/2010/01/31/world/middleeast/31missile.html?hp (30 January 2010).

71   In June 2009 the author failed to access Islamonline.net from several locations in Tunisia. Access to Al-Jazeera.net was not similarly blocked.

72   I participated in a tour of Al-Jazeera headquarters in March 2008. 'Reporters without Borders outraged at bombing of Al-Jazeera offices in Baghdad'. Online. Available http://www.rsf.org/article.php3?id_article=5945 (8 April 2003).

73   Cole, *Engaging the Muslim World*, p. 108. Also, Juan Cole 'Did Bush plan to bomb Al-Jazeera?', Salon.com. Online. Available http://dir.salon.com/story/opinion/feature/2005/11/30/al_jazeera (30 November 2005).

CHAPTER 7

1   Michael Herb, 'No representation without taxation? Rents, development and democracy', *Comparative Politics*, 37/3 (April 2005), p. 299.

2   'Qatar to impose income tax', Reuters.com. Online. Available http://www.reuters.com/article/hotStocksNews/idUSLH60897120091117 (17 November 2009).

3   M. Herb, 'No representation without taxation?', p. 301.

4   'Oil's drop squeezes producers', *The Wall Street Journal*, 10 October 2008, p. A3. See the chart published with the article.

5   Terry L. Karl, *The Paradox of Plenty: Oil Booms and Petro-States* (Berkeley, 1997).

6   Jill Crystal, *Oil and Politics in the Gulf: Rulers and Merchants in Kuwait and Qatar* (Cambridge, 1990), pp. 6–7.

7   'Does oil hinder democracy?', *World Politics*, Vol. 53 (April 2001), pp. 356–7.

8   M. Herb, 'No representation without taxation?', p. 297.

9   Ibid, p. 299.

10   Crystal, *Oil and Politics in the Gulf*, p. 2.

11   Boston: Houghton Mifflin Co., 1934, p. 46.

12   M. Herb, 'No representation without taxation?', p. 306.

13   William G. Palgrave, *Narrative of a Year's Journey*, Vol. II (England, 1968), p. 232.

14   M. G. Rumaihi, 'The mode of production in the Arab Gulf before the discovery of oil', in Tim Niblock (ed.), *Social and Economic Development in the Arab Gulf* (London, 1980), p. 57.

15   Crystal, *Oil and Politics in the Gulf*, p. 5.

16   The song and the Asian Games performance on YouTube is extremely popular with Qataris. I was shown it several times by students at Qatar University, who

seemed especially proud that it was Qatari women, rather than foreign performers as is usually the case with such cultural performances, who were showing Qatar's traditions to the world.

17 Richard Bowen, 'The pearl fisheries of the Persian Gulf', *Middle East Journal*, Vol. 5, No. 2 (Spring 1951), p. 165.

18 Muhammad Jassim al Khulaifi, *Al Khor Museum* (Doha, Qatar, 1990), p. 15.

19 'Apparently most of the divers from the Jowasim area were slaves. In the boats putting out from the Qatar ports, however, the crews were free tribesmen, often from the interior.' Louise Sweet, 'Pirates or polities? Arab societies of the Persian or Arabian Gulf, 18th century', *Enthnohistory*, 11/3 (Summer 1964), p. 272.

20 J. G. Lorimer, *Gazetteer of the Persian Gulf*, Vol. 1, Part II, p. 2288.

21 Bowen, 'The pearl fisheries of the Persian Gulf', p. 171.

22 The existence of cultured pearls did not initially mean the death of traditional pearling. However, the difficulty of distinguishing cultured pearls and real pearls, and even the preference among some for uniform cultured pearls, cut the value of pearls to about a tenth of what it had been before.

23 Jassim al Kahyat, *Marine Revolution* (Dubai, 2005), p. 89.

24 *Travels in Arabia* (London, 1838), p. 264.

25 Al Kheat, *Marine Resources* (Doha, 2005), pp. 89–102. Lorimer also discusses the extent of pearl-fishing in some detail in in his *Gazetteer of the Persian Gulf*. Only estimates of the number of pearling ships, however, have been made. In 1896 M. Zwemer estimated that Qatar had only some 200 boats: *Cradle of Islam* (New York, 1900), pp. 100–1.

26 Qtd. in Jill Crystal, *Oil and Politics in the Gulf*, p. 117.

27 Ibid.

28 Bowen, 'The pearl fisheries of the Persian Gulf', p. 162.

29 Saleh Hassan Mohammed Abdulla, 'Labor, Nationalism and Imperialism in Eastern Arabia: Britain, the Sheikhs and the Gulf Oil Workers in Bahrein, Kuwait and Qatar, 1932–1956', PhD dissertation (Michigan, 1991).

30 http://markets.on.nytimes.com/research/markets/commodities/commodities.asp (10 June 2009).

31 'Oversupply in housing likely by next year', *The Peninsula*, 6 September 2009.

32 http://www.marketresearch.com/Business-Monitor-International-v304/Qatar-Real-Estate-Q3-6459719 (20 September 2011).

33 'Real estate market stabilizing', *The Peninsula*, 6 September 2009.

34 'Summary of landmark advisory report', http://www.landmark-dubai.com/lmp_advisory_press_0608_eng.php (6 October 2009).

35   http://www.onlineqatar.com/jobs/136-High-rate-of-unemployment-among-Qatari-women,-reveal-expert.htm (6 October 2009).

36   *The Wall Street Journal*. Online. Available http://online.wsj.com/article/BT-CO-20090922-708315.html (22 September 2009).

37   'Qatar finmin says economy to grow 7–9% in '09 –CNN', Reuters.com. Online. Available http://in.reuters.com/article/oilRpt/idINLQ65481020090726 (1 August 2009).

38   The decline of the car industry, and Porsche in particular, has revealed the perils of such luxury investments. 'Porsche casts Macht in "survival mode" as CEO departs', bloomberg.com. Online. Available http://www.bloomberg.com/apps/news?pid=20601100&sid=aLxPNEKVpQEQ (1 August 2009).

CHAPTER 8

1   'Ibn Thani is a merchant prince, he derives his power from wealth accumulated by his father and grandfather from pearling and trading.' Dickson, qtd. in Jill Crystal, *Oil and Politics in the Gulf: Rulers and Merchants in Kuwait and Qatar* (Cambridge, 1990), pp. 113–14.

2   Jill Crystal, 'Coalitions in oil monarchies: Kuwait and Qatar', *Comparative Politics* (July 1989), pp. 427–43, 440.

3   Michael Herb, *All in the Family: Absolutism, Revolution and Democracy in the Middle Eastern Democracies* (New York, 1999), p. 31, Table 2.1.

4   'The world's richest royals', Forbes.com, 8 August 2008. Online. Available http://www.forbes.com/2008/08/20/worlds-richest-royals-biz-richroyals08-cz_ts_0820royal_slide_8.html?thisSpeed=15000 (14 June 2009).

5   Transparency International, *Corruption Perceptions Index* (2009). Online. Available http://www.transparency.org/policy_research/surveys_indices/cpi/2009

6   This was about average for the region according to Vahan Zanoyan, CEO of the Petroleum Finance Company of Washington. See Gary Sick, 'The coming crisis', p. 21, In 2008 at the opening of the 37th session of the Advisory Council, a body composed of mainly non-royal Qatari tribal representatives, the Emir remarked, 'A number of bottleneck areas have risen in the economy, caused by the big increase in expatriate labour'. Online. Available http://www.diwan.gov.qa/english/the_Emir/the_Emir_speeche_83.htm (14 June 2009).

7   'Qatar resolves citizenship issue', *BBC News*, 9 February 2006. Online. Available http://news.bbc.co.uk/2/hi/middle_east/4698152.stm (1 October 2009).

8   Gerd Nonneman, 'Political reform in the Gulf monarchies: From liberalization to democratization? A comparative perspective', in Anoushiravan Ehteshami and Steven Wright (eds), *Reform in the Middle East Oil Monarchies* (London, 2008), pp. 3–47, 34; *CIA Factbook*. Online. Available https://www.cia.gov/library/publications/the-world-factbook/geos/qa.html (30 October 2009).

9   Nathan Brown, *The Rule of Law in the Arab World: Courts in Egypt and the Gulf* (Cambridge, 1997), p. 183, Qtd in *Bedouin of Qatar*, p. 49.

10 Jill Crystal, p. 6.

11 'Qatar's new supreme court has potential to force modernization of legal system', *Jurist*. Online. Available http://jurist.law.pitt.edu/hotline/2009/10/qatars-new-supreme-court-has-potential.php (5 October 2009).

12 Mehran Kamrava, 'Royal factionalism and political liberalization in Qatar', *Middle East Journal*, 63/3 (Summer 2009), p. 401.

13 Douglas North, *Institutions, Institutional Change and Economic Performance* (Cambridge, 1990). There have been some recent endeavours to understand better the exact role of informal institutions in the state. See Gretchen Helmke and Steven Levitsky, 'Informal institututions and comparative politics: A research agenda', *Perspectives on Politics*, 2/4 (2004), pp. 725–40.

14 Joseph Stigliz, 'Formal and informal institutions', in Ismail Serageldin, and Partha Dasgupta (eds), *Social Capital: A Multifaceted Perspective* (Washington, DC, 2001), pp. 59–71.

15 Daniel Brumberg, 'Democratization in the Arab world? The trap of liberalized autocracy', *Journal of Democracy*, 13/4 (October 2002), p. 59.

16 'The national'. Online. Available http://www.thenational.ae/apps/pbcs.dll/article?AID=/20090620/FOREIGN/706199868/1408/FORIEGN (21 October 2009).

17 Herb, *All in the Family*, p. 111.

18 Ibid, p. 109.

19 Rosemarie S. Zahlan, *The Making of the Modern Gulf States*, revised edition (London, 1998), p. 104.

20 J. C. Hurewitz, *Middle East Politics: The Military Dimension* (New York, 1974), p. 18.

21 Michael Knights and Anna Soloman-Schwartz, The broader threat from Sunni Islamists in the Gulf', *Policy Watch*, No. 33 (Washington Institute for Near East Policy, 19 July 2004).

22 Mehran Kamrava, 'Royal factionalism and political liberalization in Qatar', p. 401.

23 'Qatar energy Minister replaced', *Wall Street Journal*. Online. Available http://online.wsj.com/article/SB10001424052748703954004576090843270084546.html (Online 20 September 2011).

24 Ali al-Shawi, 'Political Influences of Tribes in the State of Qatar: Impact of Tribal Loyalty on Political Participation', PhD dissertation (Mississippi, 2002).

25 Rosemarie Said Zahlan, *The Creation of Qatar* (London, 1979), p. 115.

26 See the list of Advisory Council members. Online. Available http://www.qatarembassy.net/advisory.asp (30 October 2009).

27   Mehran Kamrava, 'Royal factionalism and political liberalization in Qatar', p. 403.

28   Ibid, p. 413.

29   Crystal, *Oil and Politics in the Gulf*, p. 9.

30   *On Morality and Society*, p. 70.

31   J. G. Lorimer, *Gazetteer of the Persian Gulf, Vol. II: Oman and Central Arabia* (Westmead, UK, 1970), p. 1515.

32   Zahlan, p. 21.

33   Extract from the diary of the Political Agent, Bahrain, 13 December 1907, *Ruling Families of Arabia*, Vol. 1, p. 195.

34   Rosemarie Said Zahlan, *The Creation of Qatar*, p. 17.

35   A. Montigny-Kozlowska, 'Histoire et changements sociaux au Qatar', in P. Bonnenfant (ed.), *La Péninsule arabique d'aujourd'hui*, Vol. 2 (Paris, 1982), p. 501.

36   *Records of Qatar*, p. 603.

37   *Ruling Families of Arabia, Qatar*, p. 236.

38   Ibid, p. 203.

39   Ibid, p. 255.

40   Jill Crystal, *Oil and Politics in the Gulf*, pp. 143–4.

41   'Qatar studies new law to tackle human trafficing', *Gulf News*. Online. Available http://gulfnews.com/news/gulf/qatar/qatar-studies-new-law-to-tackle-human-trafficking-1.183920 (12 June 2007).

42   'Qatar: A possible coup attempt?', www.stratfor.com (3 August 2009).

43   *Middle East Report* blog. Online. Available http://mideasti.blogspot.com/2009/08/those-qatari-coup-rumors.html (10 November 2010).

44   Miriam Joyce, *Ruling Sheikhs and Her Majesty's Government, 1960–1969* (London, 2002), pp. 40–3.

45   Ibid, p. 41.

46   Ibid, p. 43.

47   Ibid.

48   Jill Crystal, *Oil and Politics in the Gulf*, p. 154.

49   Ahmed Saif, 'Deconstructing before building: Perspectives on democracy in Qatar', in Ehteshami, A. and Wright, S. (eds), *Reform in the Middle East Oil Monarchies* (Reading, UK, 2008), p. 113.

50   Ibid, p. 111.

51   'Secretariat General: The Planning Council', *Civil Society Organizations in Qatar* (Doha, Qatar, 2004).

52   *Awal Bait al Dimaqratiyya fi Qatar* (Doha, Qatar, 2001).

53   Ali al-Shawi, 'Political Influences of Tribes.in the State of Qatar: Impact of Tribal Loyalty on Political Participation', PhD dissertation (Mississippi, 2002).

54   A. Montigny-Kozlowska, 'Histoire et changements sociaux au Qatar', p. 493.

55   Marina Ottaway, 'Evaluating Middle East reform: How do we know when it is significant?', *Carnegie Papers, Middle East Series*, No. 56 (February 2005), pp. 3–5.

56   Thomas Carothers, 'The end of the transition paradigm', *Journal of Democracy*, Vol. 13 (January 2002), pp. 4–21.

57   'Natural gas glut overwhelms speculators, defies rally', Bloomburg.com. Online. Available http://www.bloomberg.com/apps/news?pid=20601109&sid=agwUppniRIgE& pos=14 (30 November 2009).

58   Ibid.

59   Ministry of Endowments and Islamic Affairs, *18th Annual Report, 2006–2007* (Doha, Qatar), p. 22.

60   Jill Crystal, *Oil and Politics in the Gulf*, p. 3.

61   'Education: Government struggles to sell school reform', *Financial Times*, 18 November 2009.

62   'Spending on education at all-time high', *The Peninsula*. Online. Available http:// www.thepeninsulaqatar.com/Display_news.asp?section=Local_News&subsecti on=Qatar+News&month=December2009&file=Local_News2009121251732. xml (12 December 2009).

CONCLUSION

1   Council on Foreign Relations Press, 1994.

2   New York, 2008.

3   'Laid-off foreigners flee as Dubai spirals down', *The New York Times*. Online. Available http://www.nytimes.com/2009/02/12/world/middleeast/12dubai. html?scp=3&sq=dubai%20&st=cse (1 August 2009).

4   New York, 1995.

5   Gary G. Sick and Lawrence G. Potter (eds), *The Persian Gulf at the Millenium: Essays in Politics, Economy, Security and Religion* (New York, 1997), pp. 11–31. Gary Sick, however, may prove correct in his statement (p. 12): 'Widespread agreement about the political realities of any set of countries always warrants a measure of skepticism, and that has been particularly true in the turbulent waters of the Persian Gulf, where assuring perceptions of stability have had an unpleasant habit of giving way to unpleasant and unpredictable political surprises.' As Sick notes, the new consensus does seem to support the theory of sustainable monarchy in the Gulf and the 'burden of proof' is now on those who say the 'sky is falling' (p. 13).

6 Montigny-Kozlowska, 'Histoire et changements sociaux au Qatar', pp. 475–517, 476.

7 Lisa Anderson, 'Absolutism and the resilience of monarchy in the Middle East', *Political Science Quarterly*, 106/1 (Spring 1991), pp. 1–15.

8 State University of New York Press, 1999, p. 3.

9 Stanford University Press, 2007. The anecdote of a recent historical re-enactment of the meeting between FDR and the Saudi king is most illuminating.

10 'Poetics and politics of newly invented traditions in the Gulf: Camel racing in the United Arab Emirates', *Ethnology*, 39/5 (Summer 2000), pp. 243–61.

11 http://www.cansultmaunsell.com/MarketsAndServices/52/83/index.html, AECOM, the company developing and designing the Cultural Village, is based in Los Angeles, California.

12 Prince Charles's letters to Sheikh Hamad seem to have had their desired effect, as *Prospect Magazine* reports in 'Paying the price for grand designs', Vol. 161 (August 2009): 'This June [2009], the architects Rogers Stirk Harbour were unceremoniously sacked from a job designing a multi-billion pound housing project on the site of the former Chelsea Barracks. The reasons were not fully explained, and there may have been more than one, but the most obvious was that Prince Charles had written privately to the site's owners, the Qatari Royal Family, urging them to reject the Rogers design.' Online. Available http://www.prospect-magazine.co.uk/article_details.php?id=1093 (22 July 2009).

Bibliography

Note: This is not meant to be a comprehensive bibliography on Qatar. Cited here are representative works that were used in the writing of this book.

al-Abdulla, Yusuf Ibrahim (2000). *A Study of Qatari-British Relations 1914–1945*, Doha.

Abeer, Abu Saud (1984). *Qatari Women: Past and Present*, London.

Abulfatih, Hussain, et al. (1999). *Desertification and Natural Resources in Qatar*, Qatar: University of Qatar.

Aburish, Said (1995). *The Rise, Corruption and Coming Fall of the House of Saud*, New York: St Martin's Press.

Alderson, A. D. (1956). *The Structure of the Ottoman Dynasty*, Oxford: Oxford University Press.

ali Saleh, Kamal (nd). *Development of the Qatar Economy from Pearl Fishing to Oil Production 1860–1949*, Qatar.

Anderson, Lisa (Winter 1991). 'Absolutism and the resilience of monarchy in the Middle East', *Comparative Politics*, 20/1, pp. 1–15.

———— (1999). 'Politics in the Middle East: Opportunities and limits in the quest for theory', in Mark Tessler, Jodi Nachtwey and Anne Banda (eds), *Area Studies and Social Science: Strategies for Understanding Middle East Politics*, Bloomington, IN: Indiana University Press, pp. 1–10.

Anderson, Perry (1974). *Lineages of the Absolutist State*, London: Verso.

Arabian Treaties, 1600–1960 (1991). Penelope Tuson and Emma Quick (eds), Oxford.

Arjomand, Said (1992). 'Constitutions and the struggle for political order: A study in the modernization of political traditions', *Archives Europeennes de Sociologie*, 33/1, pp. 39–82.

Arkoun, Mohammed (1987). *Rethinking Islam Today*, Occasional Papers Series, Center for Contemporary Arab Studies, Washington DC: Georgetown University, pp. 1–25.

Bahry, Louay (June 1999). 'Elections in Qatar: A window of democracy opens in the Gulf', *Middle East Policy*, 6/4.

Bahry, Louay and Marr, Phebe (2005). 'Qatari women: A new generation of leaders? *Middle East Policy*, No. 12, pp. 104–19.

Balfour-Paul, Glen (1991). *The End of Empire in the Middle East: Britain's Relinquishment of Power in Her Last Three Arab Dependencies*, Cambridge: Cambridge University Press.

Bates, Robert H. (March 1991). 'The economics of transitions to democracy', *PS: Political Science and Politics*, 24/1, pp. 24–7.

Beblawi, Hazem (1990). 'The rentier state in the Arab world', in Giacomo Luciani (ed.), *The Arab State*, Berlekey, CA: University of California Press, pp. 85–98.

Belgrave, Chalres (1967). 'Persian Gulf: Past and present', *Speech at Royal Central Asian Society*, 28 June 1967.

Belgrave, Daltrymble (1934). 'Pearl diving in Bahrain', *Journal of the Royal Central Asian Society*, Vol. XXI.

Belgrave, James (1965). *Welcome to Bahrain*, 5th edition, London: The Augustan Press.

Berrebi, Claude, Martorell, Francisco and Tanner, Jeffery (Summer 2009). 'Qatar's labor markets at a crossroad, *The Middle East Journal*, 63/3, pp. 421–42.

Blanchard, Christopher (2008). *CRS Report for Congress: Qatar: Background and U.S. Relations*, Washington, DC.

Bowen, Richard (Spring 1951). 'The pearl fisheries of the Persian Gulf', *Middle East Journal*, 5/2, pp. 161–80.

Brumberg, Daniel (October 2002). 'Democratization in the Arab world? The trap of liberalized autocracy', *Journal of Democracy*, 13/4.

Central Intelligence Agency (1988). *OECD Trade with Middle East: A Reference Aid*, Langley, Virginia.

Cole, Donald P. (1975). *Nomads of the Nomads: The Al Murrah Bedouin of the Empty Quarter*, Chicago: Aldine Publishing.

Cole, Juan (2009). *Engaging the Muslim World*, New York.

Cordesman, Anthony (1993). *After the Storm: The Changing Military Balance in the Middle East*, Boulder, CO: Westview.

——— (1997). *Bahrain, Oman, Qatar, and the UAE: Challenges of Security*, Boulder, CO.

Cottrell, Alvin J. (1980). *The Persian Gulf States*, London.

Crystal, Jill (1990). *Oil and Politics in the Gulf: Rulers and Merchants in Kuwait and Qatar*, Cambridge: Cambridge University Press.

——— (1994). 'Authoritarianism and its Adversaries in the Arab World,' *World Politics*, 46/2, pp. 262–289.

Davidson, Christopher (2008). *Dubai: The Vulnerability of Success*, New York.

de Cardi, Beatrice (1979). *Qatar Archaeological Report*, Oxford: Oxford University Press.

Development Plans of the GCC States, 1962–1995, (1994) 14 vols., Ed. Archive Editions, London: Archive Editions.

Al-Diwan al-Sha'abi (2005). 'Aid al Kabisi (ed.), Doha.

Durkheim, Émile (1951). *Suicide, A Study in Sociology*, New York: The Free Press.

The Economist Intelligence Unit, *Country Reports: Qatar*, 1990-Present. Online. Available http://db.eiu.com/composite.asp?topicid=QA&desc=Qatar (September, 2011).

Ehteshami, Anoushiravan and Wright, Steven M. (2007). 'Political change in Arab Gulf monarchies: From liberalization to enfranchisement', *International Affairs*, 83/5, pp. 313–932.

——— (2007). *Reform in the Middle East Oil Monarchies*, London: Ithaca Press.

Eickelman, Dale (Winter 1984). 'Kings and people: Oman's state consultative council', *Middle East Journal*, 38/1, pp. 51–71.

el Kassas, Ibrahim (1987). *Bibliography on the Use of Aerial Photography ... in The State of Qatar*, Qatar: University of Qatar.

Fain, W. Taylor (2008). *American Ascendance and British Retreat in the Persian Gulf Region*, New York: Palgrave Macmillan.

Fenelon, K. G. (1967). *The Trucial States, Middle East Economic and Social Monographs*, No. 1, Beirut: Khayats.

Ferdinand, Klaus and Nicolaisen, Ida (1993). *Bedouins of Qatar*, New York: Thames and Hudson.

Field, Henry (Spring 1951). 'Reconaissance in Southwestern Asia', *Southwestern Journal of Anthropology*, 7/1, pp. 86–102.

Field, Michael (1985). *The Merchants: The Big Business Families of Saudi Arabia and the Gulf States*, Woodstock, NY: Overlook.

Freedom House, (2005). 'Women's rights in the Middle East and North Africa – Qatar', UNHCR REFWORLD. Online. Available www.unhcr,rg/cgi-bin/texis/vtx/refworld/rwmain?docid=47387b6fc (14 October 2005).

Gause, Gregory (1994). *Oil Monarchies: Domestic and Security Challenges in the Arab Gulf States*, New York: Council on Foreign Relations.

——— (2009). *The International Relations of the Persian Gulf*, Cambridge: Cambridge University Press.

Gellner, Ernest (1990). 'Tribalism and the state in the Middle East', in Philip S. Khoury and Joseph Kostiner (eds), *Tribes and State Formation in the Middle East*, Berkeley, CA: University of California Press, pp. 109–26.

Gengler, Justin. 'Qatar's Ambivalent Democratization' *Foreign Policy Magazine*. Online. Available http://mideast.foreignpolicy.com/posts/2011/11/01/qataris_lesson_in_revolution (10 November 2011).

Ghanim, Adl Husain (1979). *Al-Tarikh al Ijtimaʿi lil-Mira Al-Qatariyya al Muʿasirah*, Doha.

Graham, Helga (1978). *Arabian Time Machine*, London.

Grunebaum, G. E. Von (1964). *Modern Islam*, New York: Vintage.

Halliday, Fred (2005). *The Middle East in International Relations*, Cambridge: Cambridge University Press.

Herb, Michael (April 2005). 'No representation without taxation? Rents, development and democracy', *Comparative Politics*, 37/3, pp. 297–316.

———— (1999). *All in the Family: Absolutism, Revolution and Democracy in the Middle Eastern Democracies*, New York: State University of New York Press.

al-Hidous, Ibrahim (2001). *Awal Bait lil-Dimaqratiyya fi Qatar*, Doha.

Holden, David (1966). *Farewell to Arabia*, London.

Hopwood, Derek (1972). *The Arabian Peninsula*, London.

Huss, Abd al-Rahman (1962). *Qatar Mundhu al 'ahd al-'Uthmani ila 'ahd shuyukh al Thani*, Beirut.

Kamrava, Mehran (Summer 2009). 'Royal factionalism and political liberalization in Qatar', *The Middle East Journal*, 63/3, pp. 401–20.

———— (2011). *International Politics of the Persian Gulf*, Syracuse, NY: Syracuse University Press.

Kéchichian, Joseph (2008). *Power and Succession in Arab Monarchies: A Reference Guide*, Boulder, CO: Lynne Rienner.

Keddie, Nikki R. (1992). 'Material culture, technology, and geography: Toward a holistic comparative study of the Middle East', in Juan Cole (ed.), *Comparing Muslim Societies: Knowledge and the State in a World Civilization*, Ann Arbor, MI: University of Michigan Press, pp. 31–62.

Kerbage, Toufic (nd). *The Rhythms of Pearl Diver Music in Qatar*, Qatar: State of Qatar Ministry of Information.

Khiraman, Uma (nd). *Economic Activities of East Arabia between 1900–1930*, Qatar: Qatar University.

al-Khulaifi, Muhammad Jassim (1990). *Al Khor Museum*, Doha, Qatar.

al-Kirura, Muhmmad, et al. (1975). *Al Doha: Al-Madina al Duwlah*, Doha: Qatar University.

al-Kobaisi, Abdallah (1979). *The Development of Education in Qatar, 1950–1977*, Durham: Durham University.

Kostiner, Joseph (2009). *Conflict and Cooperation in the Gulf Region*, Germany: Weisbaden.

al-Kuwari, Ali Khalifa (1978). *Oil Revenues in the Gulf Emirates*, Great Britain.

Lawson, Fred (1989). *Bahrain: The Modernization of Autocracy*, Boulder, CO: Westview Press.

Looney, Robert (1990). *Structural Impediments to Industrialization in Qatar*, Kuwait.

Lorimer, John Gordon (1986). *Gazetteer of the Persian Gulf, Oman and Central Arabia*, 6 vols., London: Cambridge Archive Editions.

Michalak, L., Trocki, K. and Katz, K. (2009). '"I am a muslim and my dad is an alcoholic - what should I do?" internet advice for muslims about alcohol', *Journal of Muslim Mental Health*, Vol. 4, pp. 47–66.

Ministry of Foreign Affairs (2000). *Qatar*, London.

——— (2006). *Qatar Year Book*, Doha.

Ministry of Information (1988). *Glimpses of Qatar*, Doha.

Al-Misnad, Sheikha (1985). *The Development of Modern Education in the Gulf*, London.

Mission archéologique française à Qatar (1980). Jacques Tixier and Marie-Louise Inizan (eds), 2 Vols., Paris.

Montigny-Kozlowska, A. (1982). 'Histoire et changements sociaux au Qatar', in P. Bonnenfant (ed.), *La péninsule arabique d'aujourd'hui*, Vol. 2, Paris: CNRS, pp. 475–517.

——— (July–December 2000). 'Le territoire livré á l'arbitrage de Dieu: L'interprétation de la loi par les Al Na'im du Qatar', *Études rurales*, No. 155/6, pp. 51–73.

Nafi, Zuhair Ahmaed (1983). *Economic and Social Devleopment in Qatar*, London.

Nair, Arvind (2008). 'Experts warn of urban heat Islands as towers mushroom in Doha', *Gulf Times*, 13 April 2008.

Nakhleh, Emile A. (Spring 1977). 'Labor markets and citizenship in Bahrayn and Qatar', *Middle East Journal*, 31/2, pp. 143–56.

Niblock, Tim (1980). *Social and Economic Development in the Arab Gulf*, Exeter, UK: Center for Arab Gulf Studies.

Nomadic Societies in the Middle East and North Africa (2005). Dawn Chatty (ed.), Leiden.

Olsen, Beth M. (2003). *The Forensics of a Forgery: Bahrain's Submissions to the International Court of Justice in Qatar v. Bahrain*, Manama, Bahrain: Jabo Pub. Group.

Onley, James (2009). 'Britain and the Gulf Sheikhdoms, 1820–1971: The politics of protection', *Center for International and Region Studies Occasional Papers*.

——— (2008). *The Arabian Frontier of the British Raj*, Oxford.

al-Othman, Nasser (1984). *With their Bare Hands: The Story of the Oil Industry in Qatar*, London.

Owen, Roger (2004). *State Power and Politics in the Making of the Modern Middle East*, London: Routledge.

Palgrave, William G. (1865). *Narrative of A Year's Journey Through Central and Eastern Arabia (1862–63)*, 2 Vols., London and Cambridge: Macmillan and Co.

Qatar, Duwlat (State of Qatar) (2007). *Al-Jazira al-Rusmiyya*, Doha.

Qatar National Commission for Education, Culture and Science (January 1985) *The Educational Policy of Qatar*, Doha.

Rabi, Uzi (Summer 2009). 'Qatar's relations with Israel: Challenging Arab and Gulf norms', *The Middle East Journal*, 63/3, pp. 443–60.

Rahman, Habibur (2006). *The Emergence of Qatar*, London: Routledge.

Rush, A. De L. and Tuson, Penelope (ed.) (1991). *Ruling Families of Arabia: Documentary Records of the Dynasties of Saudi Arabia, Jordan, Kuwait, Bahrain, Qatar, UAE and Oman*, 12 vols., Tuson, London: Archive Editions.

——— (2004b). *Constitutionalism in the GCC States*, Dubai: Gulf Research Center.

——— (2008). 'Deconstructing before building: Perspectives on democracy in Qatar', *Reform in the Middle East Oil Monarchies*, A. Ehteshami and S. Wright (eds), Reading, UK: Ithaca Press, pp. 103–25.

Saif, Ahmad (2004a). *Arab Gulf Judicial Structures*, Dubai: Gulf Research Centre.

Saleh, Hassan Mohammed (1991). *Nationalism and Imperialism in Eastern Arabia: Britain, the Sheikhs and the Gulf Oil Workers in Bahrain, Kuwait and Qatar, 1932–1956*, Ann Arbor, MI: University of Michigan.

Sauer, James A. (1996). 'The River Runs Dry,' *Biblical Archaeology Review*, July/August.

Seikaly, May (1994). 'Women and Social Change in Bahrain,' *International Journal of Middle East Studies*, Vol. 26, pp. 415–426.

Al-Sharq (2007). Qatar al Madi, Doha, Qatar.

al-Shawi, Ali (2002). 'Political Influences of Tribes in the State of Qatar: Impact of Tribal Loyalty on Political Participation', PhD dissertation, Mississippi: Mississippi State University.

al-Shaybani, Muhammad S. (1962). *Imarat Qatar al-Arabiyyah bayn al Madi wal-Hadr*, Beirut.

Sick, Gary (1997). 'The coming crisis in the Persian Gulf', in *The Persian Gulf at the Millenium*, New York: Palgrave MacMillan, pp. 12–21.

Sinan, Mahmud Bahjat (1966). *Tarikh Qatar Al 'Amm*, Baghdad.

Sultan (1989). Muhammad Jabir, *Kalimat fi al-Zaman al S'ab*, Doha.

Sweet, Louise (Summer 1964). 'Pirates or polities? Arab societies of the Persian or Arabian Gulf. 18th century', *Enthnohistory*, 11/3, pp. 262–80.

Thomas, R. Hughes and Bidwell, Robin (eds) (1985). *Arabian Gulf Intelligence: Selections from the Records of the Bombay Government*. New Series, No. XXIV, 1856, Cambridge UK: Oleander Press.

United Nations Economic Commission for Western Asia (1980). *The Population Situation in the ECWA Region: Qatar*, Beirut.

Valencia, Rafael, et al. (nd) *Qatar: Cultural and Natural Heritage*, Barcelona: Gas Natural and QatarGas.

Vitalis, Robert (2007). *America's Kingdom: Mythmaking on the Saudi Oil Frontier*, Stanford, CA: Stanford University Press.

Waterbury, John (1994). 'Democracy without democrats?: The potential for political liberalization in the Middle East', in Ghassan Salamé (ed.), *Democracy without Democrats? The Renewal of Politics in the Muslim World*, New York: I.B.Tauris, pp. 23–47.

Webster, R. M. (1987). *Bedouin Settlements in Eastern Arabia*, Doctoral Thesis, Exeter: University of Exeter.

Wilkinson, J. C. 'Traditional concepts of territory in South East Arabia', *The Geographical Journal*, Vol. 149, pp. 301–15.

Winkler, Onn (2000). *Population Growth, Migration and Socio-Demographic Policies in Qatar*, Tel Aviv.

Wright, Steven (2007). *The United States and Persian Gulf Security: The Foundations of the War on Terror*, London: Ithaca Press.

Zahlan, Rosemarie Said (1979 reprinted 1989). *The Creation of Qatar*, London: Routledge.

_____ (1998). *The Making of the Modern Gulf States: Kuwait, Bahrain, Qatar, the United Arab Emirates and Oman*, London: Ithaca Press.

Index